Arts Integration

Arts Integration

Teaching Subject Matter through the Arts in Multicultural Settings

Fourth Edition

Merryl Goldberg

California State University, San Marcos

PEARSON

Boston Columbus Indianapolis New York San Francisco Upper Saddle River
Amsterdam Cape Town Dubai London Madrid Milan Munich Paris Montreal Toronto
Delhi Mexico City São Paulo Sydney Hong Kong Seoul Singapore Taipei Tokyo

Editor: Kelly Villella Canton
Editorial Assistant: Annalea Manalili
Marketing Manager: Darcy Betts
Production Editor: Janet Domingo
Editorial Production Service: Christian Holdener, S4Carlisle Publishing Services
Manufacturing Buyer: Megan Cochran
Electronic Composition: S4Carlisle Publishing Services
Interior Design: S4Carlisle Publishing Services
Cover Designer: Linda Knowles

Credits and acknowledgements borrowed from other sources and reproduced, with permission, in this textbook appear on appropriate pages within the text.

Previous editions were published under *Arts and Learning,* Copyright © 2002, 1997, 1992, Allyn & Bacon, Inc.

Library of Congress Cataloging-in-Publication Data
Goldberg, Merryl Ruth.
   Arts integration: Teaching subject matter through the arts in multicultural settings / Merryl Goldberg. — 4th ed.
     p. cm.
   ISBN-13: 978-0-13-256556-1
   ISBN-10: 0-13-256556-0
   1. Arts—Study and teaching (Elementary)—United States.   2. Multicultural education—Activity programs—United States.   I. Title.   II. Title: Arts integration: Teaching subject matter through the arts in multicultural settings.
   NX280.G65 2012
   372.5'044—dc22

2011000227

Printed in the United States of America
10 9 8 7 6 5 4 3 2 1   15 14 13 12 11

PEARSON

www.pearsonhighered.com

ISBN-13: 978-0-13-256556-1
ISBN-10:   0-13-256556-0

With lots and lots of love
to my daughter
Liana Cai—
You're one heck of
an amazing kid

About the Author

Merryl Goldberg, Ed.D.

Merryl Goldberg is a Professor of Visual and Performing Arts at California State University San Marcos (CSUSM), where she teaches courses in arts, learning, and music. She is founder and director of Center ARTES, an organization dedicated to restoring arts to education through working with the San Diego County Office of Education, arts partners, parents, and teachers. She has written numerous books, articles, chapters, editorials, and blogs. She is the recipient of many grants, including a U.S. Department of Education Innovation grant, a joint Spencer and John D. and Catherine T. MacArthur grant, Fulbright-Hays Foundation grants, and California Arts Council grants relating to her work with arts in the schools. Prior to entering academia, she recorded numerous CDs and was on the road for 13 years playing the saxophone with the Klezmer Conservatory Band.

Now that you have read the official bio, here is a little more of my personal story.

I am fortunate in that the arts have been an integral aspect of my own life since childhood. My father was a painter and in his later years dedicated to acting and directing high school students. He began "CATS," a children's theater. What an inspiration he was to me and my family as well as the hundreds of students whose lives he touched. His father, my grandfather, was a musician who played with Benny Goodman, Duke Ellington, Paul Whiteman, and the Boston Pops. My mother crafts jewelry, stationary, has worked with stained glass, and is one of the most amazing knitters I know!

I bring additional experience to this discussion as well. Since 1980, I have traveled throughout the world as a professional musician with the Klezmer Conservatory Band playing the saxophone, performing and recording ethnic music in a variety of settings including the Adelaide World Music Festival in Australia, jazz and folk clubs, weddings, and radio shows such as "Prairie Home Companion" with Garrison Keillor. At a certain point in my performing career I decided to give up the stage and applause as a full-time profession and turn my energies to education.

Though I continue to perform, my greatest moments are now spent in working with teachers, artists, and students and creating the spaces for engagement through the arts. For me, not much compares to being able to spend time with individuals as they practice being imaginative and creative, or while they are taking risks and engaging in a sense of wonder. And, when all is said and done, there is absolutely no shortage whatsoever to the potential and possibilities of all of us.

SOURCE: Sun and Moon Vision Productions.

Contents

Preface

"If you can dream it, you can do it. Always remember that this whole thing was started with a dream and a mouse."

Walt Disney[i]

Arts Integration is about children and teachers in some of their most imaginative and creative moments. It is about teachers being dream-makers opening spaces in creating a learning community committed to educational equity. It is about finding your own "mouse" and bringing it to life! It is about access to knowledge and it is about the journeys of individuals as they seek adventures in learning. An underlying premise of this book is that the artistic process is a process of learning, and that all children can, and want to, learn.

NEW TO THIS EDITION

If you are familiar with previous editions of this book you will immediately notice a title change. This new edition is titled *Arts Integration: teaching subject matter through the arts in multicultural settings*. In fact, it is the second title change since the first edition of this book was published in 1997 under the title: *Arts and Learning*. When I first wrote the book, the term "*arts integration*" was not part of the educational lexicon. In the years since, however, arts integration has become an accepted term and more importantly, an accepted educational methodology for teaching and learning.

The goal of this new edition is multifold. It was time to revisit the references and update research. I also wanted to reflect the attention to assessment and the significant role arts have with regard to assessing students' learning in the subject areas. I've strengthened the arguments concerning arts and engaging English language learners, and I have added sections describing additional programs that focus on the use of arts to teach specific skills such as reading. Here are some more specifics:

- Updated references include recent research that bolsters the need and multiple roles the arts have in the classroom are found throughout the text.

- A "top ten" list of the ways arts are fundamental to creating the space for learning including a discussion of wonder, passion, risk taking, and creating confident learners can be found in chapter 2.

---

[i] Disney Quote from thinkexist.com

- A deeper attention to the role of arts in reaching and supporting English language learners can be found throughout the text.
- Attention to the role of "visual literacy" especially with regard to the teaching of reading is highlighted in chapters 4 and 8.
- Chapter 9 which focuses on assessment is completely revamped and outlines several ways to utilize the arts to create and assess student learning outcomes. The chapter also includes and debunks several myths regarding the arts and assessment.
- Chapter 10 includes a discussion of DREAM—Developing Reading Education Through Arts Methods. This federally funded research project paves the way for using visual arts and theater as a vital teaching tool for reading.

Educators using this book need not have any arts background or familiarity with specific art techniques. The book will introduce you to the possibilities the arts hold for you and your students. Its motivating philosophy is that the arts are fundamental to education because they are fundamental to human knowledge and culture, expression, and communication. Artistic methods and activities encourage creative and critical thinking skills while at the same time enabling students to imagine possibilities, seek solutions, and be active discoverers of knowledge.

This book is unique in that it does not focus on learning about the arts. Instead, it focuses on how teaching and learning can be considerably enhanced through art-based activities. Learning subject matter in this way supports an integrated approach to curriculum development and teaching. Learning with the arts occurs when an art form is the source of a study. For example, a teacher may introduce her students to the songs of the civil rights movement as a method of studying the period, or to the paintings of Monet or Manet in studying mathematical points and sets. Likewise, a teacher might use poems written at the time of the American Revolution as a source to study aspects of the war. Learning with an art form introduces students to real-life applications of the arts in documenting humanity's most personal histories and expressions.

Learning *through* the arts employs artistic mediums as a strategy for learning. For example, students might dramatize the life cycle of a spider or butterfly to better understand it, or they might write a rap script as a way to apply and express their observations of nature. By learning through the arts, students are engaging with ideas rather than reporting on them. As they work through the arts to express subject matter, they are stretching their imaginations and pursuing the challenges involved in critical thinking and learning.

The arts are indeed powerful tools for motivating students to apply their knowledge, work cooperatively, and make connections across content areas; and arts integration can become a natural tool for everyday learning. As a teaching methodology, learning with and through the arts encourages imaginative, metaphoric, and creative thinking as well as cultural awareness. Participation with the arts gives children the freedom to learn and explore subject matter, discover the world around them, and venture to new worlds. By integrating learning strategies based on the arts, teachers may tap into multiple learning styles and modes of expression, thereby fulfilling several goals of multicultural education.

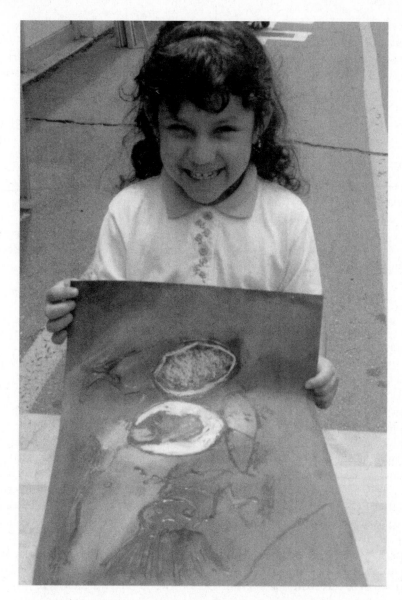

Showing off her oceanography collage, this kindergartener from Escondido, California, delightfully shares her knowledge of sea creatures.

I focus on many art forms throughout this book, ranging from rap and poetry and the power such few words can capture and convey, to the magic of movement and dance that allows us to experience how simple shapes can become intricate mathematical formulas. As you consider the ideas and activities in this book, I ask you to keep a number of things in mind. None of the activities are meant to be prescriptive, or even replicated in their reported form (although they can be). Each classroom teacher should adapt the ideas to her or his situation. Therefore, I see this book as a springboard toward developing a way of teaching and learning that can work for you and the children in your classroom, rather than as a guide for activities.

A word of encouragement as you consider integrating arts activities into your practice. Be willing to take risks. It can be a bit intimidating to try new activities, especially if you haven't had much experience with the arts. But, I have rarely been in a perfect teaching situation, and I have long gotten over the idea that everything I might do will work or that the art pieces I create will always be magnificent. Fortunately for you, your students will probably jump on the bandwagon immediately. Few children shy away from the opportunity to perform, listen to music, draw a picture, or create a sculpture. Once you get going, the unleashing of your own and your children's creativity not only will surprise you but will expand the expressive opportunities and intellectual musings in your classroom. Often, the greatest successes result from the greatest risks. Be an arts adventurer and invite your students along.

ACKNOWLEDGMENTS

Putting together each edition of this book has been a joyful adventure. I am indebted to the many people I have met along the way for their ideas and suggestions. First and foremost, thanks to hundreds of children with whom I worked in the course of gathering ideas and artwork. As well, thanks to their teachers in the SUAVE, DREAM, and AVID for Arts programs. Thanks to California State University San Marcos students who have enthusiastically learned through the arts and continually contribute to my further understandings of the arts.

I am grateful to the Spencer Foundation and the John D. & Catherine T. MacArthur Foundation for their generous support of research of the SUAVE program as well as the Department of Education Model Arts grant, the research of which is reported in this edition. A very special thanks to my original wonderful, curious, and questioning research team of Victoria Jacobs, Tom Bennett, and Laura Wendling, and especially to Patti Saraniero who is an arts education guru so far as I'm concerned, not to mention researcher "extraordinaire."

Special mention goes to the many artists, past and present, whose work makes a difference in children's lives and has been a source of inspiration for this book. And I am most grateful to the board members of Center ARTES (art, research, teaching, education, schools), a center at California State University San Marcos dedicated to restoring arts to schools. Their efforts have been an absolute inspiration to me. I especially want to thank Ruth Mangrum, Center ARTES board member, whose dedication and support of arts and children has been an inspiration to me. Ruth and I have worked together for 20 years now making and creating the spaces for children to flourish and grow. She is one very special individual! Thanks to my family (especially my mom and daughter!) and friends—it takes a village—and I'm very grateful for the villages I inhabit and visit. Thanks to the following folks for pushing my thinking: Bill Bradbury, Mtafiti Imara, Ranjeeta Basu, Marie Thomas, Vivienne Bennett, Vicki Golich, Brenda Hall, Ron Jessee,

Patti Saraniero, Carolyn Funes, Matt Funes, Larry Reitzer, and M2, a.k.a. Marla Matt, whose observations, questions, reflections, and encouragement have added greatly to this edition.

Kudos to the staff and editors at Allyn & Bacon Pearson Teacher Education for their ongoing support, especially Kelly Villella Canton, Senior Acquisitions Editor and her team: Janet Domingo, in-house production; Annalea Manalili, editorial assistant; and Kate Cebik, photo research. A big thanks as well to Christian Holdener, Project Editor, S4Carlisle Publishing Services.

I would also like to thank the reviewer for this edition: Patricia Bode, Tufts University School of the Museum of Fine Arts, Boston.

Arts Integration

Chapter 1

Art Integration: A Methodology for Learning

THE CLIFF

It stands alone in silence
never losing its strength
except sometimes a wave
will come and dig beneath
the sandstone shell

It cannot lose more than a chip
but slowly it disintegrates from
all the time the tide has come and
all the time the wind has gone

Joey Strauss, fifth grader

Reading poems like this one by Joey, a fifth grader in southern California, reminds me how fundamental the arts are to human development, expression, and communication. Joey wrote this poem after closely observing the cliffs on a beach near his school as an assignment for his science class. In teaching a unit on ecology, his teacher sought to put her students directly in touch with nature. Having them observe and document aspects of their environment—in this case, the local beach—is important, she argued, to their learning. But what makes this class unusual is that the teacher also used an art form—poetry—as a way to have the students reflect on, work with, and apply their observations. The arts provide a methodology by which her students can transform their observations into a creative form as they learn about nature. The teacher has experienced again and again that using the arts as a teaching methodology allows her students to think more deeply about subject matter.

This integrated poetry activity is representative of the potential of the arts in the construction of knowledge: that of a methodology for exploring subject matter in a deep and meaningful manner. Not only do the arts serve as an engaging medium, but they provide students with the tools to work with ideas as well. In so doing, they also expand the expressive opportunities available to children in the classroom. Whereas traditional schooling relies heavily on testing and writing as the principal modes of assessment and expression, the arts expand the modes available to children as they seek to understand and express their conceptions of the world around them.

I've never met a kid who wasn't capable or who didn't have enormous potential. What most kids need is opportunity. Sadly, children are losing opportunities to learn as schools continue to focus narrowly on reading and math instruction and on measuring student achievement via standardized test scores in those areas. Diane Ravitch (2010, p. 226) cautions that "Our schools will not improve if we value only what tests measure. The tests we now have provide useful information about students' progress in reading and mathematics, but they cannot measure what matters most in education. Not everything that matters can be quantified." Ravitch goes on to advocate for emphasis on a curriculum that educates children in becoming responsible citizens—a curriculum that includes the arts. "If we do not treasure our individualists," she contends, "we will lose the spirit of innovation, inquiry, imagination, and dissent that has contributed so powerfully to the success of our society in many different fields of endeavor" (p. 226).

In this chapter, I will provide several compelling arguments focusing on the arts as key in educating our children. Our schools are home to learning and set the stage for the ability of the next generation to become engaged citizens and participants in society.

Noted writer/entertainer Bill Cosby observes that "It matters not what our national, racial or regional differences are; we are all prone to acculturate ourselves toward using the arts to help us understand ourselves more fully and act as a motivating force in our daily lives" (qtd. in Asmal, Chidester, & Wilmot, 2003, p. 282). The following poem, written by Piero Mercanto, a seventh grader, reflects precisely the power of the arts as a source of acculturation. Piero reflects upon himself as a learner and what it is like to enter a new world. Piero arrived in the United States as a Spanish-speaking child. This poem describes his entry into his new world.

EL MUNDO

Al llegar a otro mundo,
Es como caer en un
Hoyo negro todo sin
Color y sin risas.
Es como buscar,

Algo que no se
Te ha perdido y que
Nunca podrás
Encontralo.
Cada día se va
Y ni me doy cuenta,
Como se va. Tal vez
Se lo lleva el viento,
Tal vez no.

THE WORLD

To arrive in another world
is like falling into a
black hole all without
color and without laughter.
It's like looking
for something you
have not lost and
you will never find.
Every day passes
and I can hardly account
for it. Perhaps
the wind takes it,
perhaps not.

Piero Mercanti, seventh grade, translated
by Maria Marrero
(Harvard Educational Review, 1991)

Whether learning a new language or a strategy for fitting into a new culture, the arts give students like Piero a reliable and important outlet to express their knowledge, feelings, and unfolding understandings. This is not a novel idea. In broader terms, Nelson Mandela often spoke of the importance of both arts and sports in the building of community. In writing about Mandela, Cosby puts it this way: "He [Mandela] has boldly noted that the creative, performing arts and visual arts are the most common and the most notable vehicles through which constructive cultural engagement can take place. . . . They present us with a keen insight as to who we are as well as who we wish to become" (Asmal et al., 2003, p. 283).

ARTS AND KNOWLEDGE

I consider knowledge as an evolving and nonstatic action. As we learn, we are constantly changing our understanding of the world. What I think about today will surely change as I gather more and more experiences tomorrow. Bodies of knowledge that often take priority as a focus of study in schooling should instead serve as a springboard from which children may explore ideas about their relationship to the world. In other words, bodies of knowledge are not fixed. For example, as scientists continue to explore aspects of the natural world, their theories evolve and change accordingly. In the realm of history, events and stories may be interpreted and reinterpreted according to perspective and additional documentation.

In describing knowledge, I do not mean the reiteration of someone else's great ideas. Instead, I would concur with Eleanor Duckworth (2006) when she writes, "By knowledge, I do not mean verbal summaries of somebody else's knowledge. . . . I mean a person's own repertoire of thoughts, actions, connections, predictions, and feelings" (p. 14). Accepting this premise, a teacher may play an important role in the classroom by having her students actively work with knowledge rather than simply mimicking others' knowledge. Here, the arts are important.

Having been on the beach and documented aspects of nature along with Joey (the child whose poem is at the opening of this chapter) and the other children in his class, I have witnessed students as they work toward making sense of their surroundings. Writing poetry gives them a structure through which to apply their observations. In doing this they are actively working with a knowledge base and constructing understandings of nature through an art form. The art form enables each child to apply his or her observations in an imaginative manner, creating a personal connection to the subject matter. At the same time, because students are engaged in the activity they are in a strong position to retain and apply their understandings in the future.

Placing the students directly in touch with nature is a sound pedagogical approach in and of itself, but asking the students to write poetry following their observation activities gives them an opportunity to reflect even more deeply on their work. As the students consider the complex aspects of nature, the poem is a form through which they can actively reflect upon their experiences. In his sketchbook, Joey recorded the following notes based on his observations of that day. It is fascinating to see the leaps Joey made from notes to poem.

Cliffs
    solid sandstone
    full of holes and crevices
    covered with brush
    iceplant

Waves
    forming far away
    it grows to a few feet high
    a surfer catches it
    it crashes
    and turns to foam on the sand

A Rock
    worn smooth
    dark black holes
    streaks of white

egg shaped
four small holes

Seagull
   diving
   swooping
   flying far away
   flapping
   soaring high above my head
   spies its prey and dives

It is evident from his notes that Joey paid close attention to his surroundings. As it happens, his observations are recorded in what some might consider a surprisingly poetic manner. I, too, was surprised in the beginning. But I have learned that when children are constantly engaged in thinking imaginatively, they begin to naturally apply their observations and understandings in creative ways. I have come to learn that applying one's imagination can be a practiced skill. In writing his poem, Joey has taken his observations, seriously worked with them, and transformed them into something else.

Transformation is a key to knowledge construction and acquisition. The activity of writing a poem has given Joey an opportunity for learning and an outlet for expressing his ideas and questions. At the same time, each student is engaged in "practicing" his or her imagination. By working on something in a manner that stretches his or her thinking, the child is simultaneously engaged in critical and reflective thinking. The arts allow that imaginative and critical thinking to emerge in a personal and creative manner. Consider the following poem written by Rell on the same day, after she documented the rush of incoming waves.

THE WAVE

No one is there to ride it
but the sun
who glimmers with glee
at riding
being closely followed
as it washes to shore
in turn.

Rell Parker

Whereas Joey was fascinated by the cliffs, Rell focused on the waves. Both successfully completed the nature observation assignment by carefully documenting an aspect of the beach. Both used their observation notes to create a unique poem. In this example, the teacher and I know at the very least that the students are engaged in a process of learning through applying observations to a deeper level by using them in a concentrated and serious way. As well, each child is an emerging poet and can share his or her original compositions with the class, often to the amazement of peers.

ARTS AND LEARNING

When people of previous generations think of the arts in education, they think of their own elementary music class in which they probably sang songs accompanied by a teacher on the piano, guitar, or other simple instrument. They have recollections of art class where the art teacher had them sculpt a clay bowl or draw a still life. Today's college students, however, have not been so lucky. Most of them have had very limited experiences with formal arts instruction in their public school education. Budget cuts and the No Child Left Behind legislation have effectively curbed arts education. My students, however, are keen consumers of popular culture, and have tapped into their own rich cultures that honor the value of the arts.

The arts have not always been separate subjects. Historically, when arts were introduced into education in the United States, they served a particular purpose. Music was first introduced into the public schools in an urban setting (Boston, in 1838) to promote hymn singing. Boston was also home to the first drawing program, which was introduced as a result of the Industrial Drawing Act of 1870, passed by legislators (composed and signed by manufacturers). The Industrial Drawing Act was designed to introduce drawing to children for the purpose of training individuals for work related to design in manufacturing. Since the 1950s, however, the arts have been taught as something added onto a core of "basics." Although some might argue that the arts *are* basic (as I would), for the most part the arts have remained removed from other learning.

There are three ways in which I describe the arts as integrated into learning: *learning about* the arts, *learning with* the arts, and *learning through* the arts. For many, the most common form of arts education involves a professional who teaches *about* the arts. In this familiar model, an arts specialist usually handles the job: The music teacher takes the children for an hour or so each week and teaches about music; the art teacher in his unusually colorful separate room teaches about visual arts. If you were lucky, there might have even been a drama or dance teacher in your school whom you met with on a weekly basis. Although this model has served education well, we see its importance slowly diminishing in direct proportion to shrinking educational budgets. The arts, often considered a "frill," have been cut as the basics—particularly reading and mathematics—receive attention.

Cutting the arts, besides being incredibly unfortunate for our children, is also against the law! However, only a handful of states have what I call "arts education police," whose job it is to ensure that all children receive their rightful education—one that incorporates the arts. According to the No Child Left Behind legislation of 2002, all children are entitled to a comprehensive and equitable education that includes the four arts areas of visual arts, music, drama, and dance. Furthermore, national standards in the arts address a developmentally appropriate method for teaching the arts, and nearly every state has adopted its own frameworks for arts education.

Taught as disciplines unto themselves, the arts reveal many aspects of human nature and give students multiple outlets to express their innermost thoughts. Keeping the arts separate from other subjects, however, severely limits their potential as a methodology for teaching and learning in general. As taught in traditional settings, the arts allow students to travel to places of mystery, dreams, and adventure. Kept separate from the sciences, math, social studies, or the language arts, the arts are limited in their potential and practical use in the classroom.

The emphasis throughout this book is to broaden the potential of arts in the classroom by outlining a *methodology* for learning. I define *arts* in the very broadest sense to include the performing arts (e.g., music, dance, drama) as well as the nonperforming arts (e.g., visual arts, photography, literature, sculpture). I define *methodology* as the means by which teachers engage students in learning that is meaningful to them, and that provides a forum through which they actively grapple with the complexities of knowledge.

Reflecting upon our own and others' knowledge changes us and the way we perceive the world. According to Karen Gallas (1994), "[creating knowledge] makes you powerful and gives you authority within community. It enables you to feel some control over your history as a learner" (p. 111). Using the arts as a way to teach subject matter places the learner in the position of truly working with ideas and taking control of learning in a manner that is at once intellectual, personal, meaningful, and powerful.

The arts, as a methodology for teaching and learning, provide the teacher with an expanded repertoire of actions and activities to introduce subject matter. By exercising their imaginations through subject-matter-related artwork, children are more likely to make new connections and transcend previous limitations. Imagination is an attribute that serves all people in all endeavors—not only artists. Creativity is fundamental to any field. For example, the chief executive officer of a company must be able to employ his or her imagination to stay competitive. A computer programmer must be creative to invent new programs or video games. A chef must utilize powers of imagination to create tasty, visually appealing dishes. The power of the imagination as a practiced skill must not be overlooked or lost in learning. The arts, as a teaching methodology, empower students to practice those skills. Teaching through the arts also is a keen way to open the world of learning to English language learners. A teacher in the SUAVE program (see Chapter 10) offers this:

> [Teaching through the arts] opens the floodgates of the second language, the gate that keeps [students] back, that keeps them limited and maybe questioning their own self-worth. It opens that gate because they have been actively involved and showing you they are feeling really good. It helps them so much to feel that yes, I can learn this and I can do this because they had all of this great self-expression come out and they have been validated. I think that the self-esteem thing is such a powerful piece in the classroom. (Goldberg, 2004, pp. 63–64)

The arts are humanity's expression of life itself. Viewed in this manner, they have not been used to their fullest in learning and teaching in typical North American school settings. Even though many art programs present students with important lessons concerning techniques such as perspective in drawing or singing in tune, history shows us over and over that the arts play an even greater role in capturing and promoting cultures. The arts present many kinds of knowledge, and students may learn a tremendous amount by examining their content. The songs, paintings, or poetry of a culture may represent the history of a people; drama might explore the political tensions of a community; playing with the colors in a sand sculpture might provide inspiration for the scientist who explores different combinations of molecules.

In light of the previous argument, I believe that we should evaluate the more common approach to arts in education and consider its limitations as well as its contributions. In short, I propose an expansion of the role of arts in teaching and learning such that art be more fully integrated as a methodology for learning and a language of expression in the general classroom. This approach broadens the definition of the role of the arts in learning to include their use as a medium or language to translate, reflect on, and work with ideas and concepts.

As a methodology, the arts become a *process* toward learning. This notion is parallel to one developed by Sonia Nieto (1996) as she discusses multicultural education: "Curriculum and materials represent the *content* of multicultural education, but multicultural education is above all a *process*" (p. 317). Both multicultural education and art as methodology require an ongoing and dynamic process. Both involve content, and both stress process through attention to active participation, learning environments, learning styles, culture, and language abilities in the classroom. This is played out in infinite ways.

At the university where I teach, we often have special programs. At one point we received a grant that enabled a group of musicians, Voice of the Turtle, who play Spanish Jewish music (Ladino), to be in residence for a week. The premise of their visit was to engage students in humanities, arts, and education classes with the incredible vessel of knowledge (content) housed within the songs of the Spanish Jews in exile, as documented in the Diaspora over the last 500 years. In 1492 Jews and Muslims were expelled from Spain and many traveled to Bulgaria, Morocco, Eastern Europe, Mexico, and Greece, among other countries, in a resettlement effort. During their exile, the Jewish Spaniards kept alive their language and history through songs and poetry. They also created new songs and poetry that reflected and documented their evolving history and the changes in their lives and cultures.

When the Ladino musicians performed at the university, they offered much more than entertainment and an eclectic style of music. They engaged the students in a *process* of learning. Captured in their songs was a rich series of history lessons, linguistic lessons, musical lessons, and cultural lessons. Their residency brought them to the Spanish Civilization class, where they presented a history lesson through song; to the Critical Music Listening class, where they introduced the students to instruments and music theory as it related to Spanish songs; to the Linguistics seminar, where the students compared the Spanish of 500 years ago to present-day Spanish; and to the Education class, where student teachers learned how Ladino culture could be introduced to children in multicultural classrooms.

The group also visited a fifth-grade bilingual (Spanish–English) classroom, where they interacted with students and engaged them in writing poetry to a traditional melody. After presenting the fifth graders with a few songs and stories from their repertoire, they played a haunting, melancholy song without words and asked students to create a poem to accompany the melody. Engrossed in the activity, children composed an amazing array of poems, both in English and in Spanish, which they later recited to the accompaniment of the musicians. The level of engagement was phenomenal, and the poems surprised us all. Here are two of the poems written that day.

VOZ DE LA TORTUGA

Triste me siento
No siento alegría
En mi corazón
Mi corazón se parte en dos pedazos
No me siento alegre en este día
Dejenme en paz
No estoy alegre
Me siento decaída
No quiero ver a nadie ahorita
Quiero estar sola
Sin nadie a mi lado
No quiero que nadie venga a mi lado
No quiero
No quiero más dolor
Quiero ver alegría
Mi corazón está derrotado de tristeza
La lluvia está cayendo
El sol no sale
Me siento sola
No hay pájaros en el aire
Todo está solo
No me gusta el día
El día está triste

Jovanna Flores

MY DYING SOUL

Here I am dying
all upon my own
with no one to die with
I am so lonesome so lonesome
whispers of sadness
birds made of stone
gray and black feathers
I am all upon my own
my sadness is too deep to cry
for my soul is spared

Emily Birnbaum

Students continued to talk about their experience with the musical group for months after the visit. Many chose poems from that day to include in a class publication.

The overall residency proved to be far more than entertainment, and it illustrates the depth with which the arts engage students in active learning. To each audience, the group offered specific content as well as an opportunity to connect evolving understandings through the arts to history, culture, and personal interests.

One might ask why it is any better to learn history through the songs of a people than through a history book. Learning through a people's musical culture provides an interesting array of authentic historical voices that is perhaps more inviting and aesthetically pleasing than a history text. Songs often can evoke feelings or moods more than written text through the musical language added to words. Songs often present an authentic point of view, drawing on the thoughts and experiences of real people in history. As such, song texts often provide firsthand accounts of events in history.

Using art forms such as the Ladino musicians provided can be highly effective in the classroom. Karen Gallas (1994) outlines three ways in which art experiences may be placed at the center of a curriculum: (1) the arts representing a methodology for acquiring knowledge; (2) the arts as subject matter for study, in and of themselves; and (3) the arts as an array of expressive opportunities for communicating with others—what she labels "art as story" (p. 116). In the example of the Ladino musicians, all the experiences Gallas outlines were played out. Jovanna and Emily, the fifth-grade students whose poems you just read, accessed the arts as both a methodology for acquiring knowledge and an expressive outlet. The songs and poems presented them with subject matter for study.

Next, we will look a little deeper at the role of art as a *language* for learning.

ARTS AS LANGUAGE

Art is a language of expression and communication that has always been, and will always remain, a fundamental aspect of the human condition and the perpetuation of cultures. Defining art is a challenging proposition because it can be viewed through so many cultural, theoretical, philosophical, and even geographical perspectives. This does not mean, however, that people have not tried. For our purposes, we will briefly examine how the arts—in their multiple complexities—act as languages of expression for people and cultures throughout the world.

"Art is a mirror of life" and "art imitates life" are common notions of the function of art in experience. The mirror metaphor is of special interest to me. Socrates and Shakespeare (through the voice of Hamlet) both raised the theory that "art is a mirror of reality" (in Danto, 1981). In discussing the two men's views, Arthur Danto concludes that Hamlet "made a far better use of the metaphor: mirrors and then, by generalization, artworks, rather than giving us back what we already can know without the benefit of them, serve instead as instruments of self-revelation" (p. 9).

What intrigues me about the mirror metaphor is that it incorporates the notion of reflection. If art is a mirror—which I believe it can be—it necessitates reflection. And in that reflection we often see things that are or aren't there. Our look in the mirror is discriminating. The same is true of our look at life; it is discriminating according to our experiences, culture, gender, environment, and so on. Art enables us to see things that are both there and not there; it provides us with an opportunity to imagine and reflect on our lives.

Bella Lewitzky (1989), a dancer and philosopher, writes: "Art is a language, a form of communication, a philosophy, a perception of truth" (p. 2). Although I might argue that there are no truths, only complexities (the more we learn, the more we know we have more to learn), I agree that the arts are most definitely a language and that they most certainly communicate. For example, let's think about music. Listening to a popular piece by the Beatles might evoke and communicate very different feelings and images than an Indian raga. Music in Australian traditional Aboriginal communities serves to communicate history, geography, and culture. Catherine Ellis (1985), while doing music research among Aboriginal communities, writes of an Aboriginal man who told her that "the most knowledgeable person in a tribal community was the person 'knowing many songs'" (p. 1). Similarly, when I hear Tchaikovsky's *1812 Overture* or his *Romeo and Juliet,* I sense definite feelings and images. However, each piece communicates very different images, stories, and feelings. In listening to the *1812 Overture* I can picture cannons and artillery. I imagine troops patriotically marching toward battle. In listening to *Romeo and Juliet* I sense two individuals drawn to each other, longing for each other. I see them trying to get close to one another.

Art Hodes, a jazz pianist who lived well into his nineties, wrote of the blues as a language. Hodes was well known for his playing with Louis Armstrong and Bessie Smith, performing standards—enduring jazz selections. Here Hodes (in Gottlieb, 1996) describes an early experience in his career, before he learned the language, as he puts it, of the blues.

> Many times they'd ask me to play. I was kidded plenty. Someone would holler, 'Play the blues, Art,' and when I would play they would laugh. That hurt, but I couldn't blame them. I hadn't as yet learned the idiom. I was entranced by their language but I hadn't learned to speak it yet.

Mickey Hart (1991), one of the drummers from the group The Grateful Dead, describes music as a "reflection of our dreams, our lives, and it represents every fiber of our being. It's an aural soundscape, a language of the deepest emotions; it's what we sound like as people" (p. 7). James Hoffmann (1991) argues that music not only communicates, but is a powerful tool, especially in the hands of performers. "Music, a potent social instrument from earliest times, operates not merely in imitation of society but also in dynamic interaction with it. In comprehending this, a performing musician gains power not only over his or her immediate audience, but through contemporary media, over a broader public as well—for good or ill" (p. 270). One could make a similar argument for other art forms as well.

The arts provide humankind with modes for reflecting on, expressing, and documenting experiences, as well as providing a body of knowledge from which to draw upon. The arts provide a method for expressing ourselves, while at the same time, they serve as a unique document of cultures and history. As a study, the arts offer historical, emotional, cultural, and personal sources of information and documentation. Lewitzky (1989) continues, "Art can, in the hands of great talent, make beauty which reverberates through our lives and carries us into rarified strata. It can shatter our perceptions. It can clarify our anger. It can help us to understand our sorrow. The arts are a mirror for society—critic, teacher and forecaster—and teach the value of individual differences" (p. 2).

Art can stimulate our imagination or reflect our experiences. Through creating a work in art, a person can explore the complexities of an idea or situation more fully than if they were to read about it or listen to a lecture. As a tool, the arts enable us to cross boundaries that are usually closed to us, or to join together in ways that are new. As such, it is not unusual for artists to imagine new ways of being or to invent ways of seeing something anew.

Creating art or experiencing it is an act of what Lucy Lippard (1990) describes as "a process of consciousness" (p. 9) reminiscent of Nieto's characterization of multicultural education. Maxine Greene (1991) writes of encounters with arts as "shocks of aware-ness" that may, and should, leave persons "less immersed in the everyday, more impelled to wonder and to question" (p. 27). She goes on to tell us how it is not uncommon "for the arts to leave us somehow ill at ease, nor to prod us beyond acquiescence. They may, now and then, move us into spaces where we can create visions of other ways of being and ponder what it might signify to realize them" (p. 27).

I readily admit that I love music—and many kinds of music at that. I've imagined living inside a Bob Marley reggae tune or inside a passage of Stravinsky's *Symphony of Psalms*. I can honestly say that I experience a sense of freedom when I listen to or play a piece of music that allows me to transcend everyday limitations. Music to me is, as Adrienne Rich (1993) refers to in a discussion of the arts, "a vital way of perceiving and knowing" (p. 162). As a child I spent many hours writing song after song, from the poignant to the sublime. Growing up during the 1960s, I wrote songs with lyrics rang-ing from "We need peace, we need love, all over this world, peace love peace to love" to the more whimsical notion of "Flower power is in today." Obviously, neither song made it to the Top Ten or even a Grammy nomination. However, writing these songs was a truly powerful and empowering activity. I learned to sit for long periods of time work-ing in a concentrated manner. I enjoyed the activity of creating. I was encouraged by supportive peers and adults who listened closely to my finished songs and even found opportunities for me to show them off in school cafeterias or during assemblies.

The connection to this discussion is that the language of the arts can be very pow-erful in the life of a child. Art can be a source of empowerment as children explore their world and personal potential while retaining (and, one hopes, celebrating) a sense of in-dividualism in relating to their community, be it the classroom, neighborhood, club, or family. As I have previously written (Goldberg & Phillips, 1992), "For both teachers and students, the arts can be a form of expression, communication, imagination, observa-tion, perception, and thought. The arts are integral to the development of cognitive skills such as listening, thinking, problem solving, matching form to function, and decision making. They inspire discipline, dedication, and creativity" (p. v).

Working with the arts opens the classroom to surprises and excitement. As Gallas (1994) writes, "There is an aura of excitement in the classroom engaged in the arts, and also one of serious intent. . . . What I began to see were the surprises: the ways that chil-dren could learn to read through their artworks; the potential for communication that painting offered a nonverbal child; the joy that artistic activity brought to children and teachers alike" (p. 112). I, too, am continually amazed as children work and create un-derstandings through the arts. Sometimes they make surprisingly personal statements, such as when the class bully wrote a poem about his desire to fly freely as butterfly. Through their artwork, children introduce themselves to us in deep and meaningful ways that may not ordinarily emerge otherwise.

Perhaps one of the more compelling reasons why the arts, as languages of learning, are fundamental to classroom life is that they give rise to many voices. "They can nurture a sense of belonging, of community; or, they can foster a sense of being apart, of being individual. The arts also provide a vehicle for individuals, communities, and cultures to explore their own world and journey to new ones, thus enriching their understanding of the varied peoples and cultures that exist on our planet" (Goldberg & Phillips, 1992, p. v).

Moreover, the arts can reach across boundaries. In a class where many verbal languages are spoken, the arts can be a uniting language. Although a new student from Peru might not be able to communicate in words with a child who just arrived from Vietnam, she can more than adequately communicate through her drawings and dances. Indeed, using the arts of different cultures as primary sources of learning history introduces children to the "feel" of a culture in addition to the "facts" of a culture.

ARTS AND CULTURE

"I would like us to learn things from other cultures, to sing songs from other cultures. It's wonderful. It opens up your thinking and everything else. But it should never happen to the detriment of your own" (Miriam Makeba in the book *Nelson Mandela: In His Own Words;* cited in Asmal et al., 2003, p. 279).

Art cannot be divorced from culture; it grows from individuals interacting or reacting to their world. Piero's poem at the start of this chapter poignantly illustrates this point. Through Piero's poem we can see that, as an English language learner, he arrives to not only a new language, but a new world and culture. "For some children the transition is smooth and exciting. For some the transition is filled with a sense of loss in addition to newness" (Goldberg, 2004, p. 2). Much of education involves the telling and creating of stories of our global culture. Stories are told through the spoken word, artwork, music, dance, poetry—all these languages are essential as they transmit culture both within various cultures and to people outside of the culture. It is when we begin to tell other people's stories that we must take the utmost care and respect so that our actions adequately reflect the complexities of the culture.

When students work creatively through the arts, they often begin to incorporate their culture into their work. So, too, when teachers present works of art to emphasize a point or to examine a particular issue, context must be a consideration. The arts embody culture; sometimes they even enhance it. The arts are languages that communicate; like words, they are a system of symbols that represent ideas, emotions, feelings, and history. When I first taught music, I worked at Hebrew Day School, outside of Boston. A few teachers in the school asked if I could enhance their curriculum on Jewish Eastern Europe in the 1800s. I remember feeling annoyed that I was being asked to enhance their curriculum, yet I couldn't quite figure out what bothered me. I understand better now.

The music of the Eastern European Jews in the 1800s didn't simply *enhance* life at that time; it *embodied* life. The songs reflect the hardships, the passion, the events of the time. On their own, the songs could easily be a history text—a rich one at that. The writings of Toni Morrison don't simply enhance life (though they might do that as well); they capture and embody experiences, emotions. The same can be said of Diego Rivera's paintings, Michelangelo's wall murals, Pablo Neruda's poetry, Bill T. Jones's choreography, the Black-Eyed Peas' music, and on and on.

ARTS AND CULTURE AND IDENTITY

The arts can, and often do, play a significant role in cultural and personal identity. My own daughter, to whom this book is dedicated, is of Chinese heritage and was adopted when she was a year old. Our interracial family is constantly engaged in all sorts of activities, and we spend a great deal of time each year at events for families with children from China. My daughter loves to dance, and she has learned some ribbon dancing (as have I!). We have also learned some calligraphy and been introduced to many of China's rich genres of music. These experiences acknowledge her history and offer a way for her to engage directly with Chinese customs and traditions.

Classroom teachers can similarly find ways to integrate the cultures of the children in their classrooms. In this way children can learn about many cultures and individual children will feel that they and their identity is acknowledged. On the other hand, not integrating cultures can indirectly teach children that their cultures are not valued (Goldberg, 2004). There are many openings to integrate the arts of children's cultures in your classroom. You may enlist parents or guardians of your students to help with this endeavor. It might be as simple as teaching the children a song, dance, or having an artwork hung in the classroom that was created by a child's relative.

Keep in mind that you will no doubt have children (like my own) in your class who might be adopted from cultures whose parents might or might not have a strong familiarity with the child's culture of origin. In my own case, I have found there are many community resources available to use. In San Diego we have a Chinese historical museum that offers programs and resources to teachers, schools, and families. We also have community centers for Samoan, Filipino, Mexican, and Native American communities, all of which have had wonderful working relationships with schools. The resources are available; tapping into them is often as easy as an e-mail or phone call.

Since I have brought up the subject of adoption, I believe a few more words about the topic might be helpful. As a teacher, you will have children in your class who are adopted. You will have children living with foster families, children who live in homeless shelters, and, perhaps, children living with relatives or even children of migrant workers who will spend only a few months in the area. Children will come from blended families, and families with two moms or two dads. As you approach involving children's families and guardians, be open to all these kinds of families and all they offer. When asking children to bring a photo from their childhood for a collage project, keep in mind that some might not have photos (or access to them).

A family tree assignment might cause some tension for an older child who struggles with her identity in terms of her "forever" family versus her biological family. Reframing a family tree assignment that identifies important people in one's life might be more appropriate. If you ask a child to learn a song from his mom, remember that he might not be living with his mom. For children living in nontraditional families, which, judging by my own neighborhood, is more the norm, culture and arts are a natural bridge to gaining identity and sharing it with others. As a role model, you will play a significant role in helping each child identify with the multiple cultures in your classroom and community. What a gift this will be for all of you!

ARTS AND INCLUSIVE EDUCATION: SPECIAL NEEDS, EXCEPTIONAL, AND GIFTED EDUCATION

Arts are a natural bridge for children with differing abilities, including special needs, gifted and talented, and all kinds of exceptionalities. Every child offers a unique contribution to your class and every child has strengths and needs. Every child in your class wants to be included, and the arts are a wonderful method of inclusion.

In this section I would like to highlight the role arts can play in working with many special kids that you will have in your classroom. I will begin with the value of arts to children with special needs. VSA, or Very Special Arts, is an international nonprofit organization founded in 1974 by Jean Kennedy Smith. It is an organization dedicated to raising awareness and sponsoring programs by which "people with disabilities can learn through, participate in, and enjoy the arts" (information about VSA can be found on its Web site: www.vsarts.org). This organization offers important background and advice concerning the role of arts in enhancing learning for children as well as promoting the notion that creative arts offer a venue for self-expression, communication, and independence for youth and adults with differing abilities.

According to VSA's Web site (June 2010):

VSA programming and initiatives are guided by four essential principles:

- Every young person with a disability deserves access to high quality arts learning experiences.

- All artists in schools and art educators should be prepared to include students with disabilities in their instruction.

- All children, youth, and adults with disabilities should have complete access to cultural facilities and activities.

- All individuals with disabilities who aspire to careers in the arts should have the opportunity to develop appropriate skills.

Inclusion teaches us that *all* means "all." *Everybody.* No exceptions. The arts invite people to leave familiar territory, to explore new answers and seek new questions. The arts offer a means to self-expression, communication, and independence. By learning through the arts, students become lifelong learners, experiencing the joy of discovery and exploration, and the value of each other's ideas.

VSA is committed to driving change, changing perceptions and practice classroom by classroom, community by community, until ultimately all of society has been transformed.

And I like these quotes from an earlier version of the Web site:

For hundreds of years, people with disabilities have fought negative images and stereotypes, and have often been denied equal opportunity within communities worldwide. Now, through the arts, we are breaking new ground. For people with disabilities, the arts represent a world of resources and opportunities, providing an outlet for creative expression and unlimited possibilities for personal, academic, and professional success. And, because art is an infinite and unconditional field, people with disabilities are free to express themselves without physical, social, or attitudinal barriers.

Marcel Proust wrote: "Only through art can we emerge from ourselves and know what another person sees." When we see art as the universal language that has the ability to unite all people, we understand the importance it has in the lives of people with disabilities. For a person who cannot speak, a dance performance may clearly communicate even the most complicated message. For a person with a mental disability who cannot communicate effectively through words, a painting rich with color and life may say more than verbal sentences ever could. And, for a person who has limited mobility, a song sung with emotion and spirit may elicit movement toward a state of clarity and joy. By engaging in the arts, people with disabilities are able to greatly contribute to our workplaces and communities, help extinguish old stereotypes regarding disability, and create a global culture truly representative of all people.

As VSA so eloquently states, the arts open fundamentally important and essential avenues of expression and communication for all people, including those with differing abilities. Many classrooms are inclusive classrooms, meaning that children with various abilities and disabilities can be found in a typical classroom. Through the arts, you may be more able to reach a student with special needs in a way you can't through traditional methods. You might also be able to include children with differing abilities and needs in class projects and plays, as the arts often identify strengths in individual children.

Kaleidoscope Theater is a company based in Providence, Rhode Island, that, since its inception in 1977, has integrated themes of inclusion in its plays. The theater has also included performers with differing abilities in its productions. When the movement toward mainstreaming special needs children in classrooms became the norm in the late 1970s, David Payton, director of the company, was asked to create a performance that would help children better understand the kids coming into classrooms with special needs. He created (wrote the script, and directed) a play titled, "I'm Special, You're Special." This play deals with a family with several children, one of whom has Down syndrome and who was about to be mainstreamed into the local school attended by his siblings. It is a wonderful and poignant play, and was accompanied by follow-up topics for discussion led by the actors and the teachers.

In the play, a young actor portrayed the main character with Down syndrome. As part of its work in schools, Kaleidoscope Theater asked for feedback from teachers on the effectiveness of the performances and guided discussions. Teachers, in their feedback to the company, suggested that theater members put into action what they preached and integrate actors with special needs into the performances. David Payton took the suggestion to heart and sought immediately to integrate actors with special needs into the performances. He connected with a young man with Down syndrome who took to the part immediately and acted in the play for the next twenty-five years! One day, early on, when the company was in a van traveling to a performance, the young actors were all talking about plays they would like to act in. The kids were saying, "I'd like to be a king," "I'd like to be a princess," and so on. The young actor with Down syndrome asked, "Who can I be?" It was the light bulb moment when David then realized that this young actor needn't be type-cast and could be in many other plays. It was then that Payton opened up the company to many children and young adults with special needs and integrated them into many plays and in many roles.

In a version of *Snow White and the Seven Dwarfs*, all the dwarfs wear sunglasses. One of the actors playing a dwarf is legally blind. The lights on stage hurt her eyes. In consultation with this young woman and her mom, it was clear that if the actor wore sunglasses the lights wouldn't be a bother. David then had all the dwarfs wear sunglasses. How brilliant! They have done this production several times, and no one has ever inquired, "Why are the dwarfs wearing sunglasses?!" In many of Kaleidoscope's productions, individuals with differing abilities are featured. Sometimes it is obvious to the audience and sometimes quite hidden and seamless. People who become involved with the theater company know what they are getting into and love it. It is a wonderful model for theater and community involvement.

Children with differing abilities in class might surprise you in unexpected ways. A child with a hearing impairment might *love* music and choose to take instrumental lessons. A child with a visual disability (like our dwarf above) might perform in your class play. Let children direct how they will participate and leave the options open to them. Some teachers have encouraged their students to create puppet plays about individuals with disabilities. Puppetry can be very effective in providing an opening to understanding ability and disability.

Identified gifted and talented children are to be found in many classrooms. Unidentified gifted and talented children will be in your room as well. Keep an eye open to the talents and gifts of your students and how they might benefit from drawing on these talents and gifts. This could mean that you have a creative storyteller who can lead a group of children on a science adventure, or a virtuoso pianist who can create a piece about a period of history. You can then bring in the theater and music standards and have a mini lesson on performance and creative activity. A talented artist might provide you the opportunity to address the visual arts standards and discuss aesthetics.

ARTS AND TECHNOLOGY

Technology has tremendously increased the potential of arts not only for professional artists, but for art adventurers—those who thrive on creating arts—and especially for students, using photography, computers, video cameras, tape recorders, multimedia, and so on in the classroom as a way to explore and communicate ideas. Classrooms are usually equipped with some forms of technology that can be put to use in creative ways. A tool as simple as the overhead projector can transform an ordinary spelling lesson into a creative shadow puppetry production. A pinhole camera (camera obscura) can offer a magical study of optics and the history of scientific drawing. The use of a tape recorder can add life to a dramatic performance on the subject of oceanography by adding sounds of the ocean or the slide projector or PowerPoint™ presentation can add a visual backdrop to a rap song on the subject of mathematics.

In considering what is available for computers in classrooms, visual arts packages are now quite common. Computer programs and music-writing programs are prevalent as well. The arts and music programs enable individuals to play with colors and sounds and create pieces. CD-ROMs and Web sites focusing on the works of artists, musicians, poets, sculptors, dancers, and writers are numerous, and are not only fascinating, but can be used in the classroom to teach *about* particular artists. Many arts museums post educational activities and have developed extensive curriculum materials for classrooms.

Historical Perspective

It should be mentioned that technology is not a twentieth-century phenomenon! Technology has been a tool for curious individuals and artists for centuries—well before the harnessing of electricity. For example, the phenomenon associated with the camera obscura—that when light passes through a small hole into a dark, enclosed interior, an inverted image will appear on the wall opposite the hole—can be traced back at least two thousand years to thinkers as remote from each other as Euclid, Alhazen, Roger Bacon, Leonardo DaVinci, and Kepler (Crary, 1990). Many fascinating inventions of the 1800s, such as the kaleidoscope, thaumatrope (wonder-turner), phenakistiscope (deceptive view), and zootrope, enabled images to be seen either in symmetry (as in the kaleidoscope) or in motion (early animation).[1] The study of technology in and of itself presents a wonderful view into the history (and role) of observation as aesthetic or scientific inquiry. This might be a terrific start to a scientific unit on invention.

Opening New Venues for Artists and Students

A fascinating role of technology, which we will briefly examine here, is its role in opening new venues for artists to conceptualize and enact works of art and how that parallels processes related to student learning. Technological tools broaden what is available to artists in terms of the process of working as well as the potential for presenting works. "The ongoing quest for new sounds and new ways to organize them has demanded resources that reach beyond the limits of acoustic instruments and voices," according to Elliott Schwartz and Daniel Godfrey (1993). They continue: "more than any other development since the turn of the century, electronics have expanded the techniques and materials available to composers, revolutionizing their approach to basic factors such as pitch logic, time, texture, and sound color."

Technology has provided artists with new tools and strategies for improvising and creating. Much like the traditional paintbrushes, oils, pastels, pencils, inks, or watercolors for visual artists; the piano, guitar, panpipe, and harmonica for composers; or the clay, rock, paper, or twigs for sculptors, technology has provided yet another medium for artists. Interestingly, it provides not only a new medium, but it can provide freedom as well to explore new realms of an established art form. Technology provides expanded ways to think about and work with ideas. It can be important to students' learning in that in its myriad forms, technology can offer new and expanded tools and strategies to students as they contemplate ideas and knowledge through the arts.

According to Vicki Sharp (1999), arts software such as paint programs can offer significant advantages over traditional techniques. "If the artist makes a mistake, she or he

---

[1] For more information on the early observation instruments, I would recommend Jonathan Crary's book *Techniques of the Observer* (1990). Cambridge, MA: MIT Press.

can easily correct it because there are no real paints or watercolors to spill, drip, or smear. The painter simply clicks on the mouse and instantaneously changes the picture or color, enlarges an image, or moves an object" (p. 225). With such programs, Sharp writes, students can draw shapes (including geometric shapes), create designs, and construct miniature cities. The potential for integration becomes limited only by one's imagination.

I think Sharp has an important point to make here, although I believe it speaks more to the limitations of a classroom than the limitations of the artistic process or the imagination. Many classrooms are not "wet" rooms. Therefore, the challenge of painting can be difficult at best. The computer, with its "mess-free" format, can open up avenues for explorations that a typical classroom might limit. In this sense, the computer can make available arts that might not be available otherwise.

In terms of "mistakes," the computer certainly enables students to change their work and try different images, colors, or lines with a click of the mouse. In other arts, mistakes may be harder to correct, but remain possible. In painting, for example, as soon as the paints dry, one can easily paint over a mistake. But the larger issue here concerns the notion of a mistake in and of itself. Some of the most important discoveries made by individuals stem from mistakes! Artists thrive on what others might call mistakes. The "mistakes" often give birth to wonderful and new ideas. As such, I ordinarily encourage my students to pay attention to their "mistakes" (as do many of my colleagues) as potential sources for imagining newness and what can be.

Technology and Literacy

The use of technology is so integrated at this point with our lives and education we don't even always know we are using it. Even in the realm of writing and poetry, the computer to some has become an essential vehicle in the manipulating of words and in the process of constructing thoughts. The use of the computer helps us "think" in new ways by providing the means to expand techniques of editing, saving, transforming, reviewing, and manipulating. Some would even argue that the definition of *literacy* is changing as a result of the presence of computers and multimedia. The New London Group (1996), an internationally known group of literacy theorists and educators, suggest broadening the definition of *literacy* toward "multiliteracy." They argue that literacy pedagogy

> must now account for the burgeoning variety of text forms associated with information and multimedia technologies. This includes competent control of representational forms that are becoming increasingly significant in the overall communications environment such as visual images. . . . (p. 61)

Multimedia

In my own experience as a performer, I find myself moving into the realm of multimedia. Recently, I performed *Primary Colors,* a multimedia piece involving live and electronic music composed by William Bradbury with images fixed and transformed in conjunction with the music by Deborah Small. The use of multimedia in this piece transforms a study of the primary colors into an engaging and provocative performance with images and sounds—each manipulated and composed using multimedia techniques. *Primary Colors* is loosely based on the book of the same name by Alexander Theroux. Bradbury and Small used the writing of Theroux and others quoted in the book as their inspiration and wound up with a fascinating study of the primary colors in art, history, music, poetry, fiction, myth, religions, and everyday life. Working on this piece was not only wonderful from a performer's viewpoint, but also fascinating and provocative as I began to consider the role of primary colors in ways I never had before.

Composition (with colors and sound) through multimedia has great potential for play or improvisation. As I write about in Chapter 2, play is an essential element of child development and one of the most important structures for learning. The computer is a playground for students and artists alike. Much like musical improvisation, which enables musicians to play with sounds, the computer allows people to play with images and sounds. Furthermore, in the case of games in which characters are invented, the computer can be a vehicle for role-playing or inventing and trying on new characters (Turkle, 1995).

Turning Technology over to Students

In the classroom, computers and other technology have unlimited potential and should not be seen as mere "extensions of or replacements for the textbook, the workbook, and the pen and pencil," according to Evans Clinchy (1997, p. 139). "What they are all too often *not* being used for is to turn students loose on finding answers to their own questions or discovering interesting questions in some fascinating database and then following them up on their own" (pp. 139–140). Except in rare instances, Clinchy continues,

> We are all too often *not* turning the technology over to the students to be used for their purposes. We are, therefore, not putting the new power of these machines and software at the service of students and their process of model building and making sense of the world. Since the students—including female students—are rarely intimidated by the machines and are far less frightened of them than most of their teachers (unless they pick up the fear from their teachers), it is they who have the most motivation and can easily acquire the knowhow to make technology work for them. (p. 140)

Equity and Technology

A word about equity in education with technology: Clearly some schools are better equipped than others when it comes to technology. Some teachers are better trained, some parents are more or less informed, some children have a computer at home, and some do not. One thing is for sure, technology is a part of our lives and our children's future. Access is a key issue. According to "Falling Through the Net: Defining the Digital Divide" in the 1999 report of the National Telecommunications and Information Administration:

> Overall, we have found that the number of Americans connected to the nation's information infrastructure is soaring. Nevertheless, this year's report finds that a digital divide still exists, and, in many cases, is actually *widening* over time. Minorities, low-income

persons, the less educated, and children of single-parent households, particularly when they reside in rural areas or central cities, are among the groups that lack access to information resources. (Irving, 1999)

Even the simplest uses of technology broaden the tools and methods open to our students, while at the same time, these uses begin to bridge the gap between the digital divide. In this sense, the use of technology becomes an ethical and moral issue for our students. Our schools can have a significant role in bridging the divide. I am thinking of the potential of introducing videotaping as a tool for capturing oral history or autobiography; photography (digital or otherwise) to study nature and landscape; and the computer as a tool for publishing. These activities integrate technology and the arts in a meaningful way while banking on the natural tendencies of children to connect their lives to the world. Using technology is another way we can break down the notion that the educational process must take place within the "decontextualized confines of a school building" (Clinchy, p. 141). It can bring students to virtual worlds and places on the Web, or out into the community through video or recording projects.

Students as Tech-Directors

For some students, technology is a natural. Dramatic performances of historical events or staged readings offer an opportunity to students to be the "tech-director." This position creates a terrific responsibility for students who can thrive in this area. You will also have students who know how to illustrate or publish on the computer. These students might serve as guides to other students if you create collaborative projects. By enabling your computer-interested students to participate in arts projects this way, you might be setting the stage for them to shine!

Technology in the Workplace

A final word about the role of technology and its importance in learning about the arts is due here. In the state of California alone, it is estimated that commercial production industries have grown to earn $20 billion a year and produce jobs for an estimated 500,000 Californians (*Artswork,* 1997).

> The demand in California for individuals with arts-related skills and career orientations has been steadily growing. In addition to a pressing need for artists skilled in the use of digital media and computers, there is a strong demand for producers, writers, directors, animators, lighting and sound specialists, cinematographers, and costume designers, among many arts-related career catergories. (*Artswork,* 1997, p. 13)

Thus, the role of arts and technology is ever-increasing in its importance to industry. Students trained in this area will no doubt have many career options available to them, whether these jobs be in the entertainment industry or industry in general. For our purposes in this book, however, we will remain focused on the role of the technology in aiding the teaching and learning process.

At the end of each chapter I will highlight ways in which technology might be integrated into learning with, through, and about the arts.

WHAT ARTS BRING TO EDUCATION

The arts, as languages and expressions of cultures and peoples throughout the world, provide many concrete opportunities to educators who are dedicated to an equitable education. According to Leonard Davidman and Patricia T. Davidman (1994) (who draw heavily on the conceptions and work of James Banks, Carl Grant and Christine Sleeter, H. Prentice Baptiste Jr., and Mira Baptiste to articulate their goals), *multicultural education* is understood as a multifaceted, change-oriented process that can be outlined in six interrelated yet distinct goals: (1) providing educational equity; (2) empowering students and their caretakers; (3) valuing cultural pluralism in society; (4) promoting intercultural/interethnic/intergroup understanding and harmony in the classroom, school, and community; (5) developing an expanded multicultural/multiethnic knowledge base for students, teachers, administrators, and support staff; and (6) supporting students, teachers, staff, and administrators who think, plan, and work with a multicultural perspective.

   I have created eight principles of the role of arts in an equitable education by combining goals and strategies presented by Davidman and Davidman and incorporating notions of process as described by Nieto. These eight principles follow.

- The arts expand expressive outlets and provide a range of learning styles available to all children.
- The arts enable freedom of expression for second language learners.
- The arts open venues for inclusive education and reaching out to exceptional learners.
- The arts provide a stage for building self-esteem.
- The arts encourage collaboration and intergroup harmony.
- The arts empower students and teachers.
- The arts deepen teachers' awareness of children's abilities and provide alternative methods of assessment.
- The arts provide authentic cultural voices and add complexity to teaching and learning.

1. The Arts Expand Expressive Outlets and Provide a Range of Learning Styles Available to Children.   Integrating the arts as a forum for expression gives students whose learning styles tend toward the visual, kinesthetic, spatial, or auditory more freedom to communicate their understandings. Thus, when a teacher encourages students to work with ideas through the arts, she more fully taps into their varied learning styles and her practice incorporates student-specific pedagogy.

2. The Arts Enable Freedom of Expression for Second Language Learners.   In considering the arts as languages of expression, teachers offer bilingual and limited English students more freedom to work with ideas and express their understandings without having to depend solely on the English language. For example, the first grader who cannot yet describe in words the motions of the sun and the earth, but who can demonstrate his understanding in drawing or movement, is given an opportunity to participate in learning rather than be hampered by the limitations of a specific language.

3. The Arts Open Venues for Inclusive Education and Reaching Out to Exceptional Learners. The arts enable children with differing abilities to participate in learning. The arts provide important outlets for students in communicating and expressing their understandings of content matter and their own reflections concerning their learning. The arts provide an alternative outlet for those children unable to communicate through traditional methods of speaking or writing. The arts can give children with differing abilities the opportunity to be on the same playing field as other students in the classroom.

4. The Arts Provide a Stage for Building Self-Esteem. Over and over again, teachers who integrate the arts in learning remark on the positive effect the activities have on self-esteem. Learning becomes more enjoyable, even magical, as students share their works and ideas. Increased use of the arts can raise the self-esteem of struggling students, thereby making them more successful. Teachers also remark on their students' achievements.

5. The Arts Encourage Collaboration and Intergroup Harmony. Working together on art projects can lead to a marked increase in productive teamwork. According to Betsey Mendenhall, a fifth-grade teacher in southern California, "the cooperation that comes out of learning through the arts is great." Often, the arts enable shy students to come out of their shell. They also offer children with differing abilities another venue to not only work with ideas but cooperate with others in the class. The arts allow for greater educational equity, as more students have opportunities to work with and share knowledge. The arts offer opportunites for individuals to work cooperatively with each other, thereby furthering intercultural, interethnic, and intergroup understanding and harmony.

6. The Arts Empower Students and Teachers. The arts are empowering. When sharing art projects with each other, students gain a sense of themselves and their peers as unique individuals with interesting ideas and skills. They also begin to respect and admire others' efforts as they communicate imaginative and original work through the arts. Such experiences potentially enable students to gain confidence as self-directed learners supported in taking responsibility for their own educational growth. The discipline and dedication required in creating artworks provides students with skills for working independently and interdependently to accomplish tasks as well as tackle complex ideas.

7. The Arts Deepen Teachers' Awareness of Children's Abilities and Provide Alternative Methods of Assessment. When observing students engaged in art work, teachers gain a fuller picture of the whole child. For example, the child who often acts as the class bully might surprise the teacher by writing a sensitive love poem to his mother. The child whom the teacher thinks is distracted might draw a picture in science showing that in fact she is completely tuned into the curriculum. In these examples, not only does the teacher see the children in multiple ways but she also has a broader source of information to assess her students' understandings.

8. *The Arts Provide Authentic Cultural Voices and Add Complexity to Teaching and Learning.* The arts broaden the tools available to students as they study and seek to understand cultures different from their own. Using the artwork of a culture as a core element of a curriculum introduces students to the voices, images, feelings, and ideas of a people in a way that lends authenticity. It broadens a study while at the same time introducing students to a wider range of experiences documented by individuals through means other than "objective" reporting. Because the arts lend themselves to self-expression, by including the arts in, say, the history curriculum, they bring life to people and events studied; it offers dramatic documentation of the struggles, achievements, celebrations, and complexities of living together in our diverse global community.

METHODOLOGY FOR LEARNING

Artists see things in new and often complex ways. When an artist creates, she or he is working with an idea or knowledge base. The work of an artist involves translating an idea into a form such as painting, music, dance, and so on. In education, a test of learning is the ability to translate a notion, concept, or idea from something given to something owned and utilized. For example, in having students read a chapter in a social studies book, the true test of understanding is not their ability to retell the chapter on an essay test. The test of understanding lies in the student's ability to make that information his own—to work with it, to transform it, to be able to apply it.

The work of an artist gives us further insight into teaching and learning. This work involves deep concentration, an exercise of the imagination, and often problem solving. Some artists actually articulate aspects of their work in relation to a methodology for teaching and learning. Arnold Schoenberg, a twentieth-century classical composer, writes in the introduction to his book *Theory of Harmony* (1978), "This book I have learned from my students. In my teaching I never sought merely 'to tell the pupil what I know.'" Schoenberg's chief aim was to engage the students in a search—a search he equated with that of music itself. "I hope my pupils will commit themselves to searching!" he writes. "Because they will know that one searches for the sake of searching. That finding, which is indeed the goal, can easily put an end to striving" (p. 1). Pablo Picasso, on the other hand, in an interview on the activity of painting, exclaims, "Do not seek—find!" He declares that "to search means nothing in painting. To find is the thing" (qtd. in Goldwater & Treves, 1972, p. 416).

Both make important points as we relate their ideas to the classroom. The core activity of working with or through the arts, either as a creator or as a participant/observer, puts one on a path of engagement. Whether the path leads toward a discovery or whether the search is valuable in and of itself is debatable. For our purposes, we can reconcile the seemingly conflicting opinions of Schoenberg and Picasso by recognizing that both men turn to the arts as a spring of awareness and an opportunity for action.

In the next section, I will outline the three ways in which I believe the arts can be used as an effective methodology for learning in an integrated curriculum. (1) A student may learn *with* the arts; that is, explore subject matter with the aid of an artwork. (2) A student may explore subject matter *through* the arts by creating works of art that express his or her reflections concerning specific subject matter. (3) A student may learn *about* the arts as a subject in and of itself.

Learning *with* the Arts

Learning *with* the arts occurs when they are introduced as a way to study about a particular subject. The Spanish Civilization class at my university learned about Ladino culture *with* the arts. By using the songs and poetry of the Spanish Jews as a basis for class sessions, the students were able to learn about this group of people and their experiences.

Learning *with* the arts may involve various artistic forms. In studying mathematical sets a teacher may introduce her students to the paintings of Georges Seurat, a French impressionist who created paintings with lots and lots of points. To introduce parallel lines she may introduce her students to paintings by Mondrian, an artist who used parallel lines in many of his works. A science teacher may introduce her students to different drums when they are studying sound waves and vibrations. In each case, the students learn *with* the aid of an art form that informs the subject area.

Learning *with* the arts might be an effective method to teach a unit on the civil rights movement to a middle school social studies class. The traditional school textbook describes certain key events and dates that put the civil rights movement in a historical context. Most likely, the text includes speeches by Martin Luther King, Jr. and Robert F. Kennedy. The teacher may use the text, but in addition, she may introduce children to the songs of the civil rights movement. In the school library she finds the book *Sing for Freedom: The Civil Rights Movement Through Songs* (Carawan & Carawan, 1990), which is perfect for the study; the school library also has recordings of many of the songs included in the book. The teacher plays a number of the songs in class, and the students examine the words and listen to the melodies. The songs provide a text in and of itself, bringing yet another perspective to the civil rights movement. Children are introduced to the voices (literally) of the era in a way that is not only informative but engaging. They are learning *with* art—in this case, the songs of the civil rights movement.

Learning *through* the Arts

Learning *through* the arts is a method that encourages students to grapple with and express their understandings of subject matter through an art form. Let's return to our middle school social studies class for an example. The students have now read about the civil rights movement in their textbook and listened to many songs from that time. There has been a certain amount of class discussion, but the teacher is not sure the students have a grasp on the events and importance of the movement. She devises a way—through the arts—for her students to work with the knowledge. She invents a number of characters who could have been living at that time, each with a different perspective, and asks her students to form small groups and create a mini-drama depicting the meeting of the characters. Now the students not only have a way to work with the material, but they have a form through which to express their understandings. They are learning *through* the arts and expressing their understandings in a vibrant, creative form.

Learning *through* the arts can be used at any grade level—and probably should be. There are many examples throughout this book, from as simple as having children act out the lifecycle of a flower or butterfly to more complicated exercises such as understanding DNA through recreating it in dance/movement. At the college level, I have found many ways to teach concepts of arts integration through the arts. I have also taught educational philosophy through engaging students in creating scripts whereby writers and thinkers from different time periods meet each other. Here is one such example: After asking my students to read and study parts of Piaget's *The Child's Conception of the World* and Plato's telling of Socrates' *Meno,* I had them write a mini-drama in which Piaget and Socrates meet each other. Piaget believes that knowledge is constructed through experience. Socrates, on the other hand, believes that all knowledge is innate, that we are born with knowledge from our past lives already in our bodies and a good teacher can pull the information from us by asking clever questions. With a few guidelines, students are off creating their dramas. The following script came out of one of my classes.

SETTING: Boston Common, 1990s

CHARACTERS: Socrates and Piaget

PLOT: Socrates and Piaget happen to meet on Boston Common by the swan boats—big boats that look like swans powered by a person in the back who pedals (much like the pedaling on a bicycle) as it moves across the pond. One cannot see the person's legs as s/he powers the boat. Anyone and everyone who has grown up in Boston has ridden the swan boats; they are quite a tourist attraction as well.

SOCRATES: Is it possible that you are Piaget?!

PIAGET: Well, yes—and who are you?

SOCRATES: Well, who do you think I am?

PIAGET: I have heard of you, Socrates, but I have never experienced any of your theories of knowledge.

SOCRATES: You see that boy over there? See him sitting under that tree? What do you think he's thinking?

PIAGET: Well, let's ask him. We'll ask him questions; I know how you and I feel about questioning people, and I myself truly find asking questions exhilarating.

(The two men walk to the boy's side, sitting with him under the tree.)

PIAGET: Excuse me, young man, can you tell me of what you are thinking?

BOY: Well, nothin' really.

SOCRATES: As you sit here, what is it that you are doing?

BOY: I'm watching the swan boats.

PIAGET: How do those things work, do you think?

BOY: I don't know, with the wind I guess.

PIAGET: Oh, so you think the wind makes the swan boats move?

BOY: Yup.

SOCRATES: So, boy, when there's no wind the swan boat doesn't move?

BOY: Oh no, they still move.

SOCRATES: But what makes them move if there is no wind?

BOY: I think that person in the boat?

SOCRATES: And what does that person do?

BOY: Maybe he moves something in the boat and that makes it go?

SOCRATES: What could that something be?

PIAGET: Socrates, he doesn't know!

SOCRATES: Yes, I know he knows; I must ask more questions.

SOCRATES: Son, have you ever been on a bicycle?

BOY: Oh! I get it. The boat moves when the person in the back pedals like I do on my bike.

SOCRATES: Yes, that's exactly right! I was sure you knew how it worked.

SOCRATES: See, Piaget, this young man *did know* how the boat moved. He knew it all along.

PIAGET: Well, Socrates, I truly believe this young man still believes in his first conviction. He was obviously influenced by your mentioning the bicycle and was led by your idea.

SOCRATES: I really feel that this young fellow is aware of his knowledge now that I have asked him these questions.

BOY: Yeah, I know how that boat moves. I always knew the wind made birds move.

After hearing what usually prove to be delightful and insightful mini-dramas, such as this one, I have a sense my students are not only reading the material but are working with it and devising creative metaphors to express their understandings. In this particular case, the students are groping with the nature of knowledge and comparing the notion of knowledge as innate (from souls past)—as Socrates describes in the dialogue of the *Meno*—and constructivism—as Piaget describes in *The Child's Conception of the World,* which we were also examining in class.

It is interesting that in addition to applying their understandings, these students took a stand as to which theory they felt was more convincing. They cleverly took the position of Piaget (constructivism) and showed that even though a child might answer something in the way the questioner would like to hear, it is not necessarily what he or she truly believes. This is evident in the final line of the drama, "Yeah, I know how that boat moves. I always knew the wind made birds move." Another clever twist of dialogue is evident in line three. Rather than answering Piaget's question, Socrates asks a question instead. Here, it is clear that my students were demonstrating their understanding of Socratic questioning.

Learning *through* the arts can take on many forms in addition to drama. The students writing poetry for the science lesson in the beginning of this chapter were learning about ecology through the arts. Another science class might draw from nature as a way to examine and construct an understanding of the phenomenal details of a seashell. Second language learners might write poetry. Second graders might create a dance to express their understanding of the metamorphosis of pupae to butterflies. In all these cases, learners are actively engaged in imaginative and creative thinking as they learn through the arts and construct meaning.

Learning about the Arts

Throughout the ensuing chapters I will show how learning *with* and learning *through* the arts can lead to a desire to learn *about* the arts. For example, in Chapter 4 I discuss how second language learners become engaged in working with words and language *through* writing poetry. By learning literacy skills through writing their own poetry, children (in a fourth-grade classroom) became interested in poetry itself. After writing poetry almost all students began taking poetry books from the library on their weekly trips to choose reading material. The exercise of learning language skills through the arts led to a genuine interest in reading and interpreting poetry. Because the students were engaged in writing poetry, they had an experiential basis with which to approach poetry as an art form. They became poets, or acted as poets as a way to learn. So their interest in writing poetry evolved into something larger. They began reading and appreciating others' poetry, and sharing what they had read with their friends. As poets themselves, they also developed insights in critiquing poetry. On their own they were engaged in learning *about* poetry!

The same argument may be made for any of the art forms that are employed for the teaching and learning of subject matter. Learning *with* the arts may also lead to learning *about* the arts. After reviewing paintings to study parallel lines and sets, students often are more drawn into (no pun intended) the realm of painting, relating their knowledge of lines to Frida Kahlo, Georgia O'Keeffe, or Andy Warhol. Perhaps they might even be inspired to create their own paintings, having understood something about lines from their mathematical/art study. There is no doubt that learning *with* and *through* the arts can provide a foundation for studying *about* the arts. It can also provide an incentive for students in creating their own artworks.

SUMMARY

The arts serve as a methodology or strategy for learning—expanding traditional teaching methods into a fascinating and imaginative forum for exploration of subject matter. Using the arts as a teaching tool in the classroom broadens their function from the more traditional model of teaching *about* the arts and provides opportunities for students to transform understanding and apply their ideas in a creative form. Using art forms for working with ideas fulfills many of the goals for achieving a multicultural education and provides avenues toward its strategies. As a language of expression, art gives rise to many voices in the classroom and opens many paths for all students to work with knowledge.

The three ways in which the arts can be effectively used in the classroom are: learning *with*, learning *through*, and learning *about* the arts. In utilizing all three ways, teachers expand the role of the arts in classroom experience. However, this does not necessitate special artistic expertise on the part of the teacher. Rather, the teacher is presenting a method that broadens the acceptable modes of expression in the classroom while offering her students opportunities to engage in reflective, creative, and critical thinking.

QUESTIONS TO PONDER

1. In what ways have the arts been important in your own education?

2. In what ways are the arts important in your life? Do you think that the arts shape your thinking in any way?

3. Can you recall any instances when an experience with the arts caused you to consider something in a new way? What was the art form and experience, and how did it cause you to consider something in a new way?

4. Can you recall a specific instance or instances when you learned something in school with or through the arts? Briefly retell the experience(s).

5. What experiences have you had with arts and technology?

6. What are your state's standards for arts education? Go online and find out!

 EXPLORATIONS TO TRY

1. With a partner, listen to three songs by different groups. The groups can be as different as Black Eyed Peas, Justin Timberlake, Aretha Franklin, Dave Mathews, Nora Jones, the Beatles, Sting, and so on. What does each song tell you about life? About the songwriter? About culture? About history or an event? About yourself?

2. Write a short essay expressing your philosophy of education. What are the roles of the teacher and learner in education? What is important in education? Facts? Knowledge? Searching? Finding? After you have completed your philosophy, discuss it with a partner. How does your partner's philosophy differ from yours? In what ways are your philosophies similar?

3. Think about knowledge. How would you define it? Write a poem, draw a picture, or create a sculpture, dance, rap, or piece of music that describes your thinking about knowledge. To get started, see if you can find any artworks that deal with the same subject matter. For example, the musical group Tower of Power has recorded a song titled "A Little Knowledge Is a Dangerous Thing."

4. Log onto the Internet! Search for sites related to arts and special education. Make note of sites that can be resources to you as you begin to create lesson plans that integrate the arts.

REFERENCES

Artswork. (1997). *A report of the Superintendent's Task Force on the Visual and Performing Arts.* Sacramento: California Department of Education.

Asmal, K., Chidester, D., & Wilmot, J. (Eds.). (2003). *Nelson Mandela in his own words.* New York: Little Brown and Company.

Carawan, G., & Carawan, C. (Eds.). (1990). *Sing for freedom: The story of the civil rights movement through its songs.* Bethlehem, PA: A Sing Out Publication.

Clinchy, E. (1997). The new technologies and the continuing questions. In E. Clinchy (Ed.), *Transforming public education.* New York: Teachers College Press.

Crary, J. (1990). *Techniques of the observer.* Cambridge, MA: MIT Press.

Danto, A. (1981). *The transformation of the commonplace: A philosophy of art.* Cambridge, MA: Harvard University Press.

Davidman, L., & Davidman, P. (1994). *Teaching with a multicultural perspective.* New York: Longman.

Duckworth, E. (2006). *The having of wonderful ideas and other essays on teaching and learning* (2nd ed.). New York: Teachers College Press.

Ellis, C. J. (1985). *Aboriginal music: Education for living.* Queensland, Australia: University of Queensland Press.

Gallas, K. (1994). *The languages of learning: How children talk, write, dance, draw, and sing their understanding of the world.* New York: Teachers College Press.

Goldberg, M. (2004). *Teaching English language learners through the arts: A SUAVE experience.* New York: Allyn & Bacon.

Goldberg, M., & Phillips, A. (Eds.). (1992). *Arts as education.* Cambridge, MA: Harvard Educational Review, Reprints Series #24.

Goldwater, R., & Treves, M. (Eds.). (1972). *Artists on art from XIV to XX century.* New York: Pantheon.

Gottlieb, R. (Ed.). (1996). *Reading jazz: A gathering of autobiography, reportage, and criticism from 1919 to now.* New York: Pantheon Books.

Greene, M. (1991). Texts and margins. *Harvard Educational Review, 61*(1).

Hart, M. (1991). *Planet drum.* San Francisco: HarperSanFrancisco.

Hoffmann, J. (1991). Computer-aided collaborative music instruction. *Harvard Educational Review, 61*(3).

Irving, L. (1999). Falling through the Net: Defining the digital divide. Washington DC: National Telecommunications and Information Administration.

Lewitzky, B. (1989). Why art? University of California, San Diego Regent's Lecture, May 31, 1989.

Lippard, L. (1990). *Mixed blessings: New art in a multicultural America.* New York: Pantheon.

The New London Group. (1996). A pedagogy of multiliteracies: Designing social futures *Harvard Educational Review, 66*(1).

Nieto, S. (1996). *Affirming diversity.* New York: Longman.

Ravitch, D., (2010). *The death and life of the great American school system: How testing and choice are undermining education.* New York: Basic Books.

Rich, A. (1993). *What is found there: Notebooks on poetry and politics.* New York: W. W. Norton.

Schoenberg, A. (1978). *Theory of harmony.* Los Angeles: University of California Press.

Schwartz, E., & Godfrey, D. (1993). *Music since 1945: Issues, materials, and literature.* New York: Schirmer Press.

Sharp, V. (1999). *Computer education for teachers* (3rd ed.). Boston: McGraw-Hill College.

Turkle, S. (1995). Constructions and reconstructions of the self in virtual reality. *Electronic Culture, Technology and Visual Representation,* Aperture, 354–365.

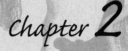

Chapter 2

What Does It Mean
to Be a Learner?

Open to new ideas, eager for
Knowledge, yearning for experience,
A learner.

Excited by change, looking for
New beginnings,
A learner.

Fulfilled by diversity,
Immersed in expression,
A learner.

Constantly seeking,
Forever evolving,
A learner.

Olivia Friddell, student teacher

"If I had influence with the good fairy who is supposed to preside over the christening of all children," writes Rachel Carson (1965/1998), "I should ask that her gift to each child in the world be a sense of wonder so indestructible that it would last throughout life." Children are natural wonderers. "Their worlds are filled with newness and as teachers we are in the unique position of keeping that wonder central to children's lives" (Goldberg, 2004, p. 6). Learning and developing children's intellect is central to what schools should be doing.

When I give talks I like to start with a top ten list of my education-related wishes for children. At the top of my list is Rachel Carson's "wonder." Here is my list.

1. *Wonder:* Educating children to wonder is a gift, one that can be cultivated through engagement with the arts, which, at their core, set the stage for wondering.

2. *Desire:* There is nothing like desire to get us motivated to do anything, including learning. How do we create a sense of desire to learn and to care about learning? I believe an arts-rich curriculum empowers children to begin to care about their learning, to invest in thinking, and to desire to learn more.

3. *Passion:* All of us have passions, including children! Creating spaces in school to unleash children's passions or to encourage new passions makes for wonderful learning experiences. Arts are often a direct line to feeling passionate! Whether or not one becomes an artist, participating in the arts opens students to the notion of embracing passion.

4. *Risk Taking:* Taking risks is at the core of what artists do on a daily basis. Taking risks teaches children to think outside their boxes and encourages innovative, inventive, and creative thinking. Isn't that what we hope children will learn in their education in addition to specific content knowledge?

5. *Confidence:* Children do not come to us automatically feeling confident. At least in my experience, confidence is something that is practiced. The arts by their nature necessitate the practice of skills, techniques, and use of the creative mind. This practice often leads a child to a place of self-confidence. In classrooms where there are high numbers of English language learners, becoming confident in use of language can be supported through arts-based methods.

6. *Complexity:* Artists rarely see things as "either/or." This view of the world enables artists to cross boundaries, try new things, and to imagine other ways of being or acting. This outlook is essential to an educated individual.

7. *Engagement:* Engagement is key to participation in democracy. School is the place that can set the stage for children to learn the skills of democracy. Arts and sports are two key areas of the curriculum that, at their core, are about engaged participation.

8. *Practicality:* Education can be meaningless if it doesn't apply to the real world or have applications in real life. Through the arts, children can engage in real-life applications of their ideas and create imaginative inventions to tackle real-life challenges. A great example of this comes to mind of when I had a backstage tour of the penguin exhibit at San Diego's Seaworld. The keepers had a real challenge in identifying the birds, so they created a wonderful bead system whereby the birds wear anklets with an intricate mathematical scheme that identifies each individual bird. Creative and fashionable!

9. *Ownership:* Taking responsibility for learning can lead to ownership of ideas and subject matter. If children feel ownership of their learning they will be engaged in learning. The arts enable students to have that feeling of ownership, especially when putting on a play or showing a finished art piece on a school gallery wall.

10. *Knowing their stuff:* I am concerned that test taking measures very little of children's actual capabilities. Furthermore, emphasis on testing has guided teaching in ways that

severely limit the possibilities of how children learn. Broadening looking at students' learning through arts-based methods (see Chapter 9) provides opportunities for kids to really work with ideas and show their understandings (or lack of understanding) of subject matter.

With my top ten list as the backdrop, this chapter explores the notion of learning itself—and how the arts can be fundamental to learning no matter what the arena or subject matter.

THEORIES OF INTELLECTUAL DEVELOPMENT

Intellectual development has been defined in a number of ways and by various people in educational circles. Eleanor Duckworth (2006) writes, "the having of wonderful ideas is what I consider the essence of intellectual development" (p. 1). She also declares that the having of wonderful ideas is essentially a *creative* affair: "When children are afforded the occasions to be intellectually creative—by being offered matter to be concerned about intellectually and by having their ideas accepted—then not only do they learn about the world, but as a happy side effect their general intellectual ability is stimulated as well" (p. 12).

Howard Gardner (1990) originally described intelligence as an *ability* "to solve problems or to fashion a product, to make something that is valued in at least one culture" (p. 16). It is interesting that Gardner's definition of creativity paralleled his definition of intelligence: "the ability to solve problems or to make something or to pose questions regularly in a domain; those questions are initially novel but are eventually accepted in one or more cultures" (p. 21). In a more recent book reflecting on his theory, *Multiple Intelligences* (2006), Gardener updates his definition of intelligence: "An intelligence entails the ability to solve problems or fashion products that are of consequence in a particular cultural setting or community" (p. 6). Gardner (2006) theorizes that intelligence does not relate to a single property or capability of the mind. Instead, he identifies 8 1/2 kinds of intelligences: linguistic intelligence, musical intelligence, logico-mathematical intelligence, spatial intelligence, bodily-kinesthetic intelligence, intrapersonal intelligence, interpersonal intelligence, naturalist intelligence, and the 1/2: spiritual intelligence. His theory has been useful to educators who have adapted their teaching styles to match the learning styles and intelligences of their students, thereby broadening the educational opportunities available to many children.

Jean Piaget (1963), known for constructivist theory and developmental stages, writes that "intelligence is an *adaptation*. . . . Life is a continuous creation of increasingly complex forms and a progressive balancing of these forms with the environment" (p. 3). He describes intelligence as an ongoing construction of knowledge, the process being one of continual adaptation. In a somewhat parallel discussion, Lev Vygotsky (1971) defines art in a similar manner. He writes, "from a social viewpoint, art is a complex process of balancing the environment" (p. 294). One wonders what kind of conversation Piaget and Vygotsky might have concerning the relationship between intelligence, art, and environment.

What interests me in comparing these three definitions of intellectual development and Vygotsky's definition of art is that each thinker emphasizes intelligence as an activity, a creative affair, or an evolving process. Whereas Duckworth and Gardner stress a resulting idea or product in relation to the activity or ability, Piaget emphasizes an action: adaptation.

I am particularly drawn to Piaget's characterization of intellectual development because he emphasizes an evolving and ever more complex process rather than a static outcome. Thinking of intellectual development as a continually evolving process enables us to consider learning as an ongoing process with a future rather than the acquisition of a knowledge base as a matter of fact—which is so often the case in education. Although intellectual development is often gauged in terms of answers reported on a test or the retelling of a historical event, these devices leave little room for assessing creative and reflective thinking. Piaget also stresses, along with Vygotsky, that the work is an effort toward balancing, and the balancing is related to one's environment.

In utilizing the arts for intellectual development, my goal is to engage students in thoughtful inquiry and reflective questioning. To that end, the art form provides a method that enables each student to represent and translate an idea. While they work through an art form—perhaps in an effort to find balance—I want students to be constantly aware and able to perceive aspects of their world from many perspectives. I want them to accept risks in their thinking and be willing to live with confusion. Finally, I want them to accept what they have learned as incomplete. After all, in both teaching and learning there is always somewhere else to go with one's ideas. Like Piaget, I believe that intellectual development is a nonending, continuous, and lifelong process.

One of the ways I encourage the intellectual development of my students is to create activities involving the arts that demand that they go beyond their everyday boundaries. For example, in a music class I teach, I ask each student to compose and notate a "kitchen piece." The assignment is to create a short sound composition using objects found in the kitchen. The piece must be performed twice, and it must be accompanied by an invented notation. The notation leads us into a discussion of representation. The activity pushes students beyond their ordinary limits to create something out of an extraordinary situation. Performances make use of pots and pans, occasionally a blender, spoons, glasses filled with water, Tupperware drums, garlic presses, whisks, and so on.

In reflecting on this exercise in her final paper for the class, one of my students, Diane Hunter (1995), wrote, "I have not, nor will I ever, complete my kitchen symphony, or my work symphony, or my bedroom symphony, etc. Everything that once created a 'noise' now has a tonal quality about it and is subject to a Hunter audition. . . . I started to pay more attention to the words of songs, to observe people as they move, and to listen to the sounds of life and the changes of tones." What delights me most about this comment is that the world has somehow changed for Diane. She is open to hearing things in a new way; her awareness of her surroundings is now an "audition" and a source of thoughtfulness rather than an accepted and unquestioned decoration. She is clearly engaged in an intellectual pursuit.

As a teacher, I feel great joy when my students leave class eager to keep on thinking and open to seeing objects and ideas in new and different ways. I love thinking that my students will continue pursuits started in class, that they perceive the class as opening up a world rather than putting the finishing touches on it. Being open to curiosity and further contemplation is fundamental to learning. A teacher can play an important role in provoking her students intellectually by continually providing occasions that engage and encourage students to be adventurers in learning. Students need not agree with the ways in which teachers pursue any given question; rather, they will critically consider what is offered to them, reflect on it, and decide for themselves how to proceed. When students accept challenges instead of answers, teachers have accomplished something important. Intellectual development, seen in this light, is not the acquisition of answers but a motivation to learn.

Unfortunately, I believe that many of us—as well as our students—have not been encouraged to think creatively or of ourselves as "creative." Instead, our intellectual development has been relegated to finding and remembering answers. Julie Horton (1995), another student, writes, "Throughout my years of schooling, I do not feel that I was challenged to think creatively. As a student, I was seldom asked about my own opinions and ideas. I think this is a sad commentary on the schools I attended. However, I know that teaching strategies can and must be changed."

Julie goes on to propose creating an inviting and secure environment where children feel they can take risks, create, and learn. Another component to this change requires placing children in positions where they can work with ideas rather than accept them. Here the arts lend us a method to do so, and an expanded form of communication to express such learning. In the following section, I will explore the ways in which the arts, through encouraging representational and reflective thinking, provide many opportunities for intellectual growth and development.

THE ROLE OF "TRANSLATION THROUGH REPRESENTATION" IN LEARNING

For some time now I have been documenting the ways in which students translate and represent subject matter content through the arts. This is more than a fascinating journey into how individuals create meaning and work with knowledge; I believe that examining the ways in which children and adults represent emerging understandings can suggest ways in which to approach education and teaching.

When a student listens to a lecture and then writes a paper or takes a test, the instructor has little information that tells her if the student understands the material—although she does know that the student can retell the story of the lecture. If the student actually does connect to the material because she or he has a basis to integrate it into her or his schemas, the student might, in fact, understand and relate to the lecture—it might even be seminal in furthering the student's thinking. In this case, the instructor has had some success.

I would argue, however, that there are relatively few times in learning when lecturing or "telling" is successful. Vito Perrone (1989) points out throughout his book, *A Letter to Teachers*, that learning is a personal matter and varies for different children, proceeds best when children are actively engaged in their own learning, and is enhanced by a supportive atmosphere. John Dewey (1959) wrote of "learning by doing." Jerome Bruner (1962) wrote of "discovery learning." Many educators have argued (and continue to argue) that students relate to information more substantially if they are enabled to work with the material and construct their own understandings (Bissex, 1980; Duckworth, 2006; Hawkins, 1978; Kamii, 1984, 1989; Piaget, 1980; Schickedanz, 1990; Watson & Konicek, 1990).

When students translate into artistic expression their emerging understanding of a particular subject, they are actively engaged in their own learning. The act of translating requires students to work with ideas as opposed to absorbing them. Often the act of translation leads to the creation of metaphor. The role of metaphors in learning has been seen as fundamental to intellectual development (Belenky et al., 1986; Berthoff, 1981; Bowden, 1993; Gallas, 1991, 1994; Goldberg, 1992; Lakoff & Johnson, 1980).

Ann Berthoff (1981) argues that metaphors "encourage us to discover relationships and how they might be articulated." (p. 7). She writes that "metaphors are heuristic in function," meaning that they lead to knowledge creation. Similarly, George Lakoff and Mark Johnson (1980) argue that metaphors form a basis for thought and action and are, in fact, pervasive in constructing "how we get around in the world and how we relate to other people" (p. 3). Metaphors are powerful tools that we all use in conceptualizing our world and our relationships (Bowden, 1993).

Intellectual development requires the ability to translate and represent ideas. Often, this includes the creation of metaphors for understanding. If a student can transform someone else's idea by creating a metaphor, or can integrate his or her own observations of subject matter—nature, for example—by creating a representation in art, then that child is truly engaged in an intellectual journey. This is a far cry from merely mimicking others' knowledge.

Artistic activity naturally encourages representation and the use of metaphors. The artist is steeped in a world of metaphoric representation as she or he begins a process of creating a form that expresses some idea or feeling set to music, put into words (in poetry or literature), or placed in a visual or tactile form. The visual artist translates ideas into visual representations and/or visual metaphors. The musician works with sound to represent ideas, emotions, even events through tones and rhythms. Indeed, the arts provide a natural structure through which students can engage in representational and metaphoric thinking. The arts not only encourage this kind of thinking, they demand it. In addition, artistic activity provides a lens through which students can look at and examine their world as well as express it.

I would argue that artistic activity as representational and metaphoric thinking embodies many of the virtues of emanicipatory education and could therefore hold a unique key to education. To that end, I offer a quote from James Baldwin (in Simonson & Walker, 1988) that addresses the purpose of education: "The purpose of education is to create in a person the ability to look at the world for himself, to make his own decisions, to say to himself this is black or this is white, to decide for himself whether there is a god in heaven or not. To ask such questions of the universe, and then to live with those questions, is the way he achieves his own identity." Baldwin goes on, however: "But no society is really anxious to have that kind of person around. What societies really, ideally want is a citizenry which will simply obey the rules of the society. If a society succeeds in this, that society is about to perish. The obligation of anyone who thinks himself responsible is to examine society and try to change it and fight it—at no matter what risk. This is the only hope society has. This is the only way that societies change" (p. 4).

Baldwin might have also been addressing an aspect of the artist in society. Let me re-phrase his words: "An artist is a person with the ability to look at the world for her- or himself, to make her or his own decisions, to say to her- or himself that this is black or this is white, to ask her- or himself whether there is a god in heaven or not. To ask questions of the universe, and then to live with those questions, is the way the artist achieves her or his own identity." As to when society does not seem terribly eager to have the artist around, we have examples of that as well. Reactions against the work of various artists who have received grants through the National Endowment for the Arts attest to this.

The artist can be an autonomous agent, but usually is closely connected to society and reacts to it in some way—through a representational expression. What the artist does through artistic activity is what emancipatory educators encourage: critical, reflective, and creative thinking in the context of society, coupled with expression. That expression might be an attempt to change society or to simply explore its complexities.

When we think of knowledge, as Baldwin does, we must consider *whose* knowledge we are talking about and *who* decides what that knowledge is. There are many ways to perceive the world and many lenses through which to examine it. Is it the school's job to prepare future workers who subscribe to one point of view, or should the school be preparing students to consider multiple points of view and ways to interact as adults within an economically based society? Participatory democracy—or democratic education, in theory—would prepare students to think for themselves and debate critical issues in a process that bears on a society. Through the arts, students may have more opportunities to practice some of the skills necessary to becoming concerned, reflective thinkers and citizens.

Because artists are so steeped in representational transformation, they often see things in unusual ways; they rarely see things as either/or. The following poem by Mitsuye Yamada is a good example. Yamada was born in Japan and emigrated to the United States with her family. During World War II, she was interned at the Minidoka War Relocation Center in Idaho. This poem is from her book, *Camp Notes and Other Poems* (1976).

> MIRROR MIRROR
>
> People keep asking where I come from
> says my son.
> Trouble is   I'm american on the inside
>   and oriental on the outside
> No Kai
> Turn that outside in
> THIS is what American looks like.[1]

Here, Yamada implores the reader to examine what it means to be an "American." She surprises us with the lines "Turn that outside in /THIS is what American looks like." She deliberately urges us to consider the relationships of culture as we think about ourselves or others.

---

[1] "Mirror Mirror" by Mitsuye Yamada, in *Camp Notes and Other Poems* by Mitsuye Yamada. Brooklyn, NY: Kitchen Table: Women of Color Press, 1992, p. 56. Reprinted by permission of the author and of Kitchen Table: Women of Color Press, Box 40-4920, Brooklyn, NY 11240.

Whereas the artist expresses ideas through a medium such as poetry, music, dance, sculpture, or photography, traditional education has concerned itself with expression via words. Historically, the notion of art as fundamental to experience and knowledge has been discussed with depth and rigor (Coomaraswamy, 1934/1956; Dewey, 1959; Storr, 1988), although it rarely enters into mainstream educational discussions and practice with equal rigor.

When students create a poem, sculpture, or dance to express their evolving ideas, teachers know at the very least that these students are interacting with the material. They are taking ideas, working with them, and translating or transforming them into another medium. Artistic translation and representation involve active participation, thereby enabling students to develop both intellectually and emotionally as they construct greater understandings of subject matter.

STANDARDS AND ARTS EDUCATION

In earlier editions of this book I barely touched on standards and arts education. However, it is crucial to be aware that national and state standards for arts education not only exist but are in many cases mandated. According to the No Child Left Behind Act, the arts should be regarded as core academic subjects to which all children are entitled in an equitable and comprehensive education. National standards in the arts (which can be accessed on the Web at www.ed.gov/pubs/ArtsStandards.html) revolve around five basic competencies, what students should know and be able to do having completed secondary school.

- *They should be able to communicate at a basic level in the four arts disciplines—* dance, music, theater, and the visual arts. This includes knowledge and skills in the use of the basic vocabularies, materials, tools, techniques, and intellectual methods of each arts discipline.

- *They should be able to communicate proficiently in at least one art form,* including the ability to define and solve artistic problems with insight, reason, and technical proficiency.

- *They should be able to develop and present basic analyses of works of art* from structural, historical, and cultural perspectives, and from combinations of those perspectives. This includes the ability to understand and evaluate work in the various arts disciplines.

- *They should have an informed acquaintance with exemplary works of art from a variety of cultures and historical periods,* and a basic understanding of historical development in the arts disciplines, across the arts as a whole, and within cultures.

- *They should be able to relate various types of arts knowledge and skills within and across the arts disciplines.* This includes mixing and matching competencies and understandings in art-making, history and culture, and analysis in any arts-related project.

As a result of developing these capabilities, students can arrive at their own knowledge, beliefs, and values for making personal and artistic decisions. In other terms, they can arrive at a broad-based, well-grounded understanding of the nature, value, and meaning of the arts as a part of their own humanity.

In addition to the national standards, nearly every state has adopted its own standards for arts education, and arts interest groups such as the Music Educators National Conference (MENC) have also put forward standards, specifically for music education. In the state of California where I live and teach, the standards are in place for each of the four arts areas—music, visual arts, dance, and drama—and revolve around five strands: artistic perception, creative expression, aesthetic valuing, historical and cultural connections, and connections and applications across disciplines. They are clearly written out, grade by grade, with brief examples of ways to introduce the standards. I have found they are easy to follow and a great guide, especially for reluctant classroom teachers. You will probably notice if you begin to look at your state standards that you are already achieving much of what is stated.

WHAT DOES IT MEAN TO BE A LEARNER?

Every fall after about four weeks of working together, I ask my preservice student teachers, "What does it mean to be a learner?" I teach a course in which we explore teaching and learning relationships, how knowledge is constructed, learning through the arts, and the role of metaphors in understanding, among a number of related topics.

Leading up to this question, I ask my students to do several exercises in which they follow other people's understandings of a simple mathematical problem and a poetry exercise. The exercises are based on clinical interviewing techniques discussed by Eleanor Duckworth in *The Having of Wonderful Ideas* (2006), which is based on her own experiences working with Jean Piaget during the 1960s. Inevitably, my students discover that people think about things in ways that are very different from the way they think—an often surprising and moving discovery. This is a revealing lesson no matter what age!

Once students have gotten over the shock of discovering that people figure out problems in a variety of ways (ones different from their own, in particular), we begin to explore the multiple ways in which people can express knowledge. To do so, I ask the students to represent ideas concerning metamorphosis through the arts. Most students have not had the opportunity to create artistic representations, and at first they tend to be hesitant. I usually begin by asking them to describe various metamorphoses and life cycles. To get started, we look at a list of metamorphoses generated by first graders (Gallas, 1991). The list includes egg-baby-grownup-death-dirt; wind-tornado-cyclone-waterspout; egg-tadpole-frog; and egg-caterpillar-cocoon-moth. We also read about how the first-grade students in Gallas's class dramatized their metamorphoses.

After reviewing the first graders' list and dramatizations, I ask my university students to break into small groups and brainstorm their own list of metamorphoses. Ideas bounce into the air with great leaps. "I know," says Sherrie, "the life cycle of a dancer." Laura comes up with the metamorphosis of a salad, from seeds to seedlings, to vegetables, to stores, to homes, to dinner plates, to compost, to dirt, and then the process begins again. Angie asks, "How about the life cycle of a spider? How does that work?" From the other corner I hear Christina ask, "How about the metamorphosis of the women's movement over the last ten years?!"

Soon my students are working in groups to create artistic renditions of their ideas. Later they will present their work to the rest of the class. Sherrie and her group decide to make a mobile of dancers of different ages and the changes they experience. They choose the mobile because of its inherent movement is dancelike. They page through magazines looking for dancers and stumble on pictures of budding flowers. They decide that the buds are a "neat" way to describe the beginning of a dancer's career. One person in the group has the idea of hanging the pictures with different colored ribbon: The colors represent stages in a dancer's life—white signifies purity and newness, the beginning dancer; pink represents the intermediary stage of the dancer's career; and gold represents achievement.

As the activity continues, ideas arise, are discussed, are employed. Students are actively engaged; they are searching for ways to work with their ideas and express them. I sense excitement as a student finds another picture in a magazine. "This is perfect!" Lynn calls out. "We can use it for an older dancer who is now looking back on her life."

From the other side of the room I overhear a conversation about composting. Laura is describing to Julie what she knows about the role of worms in compost heaps. Then Ruthanne asks what the worms actually do. The three launch into a very scientific discussion of composting, all the while coming up with questions they would like to know the answers to, sparking their curiosity to understand more about this increasingly complex metamorphosis. From Angie's group I hear lots of laughter. They have decided to dramatize the spider and realize they don't know where the web comes from and how the spider actually can manage such a feat. "Does it come from the spider's mouth? From somewhere else? How can it actually do that?!"

The classroom is abuzz with excitement and laughter as students create their representations. I often stroll around to see what is going on, only to find that students are so engrossed in what they are doing that my presence remains unnoticed. This is quite different from a more traditional classroom, where the teacher talks or gives instructions and the students figure out how to follow. Being out of the limelight, in fact, took some getting used to in my own case because being at the center of attention can be fun. Letting go of being the center of attention as the teacher is probably one of the most challenging aspects of giving students the freedom to search for knowledge.

If Sherrie, Laura, Ruthanne, or any other student at any grade level were to simply read a chapter about metamorphosis in a school textbook, or were to listen to a lecture and then answer questions on a test, I would be hard-pressed to know if they really understood the material. On the other hand, when they create a mobile or a dramatic rendition representing a metamorphosis, I sense that they have taken the material and translated it into a different context. I can also assess the degree to which they understand the particular concepts or ideas, and then I can proceed from there.

The next week held more surprises. Sue Ann, a student in the "spider group," came to class and said she had had the most incredible experience; she had really observed a spider, and it was unbelievable. She described a web-making event to the entire class from beginning to end (with excitement!). Her appreciation for observing nature was growing and she was invested in learning about spiders. So the conversations continued, the enthusiasm grew, and the students were doing exactly what I had hoped: They were taking learning into their own hands.

The art/metamorphosis exercise gave students the opportunity to translate their ideas into another medium. The artistic activity opened up many avenues through which they could explore and reflect upon the science topic. In addition, the materials themselves—magazines, paper, scissors, glue, markers—provided tools that inspired critical thinking. For example, as the dance group perused the magazines, different pictures would further their thinking or lead it in a new direction. When one of the students found the picture of flower buds, she began to consider the picture as related to her idea. Without the "tools" (in this case, the magazines), she probably would not have thought of the flower bud in relation to a dancer.

Students were also learning about "being a learner," which is the focus of this class. They were able to use their own experiences in learning as a basis for discussions concerning teaching. In fact, class discussions after the exercise focused on the role of the teacher as a facilitator of learning, as well as the role of the learner as an active being working with ideas and reworking them. Students examined their actions in creating representations and debated their usefulness in the classroom, turning to issues of solitude and collaborative learning. Discussions also addressed assessment. In viewing each other's work, each student was beginning to value what others had come to know. In that way, the students began to discuss how as teachers they can assess what a student knows.

Following the metamorphosis work, I ask my students to reflect on being a learner and to create an artistic "representation for understanding." Although I do this with university students, the same can be done with children if the teacher is interested in exploring and reflecting with them on the nature of learning. Now, having introduced the notion that people think and learn in a variety of ways, I ask my students to reflect on their own ways of learning and exploring subject matter.

Students are required to accompany their work with a brief written statement describing their art expression. At this later point in the semester, feeling more confident to apply artistic methods to express their understandings, students willingly agree to the assignment. I present the following examples because they represent a range of the responses and forms that students bring to class. These examples offer only a small slice of the inventiveness and variety found within just one class.

Priscilla came to class with a sculpture: a colorfully painted wooden plank with a broken circle of wires (like the spokes of a wheel), words adhered in different places, and this written accompaniment:

My sculpture represents how I see myself as a learner. I am in the center, as the hub of a partially constructed wheel. The hub is in a state of confusion, continually sorting and processing what the receptors are feeding into it. The hub is also where questions and curiosities are stemming from. Emanating from the hub are feelers that eventually become the spokes of the wheel. The feelers reach out into the world and become receptors for new experiences, information, and knowledge. The world is represented by the painting. The painting is abstract and colorful, implying complexity and intrigue. As knowledge is gained the wheel begins to solidify and take shape. But since there is no end to learning, the wheel is never completely formed. The knowledge transmitted back to the hub sparks new questions, or new feelers that spin out and reach for more. The sculpture evokes movement because learning to me is an active, never ending process.

The following explains the words and phrases chosen:

"Save the world?" "Population's global impact" "Conflict": Represent the very large, difficult issues of our times that through learning we must strive to answer.

"Action/Reaction": In the process of learning, I take action upon or react to new ideas and experiences.

"Balance": As a learner, I seek a balance point where my confusion gives way to comprehension.

"Discover": To learn is to discover new thoughts, ideas, ways of perceiving the world.

"Change is in the wind": Learning is about change. My perceptions change when I learn, and this kind of change is inevitable when true knowledge is attained.

The depth of thought expressed in this work is remarkable. Clearly Priscilla felt engaged, maybe even inspired. Having previously proclaimed herself a "nonartist," Priscilla surprised herself with her sculpture. She also noted how her desire to work and think was nourished by her excitement over her emerging product. I, too, was very impressed with this work. The sculpture appealed to my artistic and aesthetic senses. The theme of the piece and the accompanying explanation delighted me because it was clear that Priscilla was deeply engaged in the issues of our class. Her detailed descriptions indicated her attempt to consider learning from many perspectives (including her own) as a complex and lifelong, evolving process.

Although not all students write so extensively, unique statements and creations emerge in this process—much to the continual amazement of the students and their peers. Working on the same question, Ed came to class with a photo of a young child peering around the corner of an opened door. It was accompanied by his statement (see statement and photo on the next page).

More sparse in words than Priscilla, Ed nonetheless presented a convincing representation of what it means to be a learner. The difference between the two is not so much in the differing form of representation (which in and of itself sparked interesting remarks from the class) but in the level to which each took her or his translation and worked with it. Priscilla articulated more of the complexities of her representation than did Ed. This does not indicate, however, that Ed put less thought into his work. He thought deeply about his representation and felt it captured the very root of what it means to be a learner. He could take his thinking even further by examining the themes of exploration, honesty, tenacity, and curiosity.

In the following example, Alejandra's representation includes an original metaphor.

What is it like to be a learner? To me, *learning is like the wings of a bird or a butterfly* [emphasis added]. It gives you the ability to soar to unfamiliar territories and reach inconceivable heights. Yet even though they can be strong and powerful they are also delicate and fragile. A teacher has the power to infringe on the

"What is it like to be a learner? I like to explore what's behind all the doors in life with the honesty, tenacity, and curiosity of a child."

SOURCE: Ken Heyman.

learner's capability or give them the freedom to explore the world. With love and support, the wings of knowledge can take you far beyond your wildest dreams.

I find Alejandra's metaphor a convincing, imaginative, and reflective representation for learning. She has taken information and ideas from class, reflected upon them, and created an original metaphor through which she expresses her understandings. She has gone a step further in expanding on that metaphor by describing the places to which the flier can go and the strength with which it can maneuver, all in all a provocative representation.

Carrie took another approach. She chose a familiar object and applied reflections concerning learning to it. Taking everyday objects and examining their connections to another subject is a useful tool, especially if students are having difficulty thinking about the problem. In this case one could ask, "How is learning like an apple? a telephone? a piano? a calendar?" and so on. The exercise can pique the creative thinking of any student who is stuck. In the next example, Carrie related learning to waffle making, an analogy she devised on her own.

When asked how I view myself as a learner, I thought of waffles. I saw raw materials, each of the ingredients, as the information I receive. Information or ingredients come from a variety of sources. The mixing bowls represent the blending of information as my mind accepts it. The measuring cups show that I get information in varying amounts. The mixer is used to blend the information together, when necessary. The waffle iron is the brain where the information is processed. The waffle is the outcome of this processing. Sometimes the waffles do not come out complete, which represents the concept that learning is never complete. The green light on the iron says it's ready to do more processing. The red light signals overload. The butter and variety of syrups show the many ways I can modify or change the information. The plain waffle is the basic information. The toppings are the ways of changing the basic information for other uses or needs.

Interesting ideas are embedded in this work, and an outcome-based educator or evaluator might even enjoy the recipe! We had, in fact, discussed outcome-based education in class. When Carrie shared this representation with the class, an interesting discussion followed. "How do you know when you're ready to do more processing?" asked a peer. "Who determines what is basic information?" asked another student. Thus, Carrie's representation prompted a considerable amount of important discussion.

One student-sculptor took a unique approach, caught the attention of the class, and really made an impression on me. Sergio created a piece he titled "Broken Dream." The piece is about 6 inches high and is basically a decorated, stick-like, winged figure. The head is a cylinder with eyes, several lips, and a question mark on the back. The figure sits on a base with numerous eyes.

Sergio wrote about his sculpture:

Many students' dreams are broken by disbelief, doubt, and society. However, with the help of art, students can reach great altitudes and find greatness. The question mark on the back of the sculpture's head represents doubt; doubt that steals the dreams of students. Doubt makes many students believe that they are not capable of achieving great things in life; doubt deprives students from getting a good education. All the mouths around the head represent the negative voices that corrupt students' minds. The voices in their minds come from their parents, siblings, friends, and teachers; voices that tell them that they are not capable of doing great things in life. Voices that stay with them for a long time.

The eyes and mouth at the bottom of the sculpture represent society, a society that holds back students from getting a good education because of their culture, race, color, gender, beliefs, and learning abilities. Society can be inconsiderate with students. The text around the sculpture's body represents knowledge; knowledge obtained with no purpose. What good is all the knowledge in the world if a student does not have a purpose or reason to live for? What good is knowledge if no one believes in a student's abilities?

The wings on the sculpture represent art, for art can give students freedom to find their abilities and reach greatness. Art can be used to inspire students

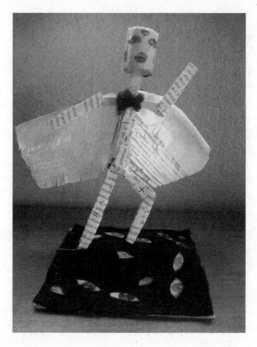

Broken Dream

with disbelief and doubt. Art can give a student purpose. With the help of art, students can reach great altitudes and find greatness.

When Sergio presented his sculpture to our class, we all fell silent. We all knew at that moment of the truth Sergio presented in such an eloquent and poignant manner through his sculpture. I thank Sergio for sharing his truth and experience. He has given me a renewed sense of urgency in arguing for the enormous capability of kids, and a passion to squelch the inadequacy of our educational system as a piece of the puzzle that serves to create doubt.

In giving this assignment, I am not expecting each student to produce a perfect or even near-perfect representation. To be honest, I am not sure what perfection would look like. The purpose of the exercise is to engage students in thinking and working with their ideas concerning learning. As such I am expecting that the lesson will give them more to consider about teaching and learning, especially by reviewing each other's ideas. We are also reminded about the complexity of learning, that it is an evolving process within ourselves as teachers and as learners, and that the process will be ongoing with our students as well.

A few more examples highlight the diversity of thinking in the class. Karen brought in a collage made of felt pasted onto a cloth background.

Learning can be as comfortable as an old pair of fuzzy slippers. This happens when the new knowledge fits well with my prior knowledge.

Learning can be as fun as a bright pair of boots. Sometimes the concepts are so exciting that I want to dance with enthusiasm.

Learning can also feel as awkward as a pair of 3-inch heels. The concepts seem so scary that I hesitate to try them out.

Here again, we have an example of a student working with something familiar to create an analogy to learning. Karen explored how different kinds of shoes are analogous to different learning situations. She applied the notion of prior knowledge and the challenge of newness in learning. Sometimes learning can be fun, sometimes scary. It would be interesting to ask Karen to delve deeper into what makes learning fun or scary, and if she is making a judgment as to the benefit of each feeling.

Sherrie brought in a geometrical art piece. In her discussion she also related the idea of prior knowledge to new knowledge. She then focused on the "bridge" that unites prior and new knowledge.

For me, being a learner means trying to fit pieces of knowledge together—making connections between new information and what I have learned previously—revising and putting all of this new information into a form that makes sense and will be useful.

But learning/understanding does not fit neatly into a particular form. It is uneven. Sometimes it overlaps and makes itself into a daring new form. Sometimes it is out there by itself, no sense about it and not useful until something bridges the gap and makes it comprehensible.

Using my creation to portray these ideas, I have used various shapes to show how the information learned is all over the place. There are pieces that connect to other pieces and form a unit of understanding. There are new items as symbolized by the paper cut-outs as well as established knowledge noted by the marking pens. They are all there, floating around, waiting for an opportunity to hookup in some sort of sensible way.

And finally, Karen's crazy quilt metaphor:

A Learner Is Like a Crazy Quilt

A "crazy quilt" is made of swatches of fabric which are remnants from other homemade garments or crafts. These pieces of fabric are arranged in such a way as to create a beautiful pattern in a quilt block. The quilt blocks are then stitched together to form a completely original finished quilt.

For the learner, knowledge and experience are like the swatches of fabric used in a crazy quilt. This knowledge and experience belongs to the learner and builds upon itself over time just as the pieces of remnant fabric which belong to the quilter are collected and added to over time. The knowledge and experience represented by the fabric combine to make a wholly unique pattern. Quilt blocks are connected to make a beautiful and useful piece of art just as a learner's knowledge and experience connect to make a beautiful and unique human being. The only difference is that the quilt has boundaries, the learner has none.

The variety in response and form is fascinating to me as the teacher and to the other students as they share in each other's thinking. It is especially important to remember that these examples come from an "ordinary" cohort of students who have no special training in the arts. Though I ask students to do this assignment every year, I am continually amazed by the representations and metaphors they create, and by the unique qualities that shine through the individual productions. This says to me that imagination and creativity are blossoming in every student. We are too ready to think that they are not. Simply given the opportunity to work through an understanding in an art form, each student can offer a unique perspective to a class. In this way, we as teachers can tap into our students' imaginative resources; and in turn, with their newfound "imaginative confidence," they can begin to apply artistic methods—or ways of knowing in their own practice—with their own students.

I believe that my students' work in exploring various ways of knowing, including artistic ways of knowing, enables them to achieve complex understandings of learning and subsequently gives them much to consider in negotiating their role in a future teaching and learning relationship. In sharing their work they are sharing something of themselves, which I believe benefits all in the learning community we call a classroom. My students were invested in their work and the work of their peers; thus, they invested in the learning and instruction issues of the class. Further, they had an experiential basis in addition to a theoretical basis on which to reflect and question teaching and learning relationships as they prepare to move into their own classrooms.

Maxine Greene (1991) reminds us how fundamental the arts can be to learning: "In truth, I do not see how we can educate young persons if we do not enable them on some level to open up spaces for themselves—spaces for communicating across boundaries, for choosing, for becoming different in the midst of intersubjective relationships. . . . That is one of the reasons I would argue for aware engagements with the arts for everyone, so that in this democracy human beings would be less likely to confine themselves to the main text. . . ." Through encounters with the arts, she continues, students may "become aware of the ways in which certain dominant social practices enclose us in molds or frames, define us in accord with extrinsic demands, discourage us from going beyond ourselves, from acting on possibility" (p. 28).

SUMMARY

By having their students create representations and metaphors for understanding, teachers are not only training children to exercise their minds by thinking but are providing a basis from which children may begin asking their own questions of the world around them. Representational and/or metaphoric thinking is a rigorous task that sets the stage for intellectual and emotional growth. The arts, being a natural structure for representational and metaphoric activity, expand children's expressive outlets as they proceed on their educational adventures. Intellectual growth begins when the student is participating in learning rather than acting as a recipient of knowledge. In this respect the arts can play a crucial role because they demand participation and awareness. Further, they enable students to pursue questions and understandings by making personal connections to knowledge.

QUESTIONS TO PONDER

1. Think of times in your own schooling when you felt intellectually challenged. What were those occasions, and what made them challenging?

2. Think of something concrete that you could do using the arts to motivate your students to use their thinking and reflective skills as a way to wrap up a daily lesson in math or reading.

 EXPLORATIONS TO TRY

1. Go to the Web and locate the national and your state's standards for arts education. What are you already doing? What do you believe you can do?

2. Create your own metaphor and representation responding to the question "What does it mean to be a learner?"

REFERENCES

Belenky, M. F., et al. (1986). *Women's ways of knowing: The development of self, voice, and mind.* New York: Basic Books.

Berthoff, A. (1981). *The making of meaning: Metaphors, models, and maxims for writing teachers.* Montclair, NJ: Boynton/Cook Publishers.

Bissex, G. (1980). *GNYS AT WRK: A child learns to write and read.* Cambridge, MA: Harvard University Press.

Bowden, D. (1993). The limits of containment: Text-as-container in composition studies. *College Composition and Communication, 44*(3).

Bruner, J. (1962). *On knowing: Essays for the left hand.* Cambridge, MA: Harvard University Press.

Coomaraswamy, A. K. (1934/1956). *The transformation of nature in art.* New York: Dover.

Dewey, J. (1959). *Art as experience.* New York: Capricorn Books.

———. (1991). Twenty-four, forty-two, and I love you: Keeping it complex. *Harvard Educational Review, 61*(1).

Duckworth, E. (2006). *The having of wonderful ideas and other essays on teaching and learning* (3rd ed). New York: Teachers College Press.

Gallas, K. (1991). Arts as epistemology: Enabling children to know what they know. *Harvard Educational Review, 61*(1).

———. (1994). *The languages of learning.* New York: Teachers College Press.

Gardner, H. (1990). Multiple intelligences: Implications for art and creativity. In W. Moody (Ed.), *Artistic intelligences: Implications for education.* New York: Teachers College Press.

———. (1993). *Frames of mind: The theory of multiple intelligences.* New York: Basic Books.

Goldberg, M. (1992). Expressing and assessing understandings through the arts. *Phi Delta Kappan,* Vol. 73.

———. (2004). *Teaching English language learners through the arts: A SUAVE experience.* Boston: Allyn and Bacon.

Greene, M. (1991). Texts and margins. *Harvard Educational Review, 61*(1).

Hawkins, D. (1978). Critical barriers to science learning. *Outlook, 29,* 3–23.

Horton, J. (1995). Unpublished manuscript.

Hunter, D. (1995). Unpublished manuscript.

Kamii, C. (1984). *Young children reinvent arithmetic.* New York: Teachers College Press.

————. (1989). *Young children continue to reinvent arithmetic—2nd grade.* New York: Teachers College Press.

Lakoff, G., & Johnson, M. (1980). *Metaphors we live by.* Chicago: University of Chicago Press.

Perrone, V. (1989). *Working papers: Reflections on teachers, schools, and communities.* New York: Teachers College Press.

Piaget, J. (1963). *The origins of intelligence in children.* New York: W. W. Norton.

————. (1980). *To understand is to invent: The future of education.* New York: Penguin Books.

Prospect Center. (1986). *The Prospect Center documentary processes: In progress.* North Bennington, VT: Prospect Archive and Center for Education and Research.

Schickedanz, J. (1990). *Adams righting revolutions.* Portsmouth, NH: Heinemann.

Simonson, R., & Walker, S. (1988). *Multicultural literacy.* Saint Paul, MN: Graywolf Press.

Storr, A. (1988). *Solitude: A return to the self.* New York: Free Press.

Vygotsky, L. (1971). *The psychology of art.* Cambridge, MA: MIT Press.

Watson, B., & Konicek, R. (1990). Teaching for conceptual change: Confronting children's experience. *Phi Delta Kappan,* Vol. 71.

Yamada, M. (1976). *Camp notes and other poems.* New York: Kitchen Table: Women of Color Press.

Piaget, Imitation, and the Blues: Reflections on Imagination and Creativity

THE SWAN

The swan gracefully flies
across the red, purple and orange
sunset. Flapping   its snow white
wings only   once or twice.
Flying   in a circle
searching   for a fish.
It dives   down and
snatches   a fish.
Struggling   to soar up
to the   clouds floating
in the sky. The swan drops the
lifeless fish and soars back
to its home . . . the sky.

Troy Geierman, fifth grader

Creativity and imagination are probably two of the most important aspects of education and spirited living. Without an ability to imagine and create, cultures would stagnate and the world would be far less interesting. In this chapter I will examine the relationships among creativity, imagination, invention, and originality from the viewpoints of both creators and participants (those who attend to a creation). First, I briefly consider a few ways in which creativity has been defined. A thorough review of creativity would fill numerous volumes and could not adequately be covered here. In its place, I focus on a few key elements of creativity and the creative process.

CREATIVITY

In Western cultures, creativity is generally viewed as an attribute that few individuals possess. A person is either creative or not. This is usually determined by something the person has made or invented, some problem solved, or some mystery cracked. Jerome Kagan (1967) is quite clear when he writes, "creativity refers to a product, and if made by [a person], we give him [or her] the honor of the adjective" (p. viii). In essence, creativity has become an elitist notion. Only a select, talented few are considered to be among the "creative," and the determination of their creativity is based on the judgment of an outcome or product they have put forth. Unfortunately, this view is considerably limiting.

According to R. G. Collingwood (1958), "to create something means to make it nontechnically, but consciously and voluntarily" (p. 128). Jerome Bruner (1962) defines creativity as "an act that produces *effective surprise*," what he calls the "hallmark of a creative enterprise" (p. 18). Howard Gardner (1993), to whom we will return later in this chapter, defines a creative individual as a person "who regularly solves problems, fashions products, or defines new questions in a domain in a way that is initially considered novel but that ultimately becomes accepted in a particular cultural setting" (p. 35).

Mikhalyi Csikszentmihalyi, the Chicago psychologist who has written several books on the subject of creativity, including *Flow*, describes creativity as "crossing boundaries." He also describes what he calls "optimal experience," which translates to the feeling of being fully aware and in control of experiences within the context of a world where many of our experiences are not within our control (for example, who we are born to and when, how tall we will grow, or how intelligent we are, etc.), when we feel a sense of "exhilaration, a deep sense of enjoyment." Creativity is something that we *make* happen.

> It is what the sailor holding a tight course feels when the wind whips through her hair, when the boat lunges through the waves like a colt—sails, hull, wind, and sea humming a harmony that vibrates in the sailor's veins. It is what a painter feels when the colors on the canvas begin to set up a magnetic tension with each other, and a new thing, a living form, takes shape in front of the astonished creator." (Csikszentmihalyi, 2008, p. 3)

Daniel Pink echoes Csikszentmihalyi's notions in his popular book, *A Whole New Mind* (2006). He describes boundary crossers in much the same way he does artists: "Boundary crossers reject either/or choices and seek multiple options and blended solutions" (p. 136). Richard Florida (2004) argues that "creativity is *essential* to the way we live and work today" (p. 21) and declares that it is an economic force, multifaceted and multidimensional in nature. "It is a mistake to think, as many do, that creativity can be reduced to the creation of blockbuster inventions, new products, and new firms. In today's economy, creativity is pervasive and ongoing" (p. 5).

I would like to submit the following perspective for consideration. Creativity is *innate*. Everyone is creative; we are born not only ready but anxious to act upon the creative proclivity within us. In other words, humans are born creative; and as I will show in this chapter, we act creatively throughout infancy and childhood as a process of natural maturation. Our development is dependent upon creative acts. Our ability to journey through the world and communicate our understandings of it are dependent upon everyday acts of creativity. Unfortunately, once we leave childhood, most of us are effectively taught to think that we are not creative and that creativity is something only a few talented souls possess. What a tragedy this is, especially as we consider the role of creativity in educational settings.

Whereas many people focus on a great painting, work of literature, or piece of music as the defining element of a creative person, we will turn to creative work that may or may not culminate in the achievement of a painting, book, song, computer program, or unique perspective on an everyday activity. Assigning a definition to creativity proves challenging in part because of its complexity and multiple manifestations. In its place, some have argued, as David Perkins does in *The Mind's Best Work* (1981), that we study the process and ask "how the creative person thinks, not what the creative person is" (p. 5).

Characterizing the work of a creative person in terms of a *process* or *action* that has a number of associated qualities opens many possibilities. Definitions of creativity that rely on the completion of a product or the solving of a problem require us to judge and develop criteria for the judgment calls. This is limiting. In characterizing creativity as an action, we can focus on the activity of creating rather than the outcome, thereby eliminating some of the problems associated with judging a product. In that light, one might contemplate the notion that it is possible for a person to be creative but not original. In formulating a characterization of creativity, we should consider specific qualities. These include motivation, concentration, the making of connections that enable individuals to transcend previous limitations, and reflection.

From birth, an individual is creative. One has to be in order to begin the process of development. An infant begins life with an awareness and a motivation to develop. *Motivation* is the first quality we will associate with creativity. At its most basic level, this motivation manifests itself through a desire to be nourished—both physically and mentally. Next we see the child motivated to imitate the actions of its caregivers or the actions of things around him such as the movement of a mobile in his crib. The work of an infant is to constantly *make connections* that empower him to transcend the limitations of what he already knows and has integrated into his experience. Thus, in order to imitate the action of a parent, a baby must work hard—and creatively—to transcend previous limitations of his actions. This continues as an active process well into the first year of a child's life. The ability to *transcend previous limitations* while constructing and adding new schemas to one's repertoire is another quality associated with the creative process.

Following infancy, play occupies the bulk of a child's physical, intellectual, and emotional development. A huge part of playing involves representation—the ability to use symbols. Play also leads us toward identifying a core quality associated with creativity—making connections. In play children are constantly engaged in creating games, fantasies, dramas, new ways to run on the playground, and so on. They are also engaged in trial and error as they try to create skyscrapers with their blocks or figure out ways to keep a kite afloat in the air. Play, viewed as an ongoing process, is essentially a creative activity through which children make connections to what they know and use those connections to explore further. Through play they develop an ability to represent their world.

As children grow older and gain experiences from which to draw in their intellectual and emotional lives, concentration and reflection assume an increasingly important role in the process of development. A creative person considers and even questions the actions he or she performs. The reflective nature of the creative person sets her aside from the person who mechanically carries out an assignment or follows through on a task. *Reflection,* then, is another quality associated with creativity.

Creativity permeates every aspect of living and human development and is not limited to early childhood. As I mentioned in a previous chapter, Eleanor Duckworth (1996) considers the essence of all of intellectual development a "creative affair." She argues that the having of wonderful ideas is fundamental to the intellectual development of both children and adults, and that instead of emerging from some mysterious place in the universe, "wonderful ideas are built upon other wonderful ideas" (p. 7). She writes that there are two aspects to providing occasions for wonderful ideas: "One is being willing to accept children's ideas. The other is providing a setting that suggests wonderful ideas to children—different ideas to different children—as they are caught up in intellectual problems that are real to them" (p. 7). Here the arts play an important role. They can provide a methodology and setting for children to work through problems and questions. Further, they provide multiple forms through which children may express and communicate their wonderful ideas.

To emphasize the point that creativity is an innate quality in all human beings, rather than a special ability of a lucky few, I will turn to language and literacy. Although linguists such as Noam Chomsky (1980) argue that humans are preprogrammed for language (universal grammar theory), our ability to employ it is essentially an aesthetic and creative process. Consider how many words we have access to, and the myriad ways we put them together to communicate with others. It is likely that every time we speak we create a sentence that has never been spoken before. The capacity to employ everyday language is a creative ability we all possess. In using language we are constantly making aesthetic choices regarding how to express our thoughts to others. Some of us, however, do it better than others. Some of us also have more or less practice in applying language.

As children learn to read and write, they begin to manipulate letters and symbols. Prior to reading, children first develop ways to write as a form of communication. This activity is known to those who study language as "invented spelling." The phenomenon of invented spelling is well documented as a developmental activity whereby children of four or five years of age "who do not read, but who know the letters of the alphabet and their sounds, show themselves able to compose words and messages on their own, creating their own spellings as they go along" (Chomsky, 1971, p. 499). Carol Chomsky argues that this aspect of development is essentially a creative affair. She compares the work of the child inventing spelling to the work of a child drawing a picture:

> The spontaneous speller composes words, according to their sounds, figuring out for himself what comes first, next, and so on. He does this for his own purposes, as a means of self-expression. Here spelling appears to share some aspects with the activity of

drawing a picture. For example, the child who draws a person is not trying to match an arbitrary pattern or to represent what someone else will deem correct or accurate. He works from his own perceptions and chooses to put down on paper those features which in some sense strike him worthy of representation. As he matures, he represents increasingly many of these features and may organize them somewhat differently. The development from early productions to later ones is clearly visible.

This is much the way it is with spellings. The child spells independently, making his own decisions. He has no preconceptions of how the word ought to be spelled nor any expectation that there is a "right" or a "wrong" way to do it. He spells *creatively,* according to some combination of what he perceives and what he considers worthy of representation. [emphasis added] (1971, p. 500)

In speaking and reading, we tap into our ability to imagine. Words only represent objects, images, stories, ideas, emotions. They are not, in and of themselves, anything more than a representative tool. Our ability to imagine what the words represent is a creative activity that is a natural aspect of human development. Again, when we look at human development, we can make a rather convincing argument that we are, by nature, creative beings who have an innate ability to represent our world.

Now I would like to return to infancy and imitation. Viewing creativity as a process leads us on some interesting paths. One path follows the role of imitation as a creative action. Prior to studying the work of Piaget, specifically his book *Play, Dreams, and Imitation in Childhood* (1962), I thought of imitation as a means toward no good end. After all, imitation couldn't be original or creative; further, the thought of certain "imitations," such as imitation chocolate or imitation cheese, made me cringe. In the classroom I imagined that imitation would teach children to act as parrots and not a whole lot more. Imitation would mean that the students did not need to think. I was wrong. I came to this understanding through an interesting musical journey, which I will briefly relate here.

PIAGET, IMITATION, AND THE BLUES

A few years ago I decided I wanted to learn to play the blues on my saxophone. Although I am an accomplished musician in the realm of classical and folk music by Conservatory standards, I wanted to learn something new—to improvise and play the blues. I also felt that I needed to learn music more by ear than by relying on written music, which I imagined any blues teacher would force me to do.

As I began my lessons, my teacher played notes on the piano that I had to imitate on the saxophone. He would play, then I would try to play; he would play, I would try to play; and this went on for many lessons. I should emphasize "*try* to play" because imitating him was not easy. I have to say I was surprised how hard it was in the beginning.

Imitating can demand a great deal of effort. As I listened to my teacher's phrases and melodies, my own thoughts emerged: Is the melody going higher or lower? Where on my saxophone do my fingers need to fall? What is the interval between those two notes? Is it a minor or a major interval? The rhythm, what was that rhythm?! There was a lot to think about, and it wasn't easy.

I had to concentrate to identify the intervals and then translate them to the saxophone. I had to listen with extraordinary care to remember the rhythms and flow of the phrases. I had to struggle. I also felt a determination to "get it right." Away from my lessons I began to consider the job of an infant who is essentially engaged in a similar process. I imagined an infant imitating the various moves of his parent or caregiver. I began to contemplate the complexity and potential of imitation.

Imitation can be a struggle. It can be a search. Imitation can bring on a will of determination. Later in life, it can lead toward the understanding of a subject. In the case of my blues lessons, I was assigned various pieces to learn. My teacher handed me a tape of Thelonius Monk playing one of his compositions, "Mysterioso," and asked me to learn the melody. It is a wonderful, albeit surprising melody that incorporates interesting melodic twists and turns. His reason for choosing this piece was that it was composed of many intervals of sixths, a common and recurring interval in the blues tradition. He wanted me to be able to recognize and translate that interval to my saxophone.

I took the tape home, listened to it over and over, and tried to get the melody in my ear. After I thought I had it memorized, I picked up my saxophone and tried to find and match the notes. Again, like the exercises in my lessons, it wasn't easy. I had to break the melody into phrases and go back and back until I could translate them to my saxophone. Then I repeated them over and over until I was confident I had them right. As I was proceeding in this work, I realized I was imitating not only the notes that Monk had recorded but also his style and the manner in which the saxophonist on the recording, Johnny Griffin (Monk was the pianist), was breathing.

I was learning not only the notes but also the style and articulations of the piece. I was also learning something related to the mood of the music—something I would never be able to do had I learned the piece from sheet music. I began to consider how each interval fell in relation to the beat and melody. I was learning the blues, and I was learning by imitating my teachers, Thelonius Monk and Johnny Griffin. Still, I struggled until the end. It was a hard piece to learn.

After feeling that I had just about gotten "Mysterioso" under my fingers, I found myself practicing it over and over whenever I took my saxophone out of its case. I'd play it backstage while I was warming up for a concert. A fellow musician would say to me, "Oh yeah, I know that tune. It's 'Mysterioso,' right? By Monk—great tune." Soon the tune became second nature. I found that I didn't need to think about it in order to play it. What a joy to be able to pull out my saxophone and just be able to play "Mysterioso"! I even began to wonder what exactly had been so hard to learn in the first place.

Then I returned to the infant determined to imitate something new—struggling, practicing, experiencing the joy in getting it to happen and then having it become second nature. The work involved in imitating began to take on a new light, not only for me and the blues, but also for the infants I was studying in Piaget's book. I realized that imitation can be an intensely creative process whereby one is engaged in the action of making new connections. In my case, it was the process of figuring out a blues standard. In the case of the infant, it is how to re-create what is going on around him, or the ability to make an interesting thing happen over and over.

I should point out that not all imitation involves such a creative process as did my learning "Mysterioso," or every aspect of infancy as it relates to transcending previous limitations. Consider the case of music students in a third-grade classroom. The students are all learning to play the recorder. As the young music teacher with 28 students in front of her begins the lesson, clusters of sound emerge in drifts. I still have a tendency to tremble when I think of that beginning music teacher! (How did I ever cope?) The teacher plays a phrase on the recorder; the students watch her fingers and imitate the movements and sounds she creates. Actually, the sounds are secondary; the students are mostly watching her fingers in an effort to re-create what was presented to them. In general, most of the students succeed.

By comparison, the recorder lesson seems a far less demanding exercise than learning the blues. In the case of the blues, I really wanted to learn. This desire provided a motivation to succeed in working at the style and specific notes. Most of the third graders didn't care much to learn the recorder, just enough to pass the music class and move on to the xylophones! The children were not motivated, nor were they curious. Instead, they were acting mechanically. While studying the blues, I reflected on my actions; the third graders had little need or real opportunity to reflect on their actions. Finally, I made a number of connections that enabled me to transcend my own limitations. The third graders didn't have that same kind of opportunity.

Drawing some conclusions from these examples, I would argue that imitation can be a creative process and an extremely useful tool in learning if a student is motivated. Sometimes imitation (even as a mechanical act) can be used to simply get a student interested in something, such as the recorder. As a creative act, however, imitation is like a puzzle that requires motivation, concentration, struggle, reflection, and the making of connections. In successfully matching an outcome, the individual transcends previous limitations. It is interesting that imitation as a creative act does not result in an original product, which is usually the judgment of creativity. Thus, an individual can be engaged in a creative process without having to be original. The work involved in imitation is creative, although the end product is not.

IMAGINATION

In thinking about learning it seems to me that the "intangible" is the essence of knowing and a key to effective education. It is the imagination, the mysteries that engage us to learn even though the "tangible" might give us structure (or a sense of structure). The arts concern themselves with structures, yet the artistic process is by nature the uncovering of the intangible and making it present. The following ancient poem of Tao Teh Ching impresses upon us the importance of the imagination:

> Thirty spokes converge upon a single hub;
> It is on the hole in the center that the use of the cart hinges.
>
> We make a vessel from a lump of clay;
> It is the empty space within the vessel that makes it useful.
>
> We make doors and windows for a room;
> But it is these empty spaces that make the room livable.
>
> Thus, while the tangible has advantages,
> It is the intangible that makes it useful.
>
> *Lao Tzu, from the Tao Teh Ching*

Much of current schooling, in my opinion, has focused on the "tangible." However, when all is said and done, our most innovative thinkers, politicians, business people, and leaders are those individuals who have practiced imaginations and understand how to mesh the tangible with the intangible, making the world "livable" and "useful."

Daniel Pink (2006), whom I mentioned earlier in this chapter, in his book (and DVD) *A Whole New Mind* describes the importance of leftbrain/right brain to the future. He offers this observation: "The future belongs to a very different kind of person with a very different kind of mind—creators and empathizers, pattern recognizers, and meaning makers. These people—artists inventors, designers, storytellers, caregivers, consolers, big picture thinkers—will now reap society's richest rewards and share its greatest joys" (p. 1).

The relation of imagination to creativity merits attention. It could be argued that imagining is the core of creating. One must imagine in order to create, although one need not create in order to imagine. However, if creativity is viewed as an action or process, the line tends to blur. In that light, imagination could be viewed as a creative process. Perhaps the difference lies in transcending limitations. For example, if I am feeling particularly sad on any given day, I might try to lessen the sadness by imagining myself on a Cape Cod beach—a place I find peaceful. I'm working hard to get to that beach, but I'm not necessarily transcending new boundaries to get there.

Perhaps we can agree that imagination relates to an awareness or consciousness of some sort. R. W. Gerard (in Ghiselin, 1952) writes that "imagination is an action of the mind that produces a new idea or insight" (p. 226). Thus, imagining is a process by which we can perceive things in new or different ways.

Mary Warnock is a scholar who has written extensively on imagination. After critically reviewing the literature on imagination, she comes to the following interpretation. What I find intriguing is her attention to the absent as well as the present in our ability to imagine our world. Further, she posits emotion as a valid arena from which the imagination might emerge.

> There is a power in the human mind which is at work in our everyday perception of the world, and is also at work in our thoughts about what is absent; which enables us to see the world, whether present or absent as significant, and also present this vision to others, for them to share or reject. And this power, though it gives us "thought-imbued" perception (it keeps the thought alive in perception), is not only intellectual. Its impetus comes from the emotions as much from the reason, from the heart as much from the head. (Warnock, 1976, p. 196)

By imagining, a person can detach herself from the ordinary or the everyday and enter a world filled with possibilities. Though artists might be more practiced at imagining, it is an activity that all of us can do. One of the more interesting roles a teacher can play is to place her students in positions where they can actively practice their imagination. This might be in the writing of questions about the life of a raindrop: Does it know where it is falling? Do raindrops go on vacation? Do raindrops miss the ocean? Does the sun move out of the raindrop's way? Or it might be an exercise of juxtaposition, as I have created in the following poem.

> Have you ever seen music fly
> or listened closely to a painting?
> I sang a dance once and
> sculptured a poem
> in blues and deep grays
> as a touch of sandstone lifted
> each word to the stars
> shooting them outward and
> downward encircling planets
> until I caught them
> back again
> in my bare hands

In my poem, I have done at least two things. I have playfully imagined art forms in a new way, and through the poem I have implored readers to stretch their own sensitivity and understandings. I applied my imagination when I created the poem. In so doing, I entered a new arena and was engaged in a creative process. I would characterize this work as meditative. The creative process moves me into another space where I can be lost in contemplation as I work with images, ideas, and feelings. Often, after having worked in a creative manner, I look back on my work and wonder to myself, "Did I really do that?!"

Children can tap into their natural ability to be creative with ease. That being so, what ignites the creative process? What sets the stage for a child to engage in acting creatively so that the moment of discovery or transcendence occurs? First, the teacher might consider what interests particular children and piques their curiosity. Second, the teacher may be a "creative role model" and practice the activity of creativity with her students. She can do this by providing occasions for them to probe deeply into ideas. She can set up challenges—perhaps playful ones—that inspire them to engage in learning and reflective thinking that become an evolving process, not an outcome.

Here again the arts play a fundamental role in teaching and learning. They provide the challenges and opportunities for children to explore their questions. They provide a medium of expression for working with ideas and feelings. They offer the chance to stretch one's imagination and creativity. In fact, I believe that without the arts, some children would not find a way to tap into their creative potential. The arts also encourage discipline and dedication. From my own experience, that discipline and dedication can be applied to other areas of living as well. As a 10-year-old, I practiced my guitar for hours. This discipline and dedication laid the groundwork for many aspects of my work today. I am convinced that what I learned from my guitar experience enables me to sit for hours and concentrate on writing this book or to focus at some length on an idea or issue I find intriguing.

HOWARD GARDNER, CREATIVITY, AND THE CLASSROOM

Howard Gardner has written extensively on creativity, which he links to the theory of multiple intelligences. His definition of a creative individual "as a person who regularly solves problems, fashions products, or defines new questions in a domain in a way that is initially considered novel but that ultimately becomes accepted in a particular cultural setting" (1993, p. 35) has interesting implications when applied to multicultural classroom settings.

In his book *Creating Minds* (1993), Gardner expounds on his theory of multiple intelligences by trying to understand and illuminate the anatomy of creativity. He discusses seven individuals from the modern era that typify the seven intelligences—Sigmund Freud, Albert Einstein, Pablo Picasso, Igor Stravinsky, T. S. Eliot, Martha Graham, and Mahatma Gandhi—and examines them in light of being creative. He devises a framework through which to examine their creativity.

Numerous questions come to mind in considering the relationship of creativity to learning. Is in examining Gardner's framework and others who define creativity according to "things," must the distinction of creativity truly depend on the judgment of a product (or problem solved)? If so, who does the judging and who has the means to offer their product for such judgment? What is the role of the imagination in creativity? In what ways are intelligence and creativity different? Alike?

A person who creates is not necessarily consciously engaged in solving a problem or creating a product. The person creating might be the child on the playground, or the child engaged in invented spelling to communicate a message to a friend or parent. The person might have made a mistake or undertaken a playful activity whereby something interesting occurred. George Eliot, the writer, once said in a conversation with Herbert Spencer, "It has never been my way to set before myself a problem and puzzle out an answer. The conclusions at which I have from time to time arrived, have not been arrived at as solutions of questions raised; but have arrived at unaware" (qtd. in Ghiselin, 1952, p. 224).

Many people create as a result of play, stress, political urgency, or elation. Often the creative connection is discovered unexpectedly through play. For example, Sir Alexander Fleming, the Scottish bacteriologist (also from the modern era, 1881–1955) known for his discovery of penicillin, was a man who thrived on play. "I play with microbes. . . . It is very pleasant to break the rules" (qtd. in Cole, 1988, p. 16). Although it might be argued that Fleming set out to solve a problem when he discovered penicillin, it is also true that play (according to Fleming) was essential to his work in the sciences and, thus, his creative ability. It is not unusual for a child in a class to recognize that he can create something new as a result of spilling paint on a piece of paper. Nor is it unusual for a child in a class to happen upon a new word combination through playing with words, and then to incorporate that word-play into a creative poem or other expression.

As I argued earlier in this chapter, play can be an intensely creative time. It is an opportunity to break the rules, open the door of discovery, and thereby create. Many musicians and composers know this aspect of creating very well—it may lie in one's ability to improvise, that is, to play with sounds. Stephen Nachmanovich (1990) writes, "looking into the moment of improvisation, I was uncovering patterns related to every kind of creativity. . . . I came to see improvisation as the master key to creativity" (p. 6). Creativity as action (in this case, play) is a natural aspect of human development. Imagine two children meeting on the playground for the first time. "Before they have exchanged two words they are running and spinning about, inventing paths and games around the swings and trees. This is the essence of improvisation—play, a kind of free-dom that allows spontaneous creative energy" (Goldberg, 1990, p. 381). Surely, this scenario of play has a place in a definition of creativity.

An event might trigger the creative process, enabling one to make new connections or transcend limitations. In Chapter 1 I mentioned the Ladino musical group that vis-ited with a fifth-grade bilingual class. Their visit and their music triggered a powerful and emotional creative action among the children. Adrienne Rich (1993) relays a simi-lar notion in describing a poem composed by Audre Lorde, "Power": "An event may ignite a poem (which may be labeled a 'protest' poem) but not because the poet has 'decided' to address the event" (p. 71). In this case, Rich tells the reader, Lorde did not choose to fashion a poem or solve a problem. She created out of another need. Lorde her-self writes of that need, "And that sense of writing at the edge, out of urgency, *not because you chose it but because you have to—that sense of survival*—that's what the poem is out of" [emphasis added] (in Rich, p. 70).

People create out of stress or frustration, as much as they do out of elation or jubi-lation. In all cases (and all the gray areas in between), the creative act stems from a reflection of, or reaction to, experience rather than a need to solve a problem or fashion a product. My point is this: A definition of creativity that focuses on a product or prob-lem solved, as Gardner's definition does, fails to take into account a wide range of expe-riences that promote creativity. It limits the conception of creativity to products judged according to previous experiences and contexts rather than allowing creativity to be related to new actions (judged according to the individual).

Especially from the standpoint of an artist, ultimately focusing on the judgment of a product can be overly simplistic. The creative work of an artist does not lie in the sig-nature on a painting or the performance of a composition; it lies in the mixing of colors on a palette or the juxtaposition of musical notes to form an interesting chord. In fur-ther relating this notion of end product to the work of children, we come up against an interesting dilemma. It is not unusual to encounter children who create and re-create but who may not be original in their finished products. Is a child who re-creates the wheel as creative as the person who first fashioned that product? I would say yes. But the child's product is not original. Many times, we find a child thoroughly engaged in figuring out a unique solution to a problem. Could that process be considered creative even if no product emerges or the solution fails?

Questions of judgment are usually fraught with problems, particularly when the judgments are based on standards created by a club of "great minds" (traditionally, Western male-centered standards). The question of access is immediately an issue. Let me illustrate this point within the realm of Western European culture, just prior to the modern era in the mid-1800s.

George Sand was a prolific and well-known writer at that time. She adopted a male name to gain acceptance in the field. Because of her sex, she had little chance of being accepted into the judging arena. She was told by Monsieur de Keratry, a popular writer and critic, "Believe me, don't make books, make babies." This statement came after he expounded on his "theories concerning the inferiority of women and the impossibility for even the most intelligent among them to write a good book" (Sand qtd. in Barry, 1979, p. 323). If one doesn't have access to the judging club to begin with, how can one ever be judged as creative? If one is judged by the existing standards, one stands little chance of favorable acceptance. In other words, how can we be sure of a judgment of creativity when the judges are most likely biased owing to their attitudes and positions in society?

Another illustration may be drawn from the life of Muriel Rukeyser, a poet of the modern era. Rukeyser is not well known, although she was recognized late in life by a number of her peers. Her battle was not uncommon for women, then and now. Adrienne Rich (1993) describes her plight:

> . . . in the history of poetry and ideas in the United States—always difficult to grasp be-cause of narrow definitions, cultural ghettos, the politics of canon makers—she [Rukeyser] has not been seriously considered in the way that, say, the group of politi-cally conservative white southern poets known as the Fugitives or the generation of men thought to have shaped "modern poetry"—Ezra Pound, T. S. Eliot, William Carlos Williams, Wallace Stevens—have been considered. . . . Her poetry not only didn't fit the critical labels, she actually defied the going classifications. (pp. 99–100)

George Sand knew how to play the game. Perhaps Rukeyser did not. In the end, Sand might be considered creative because others in her field recognized her position as a writer. But aside from her clever way of entering the playing field, and thus the club of judgment, can we assess if she is creative? She gained acceptance by her peers, but does that acceptance equate with intelligence or creativity?

Let us come back to the present and see if things are different. In my own expe-rience as a woman saxophonist, I have experienced firsthand denial into the "clubs" where male musicians gather. One summer my musical ensemble (an internationally acclaimed performing and recording ensemble) was asked to perform at the Montreal Jazz Festival, an international festival. We were to take center stage (before a crowd of 40,000) in collaboration with a French Canadian ensemble, which was all men. When it came time to practice together, I was politely asked by the men in the brass section of the French Canadian ensemble to "lay out" of the solo sections (i.e., not play) because they had practiced this before and it was a difficult part. However, the trombone player from my band—a man—was not asked to do the same. He was immediately accepted; the French Canadian male performers did not question his ability to play. My feelings at the time were of frustration, knowing that my gender clouded their judgment prior to hearing me play.

In light of frameworks that incorporate an element of judgment by peers, I cannot help but wonder how many people are denied entry into judging arenas not only because of their sex but because of color, culture, social status, or political status. I also wonder how many individuals are not deemed "creative" because they have chosen not to share their work with their peers. How do we create standards for judging children's work? First, we must recognize that our standards may not apply to the ones set by the chil-dren themselves. Second, it is imperative to critique the work of children in a construc-tive, encouraging, and rigorous manner while at the same time finding ways to train students to critique their own work and understand that there is always room for taking an idea or question further. As children come to rely on their own abilities to reflect crit-ically on their work, they become more self-confident. In this way, they can be autonomous in their ability to forge forward rather than creating work just to please a teacher or critic. In supporting the children, the teacher may adapt her method of grading and assessment so that each child's progress is judged according to his or her previous work rather than on an arbitrary standard that applies to the class as a whole. This can be achieved, for example, through the use of student portfolios.

With regard to teaching and learning, creativity can be conceived as domain-specific, much as Gardner presents intelligences. In this regard, the boundaries of creativity might be expanded to the benefit of individual students. It is true that Gardner's definition and framework apply to some creative people. His emphasis on problem solving is something that most teachers find valuable. Indeed, I find it valuable as well, and some of my most creative moments have stemmed from solving problems. However, problem solving in and of itself needn't be a creative affair. Moreover, one can be creative without solving any particular problem.

Judgment or assessment of creativity presents interesting challenges. It is difficult to cross the boundaries of cultural standards; yet without that effort, certain children might fall through the cracks and be left unrecognized for their work. In addition, it is interesting to consider the relationship of originality to the creative process. Although Gardner's definition speaks to creativity, perhaps it speaks better to the notion of originality. Finally, it is imperative to place the role of imagination within the conceptualization of children's creativity. Imagination can have an important impact on setting up activities that underscore creative moments.

CREATIVITY AND TECHNIQUE

It is important to understand that for a creator or participant, the process of working in the arts encompasses creativity *and* technique. Creativity involves the qualities already mentioned throughout this chapter; it occurs within the context of feelings and a connectedness to, or alienation from, one's culture. Being creative is essentially a process of awareness that can open new doors and change existing perceptions. Technique is the "how-to" of any art form, ranging from how one holds the brush to how one mixes the paints.

Technique is often given more attention and recognition than creativity in Western culture. It is hard not to be impressed with the violinist who can play skillfully and with gusto. Many people consider technique and creativity as one when thinking about art. But technique is only a vehicle that enables creativity to flow with ease. Let's take an example from music. When most children practice scales and fingerings on their instruments, they are practicing technique—the "how-to" of playing their instrument. The ability to read music is technique. Once a person has some degree of technique, he or she can let the music happen. Technique provides the vehicle for music to flow through an instrument, and it is definitely fundamental in promoting creativity.[1]

---

[1] If the reader is interested in learning more about technique, especially with regard to music, I recommend Vernon Howard's work (1982, 1991, 1992).

This distinction is particularly important in terms of encouraging children to work artistically. By focusing on the act of creating rather than the judgment of a product, the teacher can encourage students to be imaginative and create an atmosphere in which a desire to create—that is, to see things in new ways and explore complexities—is celebrated. On the other hand, technique enables one to create more easily. As a musician, I am better prepared to create a song or play my instrument if I have mastered some technique. A true artist has a balance of technique and creativity and uses both.

Technique is often aided by an awareness of available tools. Consider watercolor painting: Having paper that does not repel water is essential; knowing which brush will serve one's purpose enables one to paint with ease. The same is true for learning in general. Providing students with proper tools enables them to work both technically and creatively. In the arts, tools include the implements of the art form. In general education, tools may include microscopes, rulers, dictionaries, source books, and so on. On a more basic level, students need communication tools—spoken, written, artistic, movement, and musical languages—in order to work with and express their understandings.

CREATOR AND PARTICIPANT

At the opening of this chapter I alluded to the idea of creator and participant. Let me briefly expand on that notion as it relates to education. A student can engage with the arts as a creator or as a participant (audience member). Both call for action and attention on the part of the individual involved. When an individual writes a poem, that person is engaging in a creative, reflective act representing in words, phrasing, syntax, and grammar some notion about the world. The process of writing can even clarify those understandings for the individual. When someone else reads the poem and begins to engage with it, poetry happens again. It is in the engagement that the poetry lies, not in the symbols written on the page. Though the words on the page provide the initial outline of consideration, the poem in fact comes alive only through active engagement on the part of the reader. We therefore have two levels of creation in any artwork that is shared. First is the primary artist whose work might be cathartic, an exercise, or a labor of love. Second, once the art is offered to the public, the engagement with the work takes on many other qualities.[2] A person in Alaska might see something very different in a poem written by Alice Walker than someone reading the same poem in Australia. Both might interpret things that Alice Walker intended or didn't intend, considered or hadn't considered. In either case, what matters is that the poem is pivotal as the genesis of an artistic experience for all—creator and audience.

---

[2] Roger Sessions (in Morgenstern, 1956) posits a similar notion in discussing the relationship between composers and performers. He describes composers as "primary artists" and performers as "secondary artists." While his analysis lends a hierarchical relationship to composers and performers, I make the argument that artists and audiences are on more equal footing as participants in the arts.

SUMMARY

Creativity may be characterized as a lifelong and natural process by which individuals journey to new places in their exploration, understanding, and experience of life. Certain qualities can be extracted from the creative process to describe it: motivation, reflection, and the making of connections to transcend previous limitations. Creativity is not a process reserved for artists alone. In fact, when creativity takes center stage in a classroom, members of the learning community can be transformed and inspired to develop many wonderful ideas, inventions, and solutions. The action of creating and the results of engaging in creative processes can be judged according to each individual rather than according to others. In fact, it is important to encourage students to judge themselves and create rigorous criteria by which to reflect on their work. In this way, students can be engaged in creative actions and reflective thinking as they explore all there is to learn.

 ## QUESTIONS TO PONDER

1. Read more about Howard Gardner and his theories of intelligence and creativity. In your opinion, how are intelligence and creativity related? You also might want to consider what others have written about creativity, including David Perkins, Vera John-Steiner, Jerome Bruner, Ananda Coomaraswamy, and Mihaly Csikszentmihalyi.

2. Are notions of imagination and creativity culture specific? How would you go about answering this question?

3. Do you think technology impacts the creative process? If yes, how so? If no, why not?

 ## EXPLORATIONS TO TRY

1. Observe preschool children at play with blocks. Make two lists: (1) a list of what they are doing, and (2) a list of the ways in which they are being creative in their actions. Use the "qualities" associated with creativity as your guideline for thinking about creative actions.

2. Think of some moment or time in your life when you felt creative or imaginative. What made it different from other "everyday" events in your experience? Describe your thoughts in an essay.

3. With a partner, develop a list of ways in which to create a learning community/classroom that would support imaginative, creative, and reflective thinking and actions. Be specific.

REFERENCES

Barry, J. (Ed.). (1979). *George Sand in her own words*. New York: Anchor Books.
Bruner, J. (1962). *On knowing: Essays for the left hand*. Cambridge, MA: Harvard University Press.
Chomsky, C. (1971). Invented spelling in the open classroom. *WORD, 27*, pp. 499–518.

Chomsky, N. (1980). *Language and learning: The debate between Jean Piaget and Noam Chomsky* (M. Piatelli-Palmarini, ed.). Cambridge, MA: Harvard University Press.

Csikszentmihalyi, M. (2008). *Flow.* New York: Harper Perennial Modern Classics.

Cole, K. C. (1988, November 30). Play, by definition, suspends the rules. *New York Times*, p. 16.

Collingwood, R. G. (1958). *The principles of art.* New York: Oxford University Press.

Duckworth, E. (1996). *The having of wonderful ideas and other essays on teaching and learning* (2nd ed.). New York: Teachers College Press.

Florida, R. (2004). *The rise of the creative class.* New York: Basic Books.

Gardner, H. (1993). *Creating minds: An anatomy of creativity as seen through the lives of Freud, Einstein, Picasso, Stravinsky, Eliot, Graham, and Ghandi.* New York: Basic Books.

Ghiselin, B. (Ed.). (1952). *The creative process.* New York: New American Library.

Goldberg, M. (1990). Review of Free Play: Improvisation in Life and Art. *Harvard Educational Review, 60*(3).

————. (1991). Review of *Artistic Intelligences: Implications for Education. Harvard Educational Review, 61*(3).

Howard, V. A. (1982). *Artistry: The work of artists.* Indianapolis: Hackett Publishing Company.

————. (1991). And practice drives me mad; Or, the drudgery of drill. *Harvard Educational Review, 61*(1).

————. (1992). *Learning by all means: Lessons from the arts.* New York: Peter Lang.

Kagan, J. (Ed.). (1967). *Creativity and learning.* Boston: Beacon Press.

Tzu, Lao (1997). *Tao Teh Ching,* New York: Barnes and Nobles Books.

Morgenstern, S. (Ed.). (1956). *Composers on music: An anthology of composers' writings from Palestrina to Copland.* New York: Pantheon Books.

Nachmanovich, S. (1990). *Free play: Improvisation in life and art.* Los Angeles: Jeremy P. Tarcher.

Perkins, D. N. (1981). *The mind's best work.* Cambridge, MA: Harvard University Press.

Piaget, J. (1962). *Play, dreams, and imitation in childhood.* New York: W. W. Norton.

Pink, D. (2006). *A whole new mind.* NY: Riverhead Books.

Rich, A. (1993). *What is found there.* New York: W. W. Norton.

Warnock, M. (1976). *Imagination.* Berkeley and Los Angeles: University of California Press.

Chapter 4

Communication, Expression, and Experience: Literacy and the Arts

Meteors fly like a fly
Maybe it's a butterfly
with its wings spread
high in the sky

Jaime Padilla,
fourth grader

How can the arts be fundamental to becoming literate? How does using the arts provide an effective methodology for acquiring reading, writing, comprehension, and communication skills? These are the questions with which we will begin our journey into the relationships between literacy and the arts. First I will examine ways to set a context in which a rich literary environment is created. Then I will discuss ways to learn with and through the arts. This includes teaching cursive writing through movement, and spelling and vocabulary through drawing (picto-spelling). Finally, I will examine the uses of poetry as a wonderful tool for literacy, with a special emphasis toward its use in teaching a second language.

As I outlined in Chapter 1, I view the arts as languages (visual, aural, tactile, kinesthetic) that are a part of the everyday communication available to students in a classroom. Although some students have difficulty crossing "word" language barriers, the arts can join students through a common language. Art as language provides freedom of expression for second language learners and in so doing builds bridges among students as they work collaboratively. In a class where some students speak English, others Spanish, and yet others Cambodian, verbal communication can at times be challenging. Yet those students can find common ground in painting, music, drama, movement, sculpture, photography, and so on. The arts can be uniting, providing common languages and fostering intergroup harmony.

Developmentally, the arts provide a means for children as they learn to represent images and ideas. Representation is a major focus of early learning. Through dramatic play, children develop language and communication skills. Dramatic play sets the stage for creative language and symbolic development, especially in an environment that includes a variety of materials (e.g., costumes and props) that support creative play and thinking. Children's speech patterns, which represent early communication attempts, often emerge from playing with sounds in such environments. According to Nancy Cecil and Phyllis Lauritzen (1994), "Speech play becomes more social as children mature and relate to peers. Joint conversations with creative back-and-forth turns delight participants" (p. 14).

Cecil and Lauritzen recommend providing young students with an environment that encourages literacy development: "A literary-rich dramatic play area would include pencils and papers for waiters and waitresses to write customers' orders in a restaurant that has a printed menu, and alongside the print a matching rebus menu; magazines, newspapers, and books in the playhouse; prescription pads for the doctor's office; signs for stores; notepads for a refrigerator door; stationery, envelopes, and stamps for letters to be written and delivered to the addressee; and any reading and writing materials applicable to the real-life situations being dramatized" (1994, p. 15).

A creative twist on sharing time can provide another entry into developing communication and creative speech skills. Karen Gallas (1994) discusses the use of sharing time to tell "made-up" stories. As she reflected on the different kinds of talk in the classroom, she began to question her role in influencing classroom discourse. After careful consideration, she decided to turn sharing time over to her first graders. "By removing myself from the teacher's traditional role in sharing time," Gallas writes, "I could explore what happened when the children became the primary audience, or the 'ratifiers' of the discourse" (p. 18). Her turning over of sharing time opened the door for many students not comfortable with the more traditional "show and tell" to contribute in a less formal manner. A child who was homeless with very few possessions could make up a story and travel to the imaginary place where many things are possible. This in fact happened in Gallas's class. In turn, the other children traveled thoughtfully along, asking questions and encouraging the speaker to continue the story.

LITERACY WITH THE ARTS

There are numerous ways to attain literacy skills with the arts. Perhaps the most obvious is to introduce students to quality poetry and literature—a simple but effective strategy. Utilizing published poetry and literature either instead of or in addition to traditional textbooks enhances learning and at the same time introduces students to great works of art. There are also a number of wonderful children's books that concern themselves with the arts, including biographies of artists.

I have found that students are especially drawn to reading and writing poetry. I believe they are drawn to poetry in part because it is a playful form of writing. Reading poetry can be like figuring out a puzzle; it often has interesting twists and turns, not to mention a concise quality. Not only do children enjoy playing, but as we examined in Chapter 3, playing comprises the bulk of their early learning. Consider poems by Shel Silverstein. His poems tend to be humorous, with a twist (puzzle) and to the point. Their compact nature is inviting to beginning readers and second language learners. Silverstein's poetry is not overwhelming, and its playful quality intrigues young readers.

Storytelling is a natural way to engage students in applying language. Have students examine paintings or sculptures in a museum or reproductions brought into the classroom and create a story to accompany the artwork. I observed a class of second graders as they did this exercise in a local art museum. The exhibit, titled "Revisiting Landscape," included a number of paintings about nature. The children sat around one painting and observed it closely, identifying things they noticed such as trees, reflections, water, leaves, and colors. Next the teacher asked them to think of a story to accompany the picture. The results were fascinating and imaginative. One student placed fairies in the story, another invented a game of hide and seek through the trees in the painting, and a third told a tale of a family on a summer picnic.

One could do a similar activity by choosing music for children to listen to and use as the basis of an original story. Storytelling might take the form of telling, drama, or writing. You might incorporate writing by asking children to outline a story and then expand on it by telling it out loud. Children may enjoy composing a story to accompany a movement or dance. Even a dancer who exerts the slightest movement could provide the inspiration for an imaginative tale. I often take three art prints or choose three different kinds of music and have my students write a story with a beginning, middle, and end, using the prints or the music as their inspiration.

CURSIVE WRITING THROUGH THE ARTS

In a workshop I attended with my student teachers, I was introduced to teaching cursive writing through movement. Dancer and choreographer Bella Lewitzky led this session, which we all found to be an intriguing example of learning through the arts. Lewitzky and her company were given the following problem: A group of young students with whom they were to work were having difficulty grasping cursive writing. Never afraid of a challenge, the dancers devised a way to engage the children in thinking about curves and motion with their bodies.

The dancers asked all the children to stand and begin to make large curving motions with their bodies—figure eights, half circles, and loops. Next the dancers asked the children to do the same motions, but on a slant. No problem. Now the figure eights, half circles, and loops were transformed into giant "L's," "S's," "B's," and so on. From the giant motions the dancers got the children to make the motions smaller and smaller and smaller until they were so small as to be able to fit on a piece of paper. Having experienced the movements of the cursive writing through their bodies, they were well prepared for applying those movements in making marks on a piece a paper. Since that workshop, many of my students have tried the exercise in their classes with great success.

PICTO-SPELLING LEARNING THROUGH THE ARTS

Picto-spelling is an activity that engages children in both spelling and vocabulary lessons. It involves drawing pictures that incorporate the letters of a specific word in one of two ways. In the first way, the letters are used to create the picture or meaning of a word. See Figure 4.1 by a fifth grader demonstrating *dinosaur* and *fish*. Each picto-spelling is created by using of the letters of the word.

Another creative way in which students have developed picto-spellings involves incorporating the word into a descriptive picture. Figure 4.2 shows the word *round*. The student clearly demonstrates an understanding of the meaning of the word by displaying its shape through the picto-spelling. Figure 4.3 on p. 72 shows a depiction of the word *dread*. In this clever picto-spelling, the child draws a plane going down, alluding to an enactment of the word *dread*. The *Ds* are on the wings, as is the letter *E*. The *R* is in the nose of the plane and the *A* is on the tail. "Snap," Figure 4.4 on p. 73, is a picto-spelling that shows the action of the word.

By creating picto-spellings such as the examples shown here, students engage in creative thinking as they learn specific spellings and vocabulary. As a test of their comprehension, the picto-spellings provide a concrete indication of their understanding of specific words.

Figure 4.1   Picto-spelling of *dinosaur* and *fish*.

Figure 4.2   Picto-spelling of *round*.

STORY COMPREHENSION LEARNING THROUGH THE ARTS

When children dramatize, move to, or create music to represent a story, they become actively involved in working with the ideas in the story. Their engagement with a story through the arts allows them to transform the story ideas from the medium of words to the medium of drama, movement, or dance. Through that translation, children engage with the ideas, characters, and feelings of the story. As they translate the words to art forms, each story comes to life. Indeed, the act of transforming or translating is fundamental to attaining understanding or comprehension.

When children actively engage with a book or story through the arts, they have the opportunity to gain ownership of the story rather than merely assimilating the story that is given them. Students move from being listeners to being participants in mediums that encourage the crossing of boundaries and seeing new borders. For small children, dramatizing a story helps to integrate the sequence of events. This drama opens the door to one's physical, spiritual, emotional, and intellectual modalities.

If we return to the notion of the arts as languages, we can see children's potential as they use these languages to work deeply with subject matter and ideas—in this case, a storybook.

Figure 4.3   Picto-spelling of *dread*.

The teacher introduces a book to children with the expectation that they will engage with its complexities, including the sequence of events, the thoughts and actions of individual characters, and the author's observation about human experience, or theme. In order to do this, children must make the story their own and move beyond rote memorization. By translating the story into drama, movement, or music, students have a chance to interact with the characters and work with them closely. Students are placed in a position whereby they reflect on and evaluate aspects of the story in order to communicate it to others.

A child engaging in these artistic processes of translation becomes a character in the story. This allows the teacher to follow the way in which the child understands and expresses her understanding of the character. When a child moves like the swan in the story, the teacher knows the child has integrated some idea of the swan into her thinking. When a child is able to add music to the story, the teacher knows the child is considering and reflecting on aspects of the action while playing with the book's ideas. Moreover, teaching story comprehension through the arts can add interest and involvement to the study. Approaching character understanding through the arts encourages children to become active thinkers in addition to listeners. In so doing, they begin to work with symbol systems other than written language as a way to communicate their understandings.

Figure 4.4 Picto-spelling of *snap.*

Drama

How is a child's acting out of a story different than reading it or listening to it? When a child acts out a story she has read or heard, she has the opportunity to *become* the story—to internalize the characters, action, emotions. In order to be a character, she must understand something about that character and the character's motivation. Therefore, in acting out the story, the child has the chance to actively explore the character and story. Drama can be a fundamental tool that enables children to understand the story by way of engaging with it. Reluctant readers often find ways into reading via methods such as this. Acting can also apply to particular words within reading texts. In classrooms with English language learners, miming the meaning of reading vocabulary can help develop comprehension skills, as children will retain more as they physically act out words and meanings.

Drama is a powerful tool than can increase awareness in children by bringing them to experience something they may have never experienced. Through acting, children can take on roles that make them think critically about the story and about the experiences of characters different from themselves. A bully might take on the character of a meek but kind person; a shy child might take on the role of a powerful king or community leader. These roles enable the children to experience voices different from their own, opening avenues toward thinking more deeply about persons, objects, or relationships in a new way. Drama also empowers an English language learner to practice language without being self-conscious because the child's language is that of her "character" and not hers.

Another form of drama that is especially useful in developing reading comprehension skills is puppetry. Students love watching puppet shows and creating their own puppets. Puppets can represent characters who appear in their reading texts. Incorporating puppetry into classroom instruction can be as complex as arranging for students to perform puppet shows with sets or as simple as conducting individual tabletop puppetry on students' desks. In an outreach project called DREAM (Developing Reading Education Through Arts Methods), we build on the tabletop idea by having teachers and students create a puppet of themselves, a puppet of the author, and puppets of main characters.

Simple tabletop puppets can be fashioned from toilet paper rolls decorated with faces and arms; puppets can also take on the shape of an animal (real or imagined), or even a feature of a setting, such as a tree or table. Students hold onto the puppets and move them as they read. This helps students engage with the text in a very tangible manner. Such puppets are are also terrific tools for reflection. For example, a student might be asked to manipulate an author puppet while responding to the teacher's prompt, "What might the author have been thinking when the character chooses to . . . ?"There are numerous possibilities for developing critical and creative comprehension skills using puppets!

Movement (Kinesthetic)

Moving or dancing to a story also provides an opportunity to explore it from the inside out through active participation. As the student translates words to movements, he or she is working with the story's ideas. When he or she reads, the child is taking information in; through movement and dance, the child "gives out" by bringing words to life and actively interpreting the story. Young children naturally desire to move about. Exploring reading through movement enables children's natural energy to be channeled into a positive and often fun form of personal expression. Again, this is an excellent activity for English language learners to improve their vocabulary.

Music (Auditory)

Adding music to the story, or retelling the story through music, is yet another opportunity for making the story one's own through a process of translating words to sound. Even the addition of sound to words involves active reflection on the part of the student as he or she decides what sounds are important to certain aspects of the story. Again, the arts open a venue for exploration and active participation. Music can be a magic carpet, transporting children to worlds where they can separate themselves from other characters and events.

POETRY AND LANGUAGE ACQUISITION THROUGH THE ARTS

Writing poetry is akin to play—a playing with words. Poets create puzzles, readers decipher them. Writing poetry gives children the freedom to play as they work with words and language, because in poetry they can play with the rules of grammar and syntax. They can create phrases without worrying about punctuation, complete sentences, or word order. Thus, the writer can concentrate on imagining ways to put words together rather than focusing on the conventions that guide their use in specific circumstances.

Poetry is an art form that bridges representational thinking directly with language. Through poetry, one can often easily see children's personal and emotional connections to knowing and knowledge. It can unlock resources of insight in children. Karen Gallas (1991) writes, "Poetic form is often more suited to thinking and writing of children than prose; it is spare, yet rich with sense impressions. It is a medium in which the images of wonder, curiosity, and analogic thinking which so often characterize children's thinking can flourish" (p. 44).

In the case of student-poets, we see how children can create artistic forms to reveal self-knowledge and make connections to their world. As it relates to second language acquisition, the process might be akin to invented spelling. Given the opportunity to work freely with language, children are encouraged to explore the intricacies of language use. Not having to worry so much about grammatical rules (or even spellings), students may be willing and eager to invent while they express themselves with language.

In classrooms where multiple languages are spoken, poetry can be a natural bridge in working with words. Every student can benefit from word-play, but it is especially attractive to children who are learning to play with words in a new language. Educators have suggested that writing poetry provides students a forum for exploring the dimensions of their world, expressing ideas and feelings, and working with subject matter (Dillard, 1989; Greene, 1991; Heard, 1989; Hopkins, 1972; Johnson, 1990; Koch, 1973; Livingston, 1984, 1991; Phillips, 1990; Steinbergh, 1991; Tsujimoto, 1964).

There is anecdotal evidence that poetry is particularly well suited to second language acquisition and learning (Gallas, 1991; McKim & Steinbergh, 1992; Steinbergh, 1991). Steinbergh (1991) argues that writing poetry can be particularly comforting to children who come from countries where poetry is an integral part of the culture: "Hispanic, Russian, and Asian students often feel very comfortable with the expressive mode of poetry, even before they have a facility with English" (p. 57). McKim and Steinbergh (1992) notice "children whose first language is not English wanting to find the new words for their poems" (p. 7). Data from my own research over the last few years confirm that poetry can open the door to working with words, language, and ideas. Second language students were documented working with language freely and excitedly when writing poetry.

Research in bilingual and second language acquisition has yielded a number of theories with regard to learning (Krashen, 1981). Two theories—the Acquisition-Learning Hypothesis and the Affective Filter Hypothesis—bear directly on this research. The Acquisition-Learning Hypothesis supposes that like first language acquisition, children acquiring a second language learn it for some communicative purpose. The Affective Filter Hypothesis addresses the role of "affect," or personality and motivation, in second language acquisition. The literature describes three variables as related to learners' success: (1) Low anxiety relates to motivation; the less anxiety, the more learning (Stevick, 1976); (2) motivation is an indicator related to feeling a sense of identity with another group (Gardner & Lambert, 1972); (3) self-confidence is a factor in learning: "The acquirer with more self-esteem and self-confidence tends to do better in second language acquisition" (Krashen, 1981, p. 62).

In conducting research in fourth- and fifth-grade classes in southern California, I have found that students tend to be at a low anxiety level when writing poetry. They are motivated to communicate ideas, and they display self-confidence while exploring topics through their poetry. The following list includes observations that I have found significant in researching the role of poetry in language acquisition and the study of subject matter.[1]

- Students are usually eager and excited when the activity involves writing poems. Because one may take liberties with the rules of grammar and syntax when writing poetry, children feel free to work and play with words and language. This seems especially true for second language learners.

- Students devise strategies for writing and organizing their poems. Thus, they are tapping into their logico-mathematical ability as well as their "creative" ability. Forms that emerge in the children's poems are generalizable. For example, many students organize their poems in a "sandwich" form, beginning and ending their work with the same words or phrases. Others organize according to a written shape on the page, repeating patterns, or employ punctuation in very definite ways.

- Writing poetry clearly serves to further understanding of subject matter in addition to fostering language use. The writing gives them an opportunity to apply—in words—their understandings of subject matter. Writing poems inspires children to find facts and ideas they wish to include in their writing. Students have shown interest in using reference books as they create poems; others look back into their journals and sketchbooks to review ideas they deem worthy to be included in their poems. The poetry-writing process may rekindle a curiosity in the learner and then provide a way to express that curiosity.

- I have found children eager to read poetry after experience with writing it. One student, asked why she was taking poetry books from the library, said, "Poems are better than stories. They make you happy or sad more than stories do." My documentation (over a one-year period) in a fourth-grade class indicated that, on their own, every single child in the class had taken out at least one poetry book from the library. As poets themselves, they have a much stronger entry into the world of other people's poetry.

- I have found that children's ability to read and interpret poetry can be extraordinary. This is an especially important finding because under traditional testing methods, many of the students with whom I have worked have scored low on reading comprehension. When I asked students to share poems from books they found intriguing, it was not unusual to hear poems by any number of poets. I was especially heartened on a day that a child who was a nonreader in September read to me a poem by Longfellow in March. What is especially important about this example is her comprehension of the poem. It would have been easy to assume that her comprehension level was on par

---

[1] I reported findings concerning poetry and second language acquisition in depth in a paper given at the 1995 American Educational Research Association (AERA) meeting in San Francisco, "The Role of Writing Poetry in Second Language Acquisition" (Goldberg, Doyle, & Vega-Casteneda, 1995).

with her ability to read, when actually her ability to make sense of the complex poetic puzzle indicated she had abstract thinking skills and a certain depth of thought.

- I have found that a teacher's view of individual children is continually enhanced (and perhaps changed) as she sees sides to children she had never seen before through their poetry. A teacher may acquire a more complex picture of her students as she reads their poems and is introduced to the ways in which they see and express their world. Poetry projects always manage to bring surprises into the classroom with regard to perceptions of individual children, their emerging knowledge, and their personalities.

- It is not unusual for children's views of themselves to be changed as a result of writing their own poetry and listening to the poetry written by others. Many children show confidence in sharing their written work. In my research I have noticed that this is especially true among children who were identified by their teacher as having low self-esteem.

PLAYING WITH WORDS

I would like to take the reader through a series of lessons concerning poetry writing for language acquisition. The examples used here are taken from a language transition fourth-grade class in San Marcos, California. For two years I worked in this school with a classroom teacher, Michelle Doyle, studying the role of poetry in language acquisition. Fully 96 percent of the children at San Marcos Elementary school are "minority"; 92 percent of these are labeled "Hispanic" and are of Mexican or Mexican American descent. In this particular case, with the school being only 45 miles north of the Mexican–U.S. border, most of the students are transitioning from Spanish to English. There are a few other languages interspersed, including Filipino and Chinese. Most of the students are in their first or second year of transitioning into an English-speaking class. There are a few students who speak English only.

In introducing poetry to the children, we first began by engaging them in a discussion about poetry. We asked them to describe their ideas concerning poetry, asked if any of them had written, read, or remembered any poetry, and so on. Michelle and I also read one of our favorite poems to the class. Following that, we got into the activity of writing. Prior to the session we had decided to focus on the topic of "family" for the first poem. We wanted a topic that was familiar (in one form or another) to everyone in the class.

First we had the students do a group brainstorm of words in English relating to family. As the students thought of words, Michelle and I wrote them on the board. We then asked the students to create their own list of family words on a separate piece of paper, using the words on the board as a starting point. The next step was to take the words from their list and organize them into a "word poem." Admittedly, we were not sure what we would get from this exercise. Our goal, however, was to get the class working or playing with words—to find ways to manipulate or put the words together. Much to our surprise, the children unhesitatingly went about their word organizing and created word poems that astonished both them and us.

Here are a few examples.

Topic: Family
Lesson One: Word Poems
Brainstorm: *grandma, mom, dad, sister, brother, uncle, aunt, cousin, baby, niece, nephew, grandpa, caring*

Poem
Caring grandma, grandpa,
mom, dad, aunt, uncle, cousin, niece, nephew,
sister, brother, baby

Comments: There are many noteworthy aspects to this poem. The student has organized the words from oldest to youngest. The gender is consistent: male/female in pairs (with the exception of *cousin*, which does not have a gender pairing). *Caring*, which is qualitatively different from all the other words, is placed in the beginning—separate from the people words. The organizational technique is remarkably consistent and identifiable, giving us insight into this child's ability to organize and categorize while employing language.

Brainstorm: *sister, brother, baby sister, baby brother, mom, dad, reunited, relatives, cousin, grandma, grandpa, aunt, uncle, shop owner, household chores, cooking, cleaning, shop, manager, mother*

Poem
Relatives, mother, father,
brother, sister, babybrother,
babysister, grandma, grandpa,
cousin, aunt, uncle, relatives

Comments: Note the "sandwich effect." By using the word *relatives* to begin and end the poem, this child has created a definite form. Also note the sets of relatives in generational pairs by gender: mother, father; grandma, grandpa—though the gender order is not completely consistent.

Brainstorm: *family, love, friends, aunt, cousin, baby brother, baby sister, mom, dad, grandpa, grandma, uncle, niece, pictures, babysitter, caring*

Poem
Caring, grandpa,
grandmother, uncle
niece, aunt, mom
dad, babysitter,
babysister, baby
brother, friends
picture, love

Michelle Doyle and her fourth graders in San Marcos,
California, work on their family poems.

Comments: Here is another example of "sandwich" organization using descriptive words instead of words for people (relatives), as the child in the first example used.

What surprised Michelle and me in addition to the children's willingness to compose word poems was the inventiveness with which they devised ways to organize their words. Interesting and consistent patterns emerged, such as the gender, age, and sandwich forms. The children were genuinely interested in inventing a form for their words. Having this success, we forged onward to similes.

The children were asked to create similes based on a particular family member. To introduce this notion we offered some initial models. For example, I wrote, "My grandfather is like a gift to me that I opened long ago and never forgot." We asked each child to choose one family member and create a simile based on that family member. Following that activity, we shared the similes as a class. That night the teacher and I took home all the similes and circled one word in each child's phrase. We brought them back the next day and asked the children to brainstorm and then generate more words based on the circled words. The object was to create a word bank to write a poem based on that family member. Following are a few examples of the children's initial similes, their subsequent brainstorm list, and then a draft of the poem that emerged from the work. I have underlined the word we circled on the child's paper.

Topic: Family
Lessons Two and Three: Similes
Simile: My brothers are like spider webs
Brainstorm: *spider webs, spider, tarantula, cockroach, webs, sticky, dracula*

First Draft

My brothers are like spider webs walking up
and down the house. they look like
spiders when they walk, they look like
draculas with their two front teeth
they are sticky when they eat. they
look like tarantulas when they crawl.

Second Draft

MY BROTHERS

My brothers are like
        spider webs walking up
            and down the
                house.
They look like spiders
        when they walk.
They look like draculas
        with their two
            front teeth.
They are sticky when
        they eat.

They look like tarantulas
    when they crawl.
They are cockroaches eating
    everything.
They are webs when
    they are asleep.

                    Raquel

Note the careful placement of Raquel's phrases and the spacing of the lines. This showed that she was employing organizational skills in addition to using language creatively.

Simile: My mom is like a beautiful <u>flower</u> blooming in the spring
Brainstorm: *flower*
beautiful, smell good, bloom, rose, spring, red, bouquet, pollen, bees, garden

Poem

MY MOM

My mom is like a beautiful flower blooming in the spring
she is like the beautiful red rose in a bouquet
you could plant her in your garden and
she smells so good!
Anybody would like to plant her in your garden
she is beautiful!

                  Heather Mendez

Simile: My mom is like the queen of my <u>heart</u>
Brainstorm: *heart*
pretty, beautiful, red, lovely, pumping, desire, love

Poem
My mom is like the queen of my heart
When she crowned me I never forgot the day and
now she is the queen of my heart
As beautiful and sweet as a flower.
I desire my mom's lovely heart and,
she is the queen of my heart

              Kekoa Villanuevo

Note that in addition to his original simile, Kekoa goes on to create and employ another simile in his poem: "As beautiful and sweet as a flower." In the next poem, Elizabeth not only creates one simile but strings together several.

Similes: My mom is like a gift to me; she is like cotton candy; she is like the moon in the night

MY MOM

My mom is like a
gift to me and she
is like cotton candy.
She is like the moon
in the night.

Elizabeth Cerros

Garret creates a wonderfully descriptive simile in the next example. His brainstorm includes many related words, some of which he includes in the final poem. If we devoted more time to the family poems, I would ask him if he could incorporate even more of his brainstormed words into his poem.

Simile: My dad is like a friendly <u>bull</u>
Brainstorm: *bull*
nice, brown, big, mean, white, strong, spots, runs fast, hates red, big strong horns, sharp horns, blue eyes

Poem

MY DAD

My dad is like a friendly bull
but sometimes he's not a friendly bull
sometimes he's a mad bull
but I'll like him and love him
as long as I will live.

Garret Ingram

In the last example, we find another poem concerning the most popular relative chosen by the children for this assignment: mom.

Simile: My mom is like a <u>flower</u>
Brainstorm: *flower*
beautiful, color-red-yellow-white, little, cute, special, picking, roses-black red, loolie pines, outside, garden, mom, me

FLOWERS

Flowers are cute   there color
are red, yellow, white   there
color are special for me

Roses for mothers and
colors for me
beautiful gardens and
green plants
you see flowers outside
you see flowers everywhere
and remember when you pick a
flower up that's your mom.

Adan Gonsalves

Each of these poems is representative of something known to the student-poet. The known—or the knowledge—is a perception of each one's world woven together and expressed in the words and phrasing of the poem. Each student-poet created similes to reveal and express his or her understandings. For example, Raquel created an original way to describe her twin baby brothers as spiders. Her description moves beyond the ordinary as she continues to create phrases that portray their actions, such as being "tarantulas when they crawl" or "cockroaches eating everything." Adan surprised us with his last line, "remember, when you pick a flower up, that's your mom" (commas added). The line shows an extraordinary understanding and use of language, especially for a 10-year-old whose first language is not English. In addition, for Adan it shows a depth of feeling otherwise usually hidden, perhaps for lack of an outlet.

Fourth graders with the author sharing a light moment after writing and reading original similes.

Though many of the poems may have a magical quality, there is nothing magical about the process through which each child began to write. The brainstorm activity was adapted from strategies described by McKim and Steinbergh in their book *Beyond Words: Writing Poems with Children* (1992). We introduced the class to published children's poems and specific poetic devices such as the simile. It was important that the teacher and I could write and share our own poems along with the children as a way of modeling poetic forms.

As mentioned earlier, my own "family" poem began with the line "My grandfather is like a gift to me that I opened long ago and never forgot." One can see from comparing the beginning of my poem to Elizabeth's where she might have gotten the idea to start her poem. She modeled the idea of the gift as a simile, and then she used it as a springboard for two other similes that were clearly of her own device. Other students created their own similes right away. Throughout the sessions on "family," students invented similes, "wordstormed" on key words (a "wordstorm" is a brainstorm—coming up with related words to key words), applied the words to their poems to include words from the wordstorm, edited, and re-edited their poems.

Poetry as a writing tool can be used to explore subject matter. In Chapter 6, we will revisit some of these same students as they practice literacy skills while applying their writing to topics in science. Although our work with the students was specifically designed to help with their language skills, we found that we could naturally combine language skills with subject matter exploration. The same principles applied: The children were playing with and applying words, but the topics could be drawn from other subjects throughout the day.

JOURNALS: WORKING WITH IDEAS OVER A PERIOD OF TIME

From the very beginning, we created poetry journals out of folded colored paper with white, lined paper inside. Each child decorated his or her journal and kept all in-class work there as well as any other poems they found or composed. Students were given the option of writing in their journal during morning silent reading time. Many students took advantage of this offer. Two things emerged: Children began writing poems in addition to the class assignments, and children began copying poems from books—and each other—into their journals. By periodically collecting the children's journals, I was able to document their work over time. The following was written by a second language student who, over a period of six months, played with the notion of "flying."

> Meteors fly like a fly
> maybe it's a butterfly
> with its wings spread
> high in the sky

Jaime wrote this poem in October during a class assignment in which students were to write a "science poem." I was first struck by the imagery in Jaime's poem. What a lovely image of a meteor as a butterfly! I was especially delighted because Jaime could be described as one of the class "bad boys" (written affectionately, of course). Here was another awakening for me into the reality of what was possible by a child whom I had labeled in a way that didn't match my expectations. In looking at the poem closely, I was interested in his ability to manipulate the word *fly* in three different ways. Jaime shows a sophisticated understanding of various uses of the word *fly* through his applications of the word in the poem. What becomes more evident is his desire to follow through—in writing poetry—on the idea of flying in general. In his journal, his next related poem was as follows.

> Butterfly fly like a fly
> with its wings spread high in the sky
> I don't know why
> but it can fly

Here, Jaime begins to wonder about the nature of flying. He employs some of the language and phrases from his original poem, including the lines "with its wings spread/high in the sky." The meteor is now gone, and in its place is a butterfly. In his next poem, Jaime continues to work on the flying butterfly notion but relates it more to himself, as he expresses a wish to be a butterfly.

> I like a fly cause it flys
> like a butterfly
> with its wings spread high in the sky
> I'd like to be a butterfly

The following poem was written in February around Valentine's Day. Jaime is so into contemplating flying that the Valentine cupids retell his flying theme, this time, with love.

> Valentine's day
> cupids are flying with love
> and people are caring and sharing

Finally, we see where Jaime's writing and thinking is taking him: to his wish to fly freely and be able to see things from a different perspective. Here Jaime offers a view into his inner life that does not ordinarily emerge in discussions or other ways in which we interact together.

IF I COULD FLY

> If I could fly where would I go?
> I would go across the sea and the desert
> I'd fly with the hawks, the falcons
> I'd like to fly

Another student, Anna, was interested in what I would describe as word-play. She wrote the following poem and entered it into her journal. She centered it in her journal as is shown here.

> Flowers are colors
> like purple murple
> red reddy blue lue

yellow mellow
orange growange
I like colors
especially
the color
of you

I was interested in the playfulness with which Anna employs and invents language. In addition, her final line brings forth the depth to which she is able to apply metaphorical thinking through language. Again, I believe this is an example of how the poetic form can provide an opportunity for students who are willing and eager to play with words, language, and, of course, ideas.

Each student's poem documents an organizational process of thought and reflection. Each one's willingness and ability to think metaphorically amazed us. We found that the poetic form seemed to encourage and even inspire the students to work with language. Reflecting on writing poems, a few students wrote the following in their journals: "I like writing poetry because it ryms [sic] and it has interesting words." "I do like writing poems, thats [sic] one of my best things I do." "I like writing poems because it could tells [sic] how people feel or how people would feel happy, sad, mad, confuse [sic] and puzzled." "I like [writing poems] because it captures the heart in you."

Copied Poems

In our work with the fourth graders, we encouraged them to copy poems they had read into their journals. Students whose English skills were fairly new tended to copy more poems into their journals than those more skilled, who included more original poems. A number of interesting aspects of the copying should be put forth for consideration. In order to copy poems, students must read poems and make decisions about which ones are interesting. From this we can learn about each child's ability to comprehend a poem—or at least their interest in the poem, and also their interest in reading poetry. I have found that it is not unusual for students to copy lengthy poems. Nikki, a fourth grader, copied the following poem from another student's journal:

If ever there's a moment
when you need a friend to listen,
if ever someone can reach out
to dry the tears that glisten,
I'll be there.
If ever you have special needs
and hope someone will see them
If ever you have secrets and would like a friend
to free them, I'll be there.
If you just need encouragement
to help you on the way,
if you need a cheerful voice
to pull you through the day,

I'll be there.
If you need one who cares a lot
and thinks about you often
If you need one who shares your hopes, your worries
strives to soften,
I'll be there.
If you would like to be yourself
with someone who respects you,
if you need one who understands how all of life
affects you,
I'll be there.

A lot of work went into copying this poem. Nikki not only copied a lengthy poem but paid attention to spelling and grammar as well. Her choice of poem may also indicate something to us about her thinking. What we know for sure is something about her willingness to enter poems into her journal on her own, and her attention to careful copying with regard to spelling, punctuation, and phrasing. Nikki then became interested in a poem shared by a classmate. For her next entry, Nikki chose to copy the poem into her journal.

NIGHT COMES

Night comes
leaking
out of the sky
stars come
peeking
moon comes
sneaking
silvery
Who is
a king?
Who is afraid
of the night?
not I.

Copying poems also serves as a bridge for students who are not comfortable with their writing ability. Ladianni had a truly difficult time writing a science poem. In her journal she wrote "Science—Aluminum." She just could not—or was not willing to—go beyond those two words. Finally she asked if instead of composing a poem she could find and copy a science poem from a book. She proceeded to copy a number of poems from *The Random House Book of Poetry for Children* (Prelutsky, 1983). The first poem was "The Universe" by Mary Britton Miller, concerning itself with the cycles of the moon, stars, and seasons.

THE UNIVERSE

There is a moon, there is a sun
Round which we circle every year,

And there are all the stars we see
On starry nights when skies are clear,
And all the countless stars that lie
Beyond the reach of the human eye.
If every bud on every tree,
All birds and fireflies and bees
And all the flowers that bloom and die
Upon the earth were counted up,
The number of stars would be
Greater, they say, than all of these.[2]

Ladianni's next copied poem was Michael Flanders's poem about the activities of a hummingbird. Her third entry was this one by Ogden Nash.

THE CANARY

The song of canaries
never varies
and when they're molting
they're pretty revolting[3]

The poems clearly indicate Ladianni's understanding of the poetry as it relates to science. We also glimpse Ladianni's sense of humor as we read "The Canary" by Ogden Nash. The Nash poem is an interesting choice in that the vocabulary is advanced, using the words *molting* and *revolting*. One surmises that Ladianni understands these words; otherwise, why would she include the poem that contains them in her journal? In fact, when we asked her about the poem she described its humor and restated its meaning, proving her comprehension. After copying these poems into her journal, which she enjoyed doing, she surprised us with this entry.

SCIENCE

Science is magic
sometimes it's fun
Magic is wonder
wonder is fun
fun is making experiments
experiment is thinking
thinking is smart
smart is you

What a breakthrough! Although she did not write an original poem when her classmates did, she eventually went on to write the poem "Science." In this case, Ladianni

---

[2] From ALL ABOARD by Mary Britton Miller. Copyright © 1958 and renewed 1986 by Pantheon Books, Inc. Reprinted by permission of Patheon Books, a division of Random House, Inc.

[3] From VERSES FROM 1929 ON by Ogden Nash. Copyright 1940 by Ogden Nash. Copyright © renewed. First appeared in THE SATURDAY EVENING POST. By permission of Little, Brown and Company.

A fourth grader carefully considers her word choice as she begins a new poem.

needed the time—and perhaps several models—before she could compose her own poem. It was certainly worth the wait.

KEY ELEMENTS TOWARD WRITING POETRY

In researching the role of poetry in language acquisition, I have developed a list of key elements that the reader might find useful. These few elements were constructed with Michelle Doyle, the students' classroom teacher and my partner in the poetry research project.

Wordstorming: Every time the children were to write a poem (in the class setting), they would brainstorm words as a way to get started.

Modeling: We presented the students with poems written by other children, especially in the beginning of the project. Throughout the work we always modeled brainstorming, editing, and other elements of the writing process. We often did this with overheads, being careful to clear away the poem-models quickly to avoid copying or dependence.

Editing and Revising: We encouraged the children to constantly edit and revise. Often we would spend several weeks on the same poem.

Publishing: The children's poems were "published"—either put up on a bulletin board, displayed at the local university, or given away to a friend or parent. At the end of the year, each student chose a poem to contribute to a class poetry book.

Journals: Each child had a poetry journal of her or his own—a simple construction-paper book made and decorated by the student, with plain lined paper inside. They kept all their poems in their journal and could add to it at any time.

Finding the Interests of the Students: We tried to find engaging topics based on the students' interests and the curriculum.

Timing: Guided poetry writing occurred at a specific time during the week—in our case, every Friday morning. This activity gave students something to look forward to and accorded the project importance. Students could also write on their own during their free time. In addition, their teacher gave them the option of writing during silent reading time.

Sharing: Enabling the students to share their work was empowering. Sharing also took the form of reading poems they had found in books from the library or poetry center.

SUMMARY

The arts provide many methods for gaining literacy skills while also fostering imaginative, creative, and critical thinking skills. The arts can support reading and writing skills while also reaching individual children's interests and abilities. Picto-spellings and cursive writing through movement give insight into the many creative ways through which students learn and apply their emerging literacy skills.

Poetry has an especially important function with regard to literacy. Through writing poetry, students may explore a world of words while taking liberties with the rules of grammar and syntax that might otherwise impede their willingness to compose. Other insights can be gained when children learn literacy skills through the arts. In working with fourth- and fifth-grade teachers, I continually hear expressions of surprise over how much teachers learn about their students. Teachers began to view their students in new ways as they observe their arts-related activities and read their poems. Students themselves seem to view themselves differently. Mostly they exude a sense of confidence and fulfillment in their ability to create and be creative. Children with low self-esteem come out from behind their own walls, delighting in their work.

TECH CONNECT

Technology, Arts, and Language Arts

Perhaps more so than any other area, language arts presents numerous ways in which technology broadens learning with and through the arts. The following are a few ideas to get you motivated!

- Earlier you read in the chapter about picto-spells. Abel Silvas, an artist with the SUAVE program, has suggested shadow-spell. His idea is to take spelling words from your spelling list of the week and put them on the overhead or Elmo with one missing letter. A student must pose in the form of the missing letter to form its shadow on the overhead. This could be done with the entire body or with the hands. Expand this to acting out the meaning of the word in a shadow puppetry drama.

- Use the computer to create original stories, illustrate them, and produce books for the class (publish). Images can be scanned from photographs, illustrations, or magazines; taken from the Web; or entered with a digital camera.

- Videotape autobiographies as a way to begin a writing project on autobiography.

- E-mail poem pen pals. Share poems with another classroom. (This could be for language arts or for another subject.)

- Surf the Web to access poetry, information about poets, writers, and literature.

- Use photography as a start for a writing project (see the lesson plan at end of the chapter). Either have students take photos and write narratives to accompany them or use photos that others have taken as your source.

- Present stories (original or from your reading texts) in dramatic form using slides or video as the backdrop.

- Tape sounds from nature or create new sounds and add them to stories and present them in class.

 QUESTIONS TO PONDER

1. How are art forms a kind of language? What makes them a language, or not a language?
2. Do you think the term *literacy* would be defined in the same way universally (in all cultures)?
3. What is the role of literacy in technology?
4. How can poetry, storytelling, and drama be effective tools for English language learners?

 EXPLORATIONS TO TRY

1. Brainstorm as many ways as you can to learn literacy *with* the arts. See how many ideas you come up with.

2. Brainstorm three specific ways to learn literacy *through* the arts. Choose curriculum ideas/topics/mandates that come from your school.

3. Take a weekly spelling list or vocabulary list that you will use in your class. Create a picto-spelling using one or more of the words.

4. Using the same spelling list, choose two words and brainstorm related words. Then compose a poem. Reflect on your experience: How did you brainstorm and think of new words? Did you look up any words? How did you start applying the words to a poem? Did the words give you an idea, or did an idea come to you and then you added words? Did you add words to your poem *other* than those you originally brainstormed?

REFERENCES

Cecil, N. L., & Lauritzen, P. (1994). *Literacy and the arts for the integrated classroom.* New York: Longman.

Dillard, A. (1989). *The writing life.* New York: Harper and Row.

Gallas, K. (1991). Arts as epistemology: Enabling children to know what they know. *Harvard Educational Review, 61*(1).

————. (1994). *The languages of learning: How children talk, write, dance, draw, and sing their understanding of the world.* New York: Teachers College Press.

Gardner, R. C., & Lambert, W. E. (1972). *Attitudes and motivation in second language learning.* Rowley, MA: Newbury House.

Goldberg, M., Doyle, M., & Vega-Casteneda, L. (1995, April). The role of writing poetry in second language acquisition. Paper presented at the 1995 American Educational Research Association meeting, San Francisco.

Greene, M. (1991). Texts and margins. *Harvard Educational Review, 61*(1).

Heard, G. (1989). *For the good of the earth and the sun: Teaching poetry.* Portsmouth, NH: Heinemann.

Hopkins, L. B. (1972). *Pass the poetry please!* New York: Harper and Row.

Johnson, D. M. (1990). *Word weaving: A creative approach to teaching and writing poetry.* Urbana, IL: National Council of Teachers of English.

Koch, K. (1973). *Rose, where did you get that red?* New York: Random House.

Krashen, S. D. (1981). *Schooling and language minority students: A theoretical framework.* Los Angeles: Evaluation, Dissemination and Assessment Center, California State University.

Livingston, M. C. (1984). *The child as poet: Myth or reality?* Boston: Horn Book.

————. (1991). *Poem-making: Ways to begin writing poetry.* New York: HarperCollins.

McKim, E., & Steinbergh, J. (1992). *Beyond words: Writing poems with children* (2nd ed.). Brookline, MA: Talking Stone Press.

Phillips, A. (1990). *Thinking on the inside: Children's poetry and inner speech.* Cambridge, MA: Harvard Graduate School of Education, unpublished.

Prelutsky, J. (Ed.). (1983). *The Random House book of poetry for children.* New York: Random House.

Steinbergh, J. W. (1991). To arrive in another world: Poetry, language development and culture. *Harvard Educational Review, 61*(1).

Stevick, E. W. (1976). *Memory, meaning and method.* Rowley, MA: Newbury House.

Tsujimoto, J. (1964). *Teaching poetry writing to adolescents.* Urbana, IL: National Council of Teachers of English.

SAMPLE LESSON PLANS

Language Arts

The following lessons offer a wide range of possibilities for learning through the arts. Janine Burton writes out her lesson for picto-spells, described earlier in this chapter. Vicky Fox details the use of photography as a motivation tool for many kinds of writing. Dawn McDonald's lesson on animal alliteration focuses on alliteration, adjectives, and the use of a thesaurus. Mary Caney, Sue Shepherd, Kathryn Nyberg, and Julie Horn use storyboarding and pantomine for studying and creating stories.

SUAVE Curriculum and Project Description

PROJECT TITLE: Picto-spells

TEACHER: Janine Burton

SCHOOL AND GRADE: Grade 4, Richland

DISCIPLINE AREA(S): Language Arts / Visual Arts

PROJECT GOAL(S): To help students visually represent spelling of vocabulary words, showing meaning in picture—to heighten understanding of word meanings.

PROCESS AND STEPS:

- List of current vocabulary words provided to students
- Modeling of sample picto-spellings
- Students explore various words of their choices to create visual picture of meaning
- Make students aware of spelling word correctly to create picture/object
- Students share with others in groups

MATERIALS NEEDED: List of vocabulary words, paper, pencil or pen

ESSENTIAL QUESTIONS:

1. **What skills, elements, vocabulary were taught?**

   To visually represent vocabulary word, students had to truly understand what word communicated

2. **How did you assess the children's understanding?**

   Teacher observation, talking with students during process, finished products

3. **Where could you go from here?**

   Possibly to include color or perspective—perhaps a montage with more than one word in design

SUAVE Curriculum and Project Description

PROJECT TITLE: Photograph Exploration and Writing

TEACHER: Vicky Fox

SCHOOL AND GRADE: Grade 5, Miller

DISCIPLINE AREA(S):   Language Arts / Visual Arts

PROJECT GOAL(S):   Photography as art form; careful observation of photograph; imaginative writing

PROCESS AND STEPS:

1. Students view photograph; list things they *see* in the photograph and *questions* they have about the photograph, individually on paper.
2. Share orally. Add to lists, if desired.
3. Choose and do a follow-up writing activity:
   a. Write a letter *to* someone in the photo
   b. Write a letter *as if you were* someone in the photo
   c. Write a poem relating to the photo. (Poem form[s] should already be taught.)
4. Students share aloud their writings.

MATERIALS NEEDED:

- 1 photograph and opaque projector (or) enough copies of a photo for pairs to share
- notebook paper and pencils

ESSENTIAL QUESTIONS:

1. **What skills, elements, vocabulary were taught?**
   Composition, balance, center of focus, positive/negative space, changes in point of view
2. **How did you assess the children's understanding?**
   Informal assessment of use/understanding of vocabulary, teacher assessment of writings
3. **Where could you go from here?**
   Give each student a different photo/magazine picture. Have students create a book of these photos accompanied by their writings.
4. **Other comments:**
   The poetic forms with which my students were familiar were diamante, haiku, and couplet.

SUAVE Curriculum and Project Description

PROJECT TITLE: Animal Alliteration

TEACHER: Dawn McDonald

SCHOOL AND GRADE: Grade 5, Valley Center Elementary–Upper School

DISCIPLINE AREA(S): Language Arts / Visual Arts

PROJECT GOAL(S): An animal drawn in the shape of the first letter from which the animal is spelled (Example: S = Snake)

PROCESS AND STEPS: Each student thinks of a variety of animals, but chooses one he/she would like to draw. The animal is drawn on white construction paper in the form of the first letter of the animal's name.

—Using a thesaurus, each student writes out as many adjectives as he/she can, starting with the same letter. Each adjective should describe the animal in one way or another.

—Each student then uses these adjectives to write one descriptive sentence. Example: Larry, the lordly, lurking lion lumbers lazily through the lilting, lofty leaves.

—The alliteration sentence is written somewhere along the animal (big enough so it can be read).

—As a border the student writes the name of the animal all around. Example: LionsLionsLionsLionsLions, etc.

—The student then colors the picture in bold colors.

ESSENTIAL QUESTIONS:

1. **What skills, elements, vocabulary were taught?**
   Use of the thesaurus and/or dictionary. Also, the meaning of *alliteration* and *adjective*. The drawing of an animal.

2. **How did you assess the children's understanding?**
   Whether the student followed directions in production of the art picture and alliteration sentences

3. **Where could you go from here?**
   Into an adjective unit, and/or descriptive writing

4. **Other comments:**
   All students can and did do well on this, no matter their academic level. They also seemed to enjoy the activity immensely.

SUAVE Curriculum and Project Description

LESSON/PROJECT TITLE: Pantomime Storytelling

TEACHERS: Mary Caney, Sue Shepherd, Kathryn Nyberg, Julie Horn

SCHOOL AND GRADE: Grade 3, Valley Center Lower Elementary

SUBJECT AREA: Language Arts / Visual Arts / Drama

MATERIALS: Language Arts textbook, *The Two Bad Ants*

DESCRIPTION:

1. Students read story from their reading text.
2. Students make a storyboard of the story (see attached).
3. Students model characters' emotions and actions. Practice with children.
4. Students pantomime events of story (event by event).
5. Run through, with coaching and use of storyboard (on overhead).
6. Add music, pantomime entire story without cues from teacher.

ASSESSMENT: Children should be able to remember the sequence of the story, as well as the actual pantomime techniques they've learned in order to express their emotions.

SKILLS USED: Sequencing, comprehension, interpretation, character analysis, story elements, stage presence, timing.

ENRICHMENT: Students can write their own stories to be pantomimed. They can also compare and contrast stories that they've acted out. This can be made into a presentation for other classes and/or parents.

COMMENTS: We found the writing aspect of this project to be quite valuable. As our kids wanted to have their stories acted out, they saw the need to have a plot, including a beginning, middle, and ending. They realized their need to write clear events and have a story that made sense to the readers/actors. This process brought forth quite a few discussions about writing, and a genuine interest in the writing process, as there was the possibility for this type of "publishing" at the end.

**Lesson Plan: Learning Compound Words Through Music
(from Goldberg, 2004) Written by Karen Sleichter and Sherry Reid**

GRADE: Grade 2

SUBJECT AREA: Language Arts

MATERIALS: Chart with song written in large print; tape or CD of tune "Did You Ever See a Lassie?"; paper and a variety of art supplies

PROCEDURE: This song on compounds is taught to the children after an initial introduction to compound words. When the children become familiar with the song, they can fill in the blanks with their own words. For example, "Did you ever see a *drumstick*, a *drumstick*, a *drumstick*? Did you ever see a *drumstick* go this way and that?" The words should be accompanied by movement. This technique is particularly effective with second language students. After a few days, the children can illustrate a compound word of their choice. Using a variety of art media to culminate this project adds high interest for the students and makes a nice class display.

EXAMPLES OF COMPOUND WORDS: *beehive, tapeworm, backbone, drumstick, nighttime, bookworm, eyelash, toenail, fingernail, keyboard, eyeball, basketball, football, baseball, toothbrush, toothpaste, raincoat.*

Chapter 5

The Voices of Humanity: History, Social Studies, Geography, and the Arts

VOICE OF THE TURTLE

Beauty arrives on
the wings of your song
as our hearts dance
to the beat of
our collective pasts

We dream up memories of
ancient wisdom,
wrinkled hands that
reach out to us across the
eons of time,
touch our tender souls
and speak the language of
pulsating rhythms,
melancholy words,
undeniable passion.

Praise to the enduring
spirit that allows us
young and old
to gather here to share

the cries of our ancestors
the voice of the turtle
within all of us.

    Judy Leff, fifth-grade teacher

History has taught us that we learn the rudiments of our very existence through culture. What we make through the various media in the arts and what we say in words inform those who experience our artistry, denoting who we are and what our cultural aspirations are.

    Bill Cosby (quoted in Asmal, 2003, p. 286)

"In ancient Mexico the wise man was called tlamatini, or 'he who knows,'" writes Bradley Smith (1968); "he was the repository of the collected knowledge, oral and graphic, of a rich culture. The visual records in his keeping took the form of sequential picture-symbol drawings illustrating, among other themes prosaic and profound, the creation of man, the histories of dynasties, and the laws and customs of the times" (p. 7).

"His story," or history, is a documentation and retelling of the past in some manner or form. For the *tlamatini* it took the form of pictures and symbols. For the Australian Aboriginal, it is through song. For many schoolchildren, the traditional textbook does the trick. In this chapter we will explore the relationship between the arts and social studies, and the ways in which the arts can be integrated into social studies subject matter.

In documenting and retelling our pasts, we consider, interpret, analyze, and question events and actions. We then consider the study as it relates to the present and our own lives, and we include "her stories" as well as "our stories." The arts are, and have always been, a major force in history, documenting and reflecting times and changes in our lives. Judy Leff's poem at the beginning of this chapter is representative of the power of the arts in social studies. Through her poem Judy reflects on the impact of a history lesson carried out in her classroom, a bilingual (Spanish–English) performance/workshop presented by the Ladino group Voice of the Turtle, which I mentioned in Chapter 1. Presenting songs of Spain's Jewish population in the Diaspora from 1492 to the present, Voice of the Turtle not only entertains but communicates source materials documenting the events, dreams, frustrations, passions, and hopes of a people.

The poems written that day by both Judy and the students in her class were in response to the workshop, but they hold a deeper meaning. Each poem reflects a serious attempt at integrating that day's history lesson with the everyday lives of the members of the class. Not only did students and teacher consider history as subject matter in and of itself, but through their writing they also contemplated the connections of the history lesson to their present-day experiences.

The arts serve various functions with regard to history and social studies. First, they are documents to the past through which we are introduced to individuals in every corner of the world and the ways they have expressed their perception of some part of their lives. The arts serve as voices of a people and images of their lives. As far back as rock art and cave painting, the arts have provided a venue through which people have documented their experiences and provided a tremendous source of information for interpretation to later inquiries.

The arts serve another function beyond a rich documentation of culture. They are a powerful tool for social change. Victor Cockburn is a folksong writer and singer who as a teenager attended a concert that changed his way of thinking. Pete Seeger, Odetta, and Reverend Gary Davis provided his first introduction to the power of music for social change. Cockburn (1991) writes, "the simple beauty of the music and power of the lyrics inspired me to become more deeply involved with this universal form of expression. The effect it had on the audience—bringing a large roomful of people together in song—and the information and history I learned through music motivated me to learn more about folk music" (p. 71).

While deliberating history and social studies in relation to the arts, I would like to ask you, as reader, to consider a few critical issues and questions. These are meant to guide your thinking rather than dictate a certain point of view. I take the stand that social studies is both a subject and a methodology. We can study events in our lives as subject matter, but at the same time the manner in which we consider the events is equally important. In that light, I believe social studies must be a course of action in addition to a course of study. I suggest that the focus of a social studies course is to create historians and social scientists rather than able "tellers" of the past.

If we accept that history is, in part, stories from the past, then from whose perspective will the stories be told? How will they be told? How is it decided which stories will be told and subsequently included in the curriculum? Is history more than stories? Is history a chronicle of events? If so, how should newsworthy events be chosen? Does history ever change? If so, what changes it? Finally, perhaps most critical, what is the purpose of studying and understanding history?

According to the National Council for the Social Studies, there are ten thematic strands in social studies standards (Parker & Jarolimek, 2009). The first of these strands is "culture," which focuses in part on ways to "describe language, stories, folktales, music, and artistic creations [and how they] serve as expressions of culture and influence behavior of people living in a particular culture" (p. 7). Parker (2009) makes this notion more specific:

> Encourage children and their parents to share music and art that has distinct ethnic origins or particular meanings to the family. Invite an ethnic musicologist to the class to share information about music's cultural roots. Model for children that regardless of your own ethnic or racial identification, you value many different forms of music and art. (p. 214)

Teachers moving away from a presentation of history as a list of events are using historical context as a stepping-stone toward an integrated curriculum. Stories of the past are contextualized in the interrelationships among geography, economics, politics, culture, and so on. Events of the past are used as a methodology for understanding current events. Contexts and multiple perspectives are derived from primary sources including diaries, journalism, songs, poetry, and artwork.

LEARNING WITH THE ARTS

Studying history and social change *with* the arts offers students a number of interesting issues. Art examples drawn from music, visual art, poetry, sculpture, drama, photography, and so on provide the history student with primary sources to examine. Among the benefits of using artworks as primary sources is that they provide an extra bonus in their depiction of the life of a community, person, or event. Ruth Rubin (1990) discusses this bonus in her book on the history of the Jewish people through Yiddish folksong:

> In the songs, we catch the manner of speech and phrase, the wit and humor, the dreams and aspirations, the nonsense, jollity, the pathos and struggle of an entire people. . . . These are the songs that served the needs, moods, creative impulses, and purposes of a particular environment at particular periods in the history of [Jewish communities]. (p. 9)

I might argue that the songs Rubin presents are more "authentic" than an "objective" accounting by a person documenting important events. Songs and other artworks reflect human complexities in their most personal form. They remind us that there is no such thing as a standard history of a people because events and life are experienced in multiple ways and through multiple lenses. Through their melodies, harmonies, and phrasing, songs give insight into the feelings and nuances of people and cultures that cannot be found in a more journalistic report. They contain the world's repertoire of personal accounts of life experiences, including children's songs and songs about love, courtship, marriage, customs, beliefs, events, religion, struggles, survival, and so on.

On another level, songs or other artworks can be inviting. For some students, studying an art form may be more to their liking than interacting with a history text and therefore may engage them in serious contemplation. Utilizing art forms in a historical context opens the door to many students who are interested in artistic forms and/or whose learning styles are visual or auditory.

Let me highlight a few resources to get you thinking about the possibilities of integrating the arts into history lessons. By no means should my examples be taken as the best or only sources. Rather, they are a sampling of the kinds of material available to you. We will begin with poetry.

Poetry

There are many historically based poetry books. One that is used in classrooms I have visited is *Hand in Hand: An American History Through Poetry,* which contains works collected by Lee Bennett Hopkins (1994). This particular book is based on subject matter rather than a strict chronological framework. Poems represent aspects of experiences from multiple perspectives and with multiple voices. Some were written by people living at the moment in history, and others were written by poets who have reflected on the experiences of a time or life.

In the section of the book dedicated to the social changes of the 1960s–1990s, poems concerning the civil rights movement, homelessness, John F. Kennedy's assassination, the Vietnam War, and social injustice are included. The poems serve to get students thinking about the time period, but they also act as an impetus to involve the students in questioning. The poem "en-vi-RON-ment" below, written by Lee Bennett Hopkins, is an example. It opens up a stream of consideration. It includes facts about what homeless people do. But the magic of the art form adds another dimension: It gives the reader things to think about. The poet presents a complicated image that prompts the reader to think about homelessness in many ways, including the relationship of homelessness to the environment. For me, one of the major impacts of art as history is its ability to put a face on the subject. In this case, Hopkins puts a face on homelessness and invites his readers to examine it up close. As you read this poem, consider the topics your students might tackle by way of examining current issues in your own curriculum.

en-vi-RON-ment

Homeless People
line up at 8:00 a.m.
sharp
in front of D'Agostino's
on Bethune Street
in Greenwich Village
waiting patiently
for
Automatic Door
to swing open.

They have empty cans.
Sorted.
Placed neatly in rows
in discarded
cardboard flats
or layered in
past-used plastic bags.

A good firm Pepsi is best.
A dented Bud needs
a crack of the fingers
to straighten it back
to its original shape.

A foot-flattened
Orange Crush
is no good to anyone.
(it gets carefully tossed
into the city-trash-can
on the corner.)

Empty cans are coins.

Coins add up
　to a cup of coffee
　to a bowl of soup
　to a tuna on rye.

Empty cans
are important
to
Homeless People.
They need them
to
feed Them.

And
they help Them
do their conscience-bit
to
protect
the
en-vi-RON-ment.[1]

Visual Arts

Let's now move into the realm of visual arts. Paintings can lend greatly to historical contexts and understandings. *Mine Eyes Have Seen the Glory: The Civil War in Art,* edited by Harold Holzer and Mark Neely Jr. (1993), is not, according to the editors, "an illustrated history of the Civil War, or perhaps one should say *another* history of the Civil War" (p. x). "Rather," the editors suggest, "we considered [the paintings] as a part of a great effort to comprehend the Civil War, and the opportunity for comparison offered by this approach revealed meanings in the works about which we had never read before" (p. xi). These meanings lie within emotions the paintings evoke, information the details of the images provide, and sentiments the faces in the paintings portray.

Walter Parker (2009), in his book *Social Studies in Elementary Education*, urges the use of art to enrich social studies. He writes that

> . . . historical paintings along with concepts drawn from the fine arts can be used to study major events in American history such as Howard Chandler Christy's depiction of the signing of the U.S. Constitution or Jacob Lawrence's paintings of the migration of African Americans from the south to the north after World War I." (pp. 428–434)

Especially for students who enjoy visual images, but apropos for any student, paintings provide the images to which texts can only allude. In examining paintings from the

---

[1] Reprinted by permission of Curtis Brown Ltd. Copyright © 1994 by Lee Bennett Hopkins. First appeared in *HAND IN HAND: An American History Through Poetry.* Published by Simon & Schuster.

Civil War, for example, students can see the clothes the soldiers wore, the manner in which they marched, the look and size of the guns they carried, the vastness of the fields through which they traveled, the physical features of the tents they constructed for sleeping, the size of the cannons and the way they loaded them for battle, the look of the camp along the Potomac, and even specific details of events—such as the "Presentation of the Colors to the First Colored Regiment of New York by the Ladies of the City in Front of the Old Union League Club, Union Square, New York City, in 1864" in a painting by Edward Lamson Henry (1841–1919).

Photography

Photography provides a rich arena for integrating arts and social studies and language arts. Wendy Ewald is a photographer who has written several books on using photography as a teaching tool. Pictures capture events and stories and prove an engaging medium for students, perfect for the social studies. In one of her books, *I Wanna Take Me a Picture* (2001), Ewald and her collaborators describe at length learning how to read photographs, developing literacy through photographs, and using photography in the community. Taking pictures offers students another venue for studying, and viewing pictures gives the teacher and students insight not only into subject matter such as social studies, but also into the student taking the photos.

Music

In the same way, music can provide auditory understanding and connection when used critically. There are numerous songs written in response to historical events or relating to periods and characters in history. Returning to the theme of the Civil War, Jeanette Allen, a high school teacher in Sparks, Nevada, used songs including the following to introduce her students to the origins of the Civil War and the personal struggles of individuals of the time: "Battle Cry of Freedom," "All Quiet on the Potomac," "Battle Hymn of the Republic," and "John Brown's Body."

In using the songs, Jeanette went beyond encouraging her students to develop critical listening skills. She had students compile a journal of responses. She then asked groups of students to present to the class their responses to stories of the Civil War as represented through the songs and artworks. Students also used textbooks to gather information to support their opinions in their stories. One student reported to Jeanette that he felt "more connected" to the time period, the people, and their struggles, and the enormous toll the war took on this country because of the personal flavor the arts brought to the topic.

One of my favorite collections of music for teaching about a time in history is *Sing for Freedom: The Story of the Civil Rights Movement Through Its Songs,* edited and compiled by Guy and Candie Carawan (1990). In addition to the songs (complete with musical notation) and accompanying commentary, the books include a bibliography, discography, and suggested films and videos.

Drama

Considering drama, dances, and literature from various periods in a historical perspective can be a unique opportunity to understand history and social change while also giving a "feel" for the time. Many teachers have even *become* a historical character as they present information to students. This is always an enjoyable and engaging activity. Parker (2009) suggests that teachers have students focus on "the concepts of *plot* and *character* from children's literature to better understand a social event" (p. 428). This is a nice way to truly integrate subject areas of the curriculum in a genuine and engaging fashion, and to have students become the characters in their studies.

I once became Jean Piaget for a conference on teaching and learning. A few educators—myself among them—were asked to become characters rather than discuss them. So, I (as Piaget) along with Maria Montessori and John Dewey spent an afternoon talking with each other in front of an attentive audience. We even took questions from the audience about our theories and answered them in character. It was a wonderful afternoon, and the participants had a joyful time learning about various pedagogical theories and those who espoused them. They were clearly intrigued and subsequently involved as they asked question after question. We as participants also delighted in our discussions among ourselves when we disagreed on a topic or answer. It was fun for me to take on the character and arguments of Piaget rather than to present them as I usually do. I wore a beret and carried a knapsack like Piaget did. I even learned a little French to be more convincing. But more important, the role-playing forced me to consider the thoughts and words of Piaget in a meaningful and diligent manner. After all, I wouldn't want people to go away from the session with a false idea of Piaget the person and Piaget the thinker.

Pablo Tac

A curriculum we've been developing in California presents the fourth- and fifth-grade history curriculum through drama. Fourth and fifth graders in California study California Indians and the history of the California missions. Pablo Tac was a young Luseño Indian boy who lived on the San Luis Rey Mission in Oceanside, California (southern California), just a few miles away from our university. He was the first Indian person asked to write a history of his people by the Church, and was taken to Rome for his writings. He was only thirteen when he began, just slightly older than the children in the fourth and fifth grades studying California history! Abel Silvas, mentioned earlier in this text, has been teaching the life of Pablo Tac by having the students become the characters Pablo wrote about and reenacting scenes from his life, including what life was like on the mission in the late 1800s, before Pablo was taken to Rome. It is a fascinating way to learn, and extremely memorable for all the students.

LEARNING THROUGH THE ARTS

Learning social studies and history through the arts prepares students to be social scientists and historians. As students become engaged in art-related activities, they are likely to become interested in the subject matter itself. Their authentic experiences may lead to curiosity and the asking of important questions. A historian or social scientist who merely documents events is missing out on the true value of the documentation— to better understand the human condition and the contexts in which we negotiate our lives together in a community, city, country, or even on our shared earth.

In conceptualizing a language arts/social studies unit for her students, Lynne Ogren, a second-grade teacher in Reno, Nevada, decided on biography as a theme. This nicely integrates reading and history. Students could choose a biography from several in their reading book, or they could select a biography from the library or home as long as it was at the appropriate reading level. Students were asked to read through the biography at least three times and take notes under the following topic headings: Family, Childhood, School, Talent, Job, and Interesting or Important Facts. Students were given class time to look through other source materials to find other facts about their subject.

When students had completed this work, they were asked to present something to the class that represented their character. Suggestions included wearing a costume; creating a picture, poem, diorama, or song relating to the person; or re-creating the art form of that person. Students chose for their presentations Harriet Tubman, known for her work with the Underground Railroad; Chief Standing Bear, a Lakota Indian chief; Robert Goddard, a rocket scientist; and Maria Martinez, a Pueblo potter. The child who presented Harriet Tubman came to class wearing clothes based on pictures she had seen of Tubman, and she presented a poster she had created. She told the class she knew the Railroad was not a "real railroad" and instead was a code for the path to freedom, but she wanted to make the poster "anyway." The poster was of a train representing the Underground Railroad with a quote from Harriet Tubman: "I will never run my train off the track and I will never lose a passenger." Another student, a girl, gave a talk on Robert Goddard in first person, and dressed as a man! She also made a 3-foot-tall posterboard rocket.

Lynne believed that students became more "in touch" with the subject as a result of the artwork. About several of her students she wrote in her journal, "I know it was the carrot at the end of the stick in motivating them to put together a biography." In addition, she commented, "The artwork also made the presentations much more interesting for the rest of the class to listen to." This is a point less considered, but important. If presentations are engaging, as they often are when the arts are involved, they have that much more power to keep the attention of the audience. The more attention toward the subject matter, the more likely children will remember details of the class and be interested in following up on the subject. The arts can keep not only the work interesting but the class time spent in presenting it magical as well.

Presidential Puppetry

The next story illustrates how students and teachers can be empowered through arts-based activities. It relates to Principle 5 of equitable education and the arts (p. 24). Betsey Mendenhall, an experienced fifth-grade teacher in Escondido, California, took another approach to history in her classroom. As part of the SUAVE project (a professional development program that will be highlighted in Chapter 10), Betsey had artist-educator Mindy Donner as a coach in her class working to find ways to integrate subject matter and the arts. Betsey was teaching a unit about U.S. presidents. As part of the SUAVE partnership, Betsey and Mindy decided to have students create president puppets. Hesitant at first, Betsey was worried there wouldn't be enough time for this kind of project. She also was not convinced that her students would be interested in such a project. After all, puppets are for little kids.

Mindy, drawing on her skills as a puppeteer, had students bring in as many plastic grocery bags as they could find. Using only plastic bags, rubber bands, and masking tape, the children, Betsey, and Mindy began to form shapes that resembled people. Having completed the basic shapes, students added papier mâché to form the skin and then created clothes for each puppet to wear. The students loved creating the puppets and seeing them come to life from such simple materials. Each puppet would eventually become one of the U.S. presidents.

Betsey's goal was that upon completion the puppets would talk with each other, thereby enabling the students to get into their "historical characters." Her plan was to have groups of students create scripts of the various presidents talking to one another. What actually happened was even more interesting.

To get the students started, she held up two of the puppets and asked, "What kinds of things would you like these two to talk about?" She thought students would ask questions about politics. Much to her surprise, the questions revolved around these three themes: environment, violence, and family. Some of the questions the puppets would ask included "What did you do with your trash?" "Who took care of it if there were no trash collectors?" "Where did you go to the bathroom?" "If you didn't have a hose, how did you water the plants?" "Are you afraid of dying?" "Who does the president ask if he has a problem?"

Every question created another question, and Betsey was fascinated by the enthusiasm that was growing in her classroom. She sensed that students felt much freer to ask questions when it was the puppet asking the question and not them. Because the other puppet didn't have to answer the question, students became interested in the challenge of coming up with interesting questions. Some of the questions raised interesting avenues to explore as they revealed what could be labeled as erroneous assumptions. One such question was, "How did you deal with the drug problem in 1870?"

Not having an answer to this question readily available in the textbook, students were mystified about how to find the answer. They turned to Betsey. She told them she wasn't sure there even was a drug problem in 1870—certainly she didn't know if the problem existed in the same manner that the students had it framed in the present, and she told them as much. Though she didn't have an answer for them, she said she had an idea about how to begin finding out. She was about to engage them in the detective work of historians.

Betsey soon realized that her goal of creating scripts might be put off a bit, for the students had their own agenda, and it included becoming historians. Because they had raised many probing questions, Betsey started them thinking about ways to pursue answers. She asked them to consider what their sources of information concerning various questions might be—and the students started with the drug problem of 1870. Students generated the following list of places to look for information: the library, the art museum to find paintings of the period, and grandma. One student said she had noticed that the history text contained pictures from the Civil War. If the Civil War took place in 1860, she decided there were probably pictures from the 1870s that they could draw upon. Another

Betsey Mendenhall and Zulma Acosta with their president puppets.

student wondered if they could get helpful information from hospitals. From there, students began to ask related questions, including, "Did they have band-aids then?"

This "tangent" led into a wonderful discussion of inventions in history and what contexts led to certain inventions. Students looked around the room and became curious about their immediate environment. Who thought of the rubber band and how come? Kleenex? What did they use before Kleenex? The more obvious, such as the light bulb, was skipped over; it seemed as if Thomas Edison was old hat. "Been there, done that," they declared. Betsey then told them there was an inventor among them in the class. "Who?!" the students wanted to know. "Zulma," answered Betsey. Zulma looked confused and probably thought to herself, "What is the teacher talking about?"

Betsey then pulled Zulma's president puppet from the back of the room and showed it to the class. "How did you sew the president's clothes, Zulma?" asked Betsey. Zulma answered, "I didn't; I stapled them." Zulma had invented a new way of sewing. "But that's not an invention," declared a classmate. "But she invented a new way to sew," called out another student. As Betsey had hoped, a fruitful discussion emerged. Then one of the students asked about the Happy Face logo that Betsey used when she signed her name. "Did someone invent that?" one of the students asked. This led into a discussion concerning patents and how to find out if something is patented.

The class was animated. Students were engaged and having fun. Rather than learning *about* history, students were learning to be critical thinkers and how to *be* historians. They were engaging in the activities critical to the field of history and were finding ways to pursue their questions. Rather than have them create scripts at this time, Betsey shifted her focus to match the students' interest in pursuing questions. In partners, she asked the students to choose three questions they would really like to have answered. Knowing that the students would likely think they would then have to find the answers, she devised a twist. After each pair came up with their questions, Betsey had them switch questions with another pair.

Having experienced success, Betsey has considered having a monthly "jam session of questions." She thinks she might start with volunteers in pursuing answers, and then eventually include all students. She also has not given up the idea of the presidents discussing politics with one another. What was of particular interest to her in reflecting on all this work was the enthusiasm and dedication exhibited by the students. Because the "puppets" had nothing to lose, they could ask all sorts of questions—perhaps questions that a "student" might be too shy or self-conscious to ask. Though the students' direction in the puppet activity went in a way completely unexpected to Betsey, she found that the journey was thoroughly productive, worthwhile, and engaging.

Mural Making and History

Mural making can provide an opportunity for students to develop and carry through on a timeline. Murals also relate well to math lessons concerning proportion and graphing. This works for both younger and older students. The timeline in and of itself presents interesting challenges with regard to decision-making. What time period should the mural cover? What dates should be used? What events should be highlighted? How should events be depicted?

An interesting mural/history idea comes from a project in San Yisidro, a border town in southern California. By reproducing photographs from the San Diego Historical

Society, artists working with children created twelve murals expressing the cultural vitality and evolution of the town. In this case, students learned about local history, and in doing so they interacted with local artists and applied what they were learning to a community project.

Another example is the red clay brick project in Birmingham, Alabama, where students learn to make and decorate bricks. Started as an education program through the Birmingham Museum of Art, the project involved 150 inner-city schoolchildren. After learning about how the red clay in the ground surrounding their community was used to make bricks to line steel ovens, the students were introduced to decorative uses of red clay such as eighteenth-century Wedgewood pots. Students learned about "the scientific background of clay, glazes and firing techniques, and much about Josiah Wedgewood himself, including his role as an early opponent to slavery" (Frame, 1994, p. 22). According to Anne Arrasmith (quoted by Frame), a co-director of the project, "Now the students know more about Wedgewood and the Industrial Revolution than most adults and can relate that knowledge back to Birmingham and its history as a steel town" (p. 22). As a follow-up to the project, 2,000 bricks were commissioned by the city for a mural project.

Quilts and History

Quilting and quilts provide another wonderful entry into the world of history. Susan Goldman Rubin (2004), an author of children's books on art (whom I discuss further in Chapter 8), has written about slave quilts and women's quilts as art. "Over the years, women have made quilts not only to produce something useful," writes Goldman, "but as a form of self-expression" (p. 26). Slaves had a rich tradition of quilting and designed quilts with symbols from their tribes in Africa, embroidered them with designs of local plants, and created quilts with specific purposes. Some quilts had patterns that instructed runaway slaves to follow crooked routes, indicated directions to the Underground Railroad, or signified a safe house. At the end of this chapter, there is a sample lesson on creating ancestry quilts. In various cultures, both within the United States and outside of it, quilts play a fascinating role in documenting history and culture. They are also a natural tie-in to mathematics! Quilting might provide a wonderful entry into a particular lesson in your social studies curriculum.

Geography and Papier Mâché

To conclude this chapter I would like to return to Betsey Mendenhall's class, where the geography lesson centered on making a globe. This activity turned out to be a rich forum that informed the teacher about what the students knew (or didn't know) about geography. The globes were created from balloons covered with papier mâché. This gave students the base structure. Because they had seen many flat maps, Betsey assumed her fifth graders could transfer that knowledge onto a globe. Much to her surprise, she discovered that the majority of the children had never made the leap from flat map to globe. Therefore, it was the class consensus that the points furthest from each other on the map were the two outer edges of the paper. The thought of rounding the paper to meet the ends was not a part of their conceptual framework.

Unfinished president puppets seem to take a rest next to the papier mâché globe.

Students' ideas about "East" and "West" were based on their conception of California as being the "West Coast." Therefore, the idea that the Appalachian Mountains were west of the East Coast was difficult to grasp. When they started looking carefully at the maps, they discovered that the United States was not the largest country in the world—a big surprise! "When they made the globes, they created their own experiences," reported Betsey. "It was their lesson to learn, and they needed to do it themselves."

While creating their globes through the arts, students were finding ways to think about geography. They were working with knowledge and confronting assumptions, rather than taking in information given to them. The exercise not only got them directly involved with the subject matter, but also provided their teacher with information concerning their understandings and interests. The children were participants in the geography lessons and were given the opportunity to make decisions. After creating the continents and oceans, students decided to add other features such as rivers, mountains, states, and capitals.

SUMMARY

In addition to enhancing a social studies/history curriculum, the arts can be a core element of a program in two ways. First, the arts set a historical context for any study through their documentation of events, eras, cultures, landscapes, and people. In and of themselves, the arts are a rich historical text that offers the student of history authentic voices from which to study (see Principle 7 of equitable education and the arts on p. 23). In their authenticity, often the works of artists communicate much more than a typical text because embedded in the words, images, or movements of an artist are questions as well as answers, contemplation as well as fact.

Second, the arts lend a framework for the action of being a historian or social scientist. The effort involved in creating an artwork lays the groundwork for the effort in which the social scientist engages. As the students in Betsey Mendenhall's class started contemplating what the president puppets would say to each other, they began to engage in the core activities of social scientists and asked the kind of questions historians pose. Moreover, for several reasons the making of artwork opens possibilities through which students may be more willing to travel. In the first place, arts are engaging and can speak to the interests of many children. Second, as we saw with the puppet example, students felt more comfortable dreaming up and asking questions when it was the puppet asking and not them directly, giving the children a greater opportunity to explore a broad range of issues.

Returning to the California framework, which states that "a strong history–social science program at the elementary level helps all students to develop their full potential for personal, civic and professional life," we can see how the arts—through their engaging and hands-on learning qualities—can prepare such individuals.

TECH CONNECT
Technology, Arts, and Social Studies

- Have your students interview local community members and videotape the oral histories. They will learn interview techniques and find out that their community is a magnificent source for understanding local history. Students might put together a photo-documentary of the community by taking pictures, interviewing, and writing up a one-page history of various individuals.

- Dramatize events in history using archival photographs as backdrops.

- Have students create comic strips on the computer as an alternative to dramatizing events.

- Have students create an animated version of a historical event by using "stop action" or creating clay figures or drawings. Tape to create a mini-movie.

- Project historical images (e.g., a covered wagon) on the overhead or Elmo. Have students write question poems concerning the events related to the projected object/image.

QUESTIONS TO PONDER

1. In considering events and ideas in history, how do we know what is the "truth"? Is there any one truth in history? If there is truth, how do we determine it? If there isn't, how should we approach history?

2. What are the reporting tools of a historian or social scientist? Do the tools vary according to cultures, times, economy?

3. Are you familiar with your own family's past? What are the ways in which it is told?

 ## EXPLORATIONS TO TRY

1. Identify three songs and/or poems that reflect any period in history. They may be three different periods. What aspects of history does each relate? What makes these particular pieces different from history texts with which you are familiar?

2. If you could be any character in history, who would you be? With whom would you like to interact? With a partner, create a script focusing on a specific theme wherein the two characters interact and converse with each other. They may be from different time periods. Reflect on your script. What knowledge have you gained from this experience?

3. Create a "sound" map whereby people in your classroom can navigate from one point to another using only sounds, not a visual map. What other kinds of "maps" might be created? What uses might they have?

REFERENCES

Asmal, Kader, Chisdester, David, Wilmot, James (eds.) (2003). *Nelson Mandela: in his own words,* NY: Little Brown and Company.

Carawan, G., & Carawan, C. (1990). *Sing for freedom: The story of the civil rights movement through its songs*. Bethlehem, PA: A Sing Out Publication.

Cockburn, V. (1991). The uses of folk music and songwriting in the classroom. *Harvard Educational Review, 61*(1).

Ewald, W., & Lightfoot, A. (2001). *I wanna take me a picture*. Boston: Beacon Press.

Frame, A. (1994, August 7). Building arts programs, brick by brick. *New York Times.*

Holzer, H., & Neely, M. E. (1993). *Mine eyes have seen the glory: The Civil War in art*. New York: Orion Books.

Hopkins, L. B. (1994). *Hand in hand: An American history through poetry*. New York: Simon and Schuster.

Parker, W. (2009). *Socials studies in elementary education* (13th ed.). Boston: Allyn and Bacon, Pearson.

Parker, W. C., & Jarolimek, J. (2009). *A sampler of curriculum standards for social studies: Expectations of excellence*. Boston: Allyn and Bacon, Pearson.

Rubin, R. (1990). *Voices of a people: The story of Yiddish folksong*. Philadelphia: Jewish Publication Society.

Rubin, S. (2004). *Art against the odds: From slave quilts to prison paintings*. New York: Crown.

Smith, B. (1968). *Mexico: A history in art*. New York: Harper and Row.

SAMPLE LESSON PLANS

Social Studies

The lesson plans here include a directed drawing and poetry activity focusing on westward movement by Sandra Parviz, a mosaic activity of geographical regions developed by Jennifer Murphy Nelson, a community puppet unit by Sheri O'Campo, and an ancestor quilt project by Nancy Swan.

SUAVE Curriculum and Project Description

ACTIVITY TITLE: Directed Drawing and Poetry (Westward Movement Lesson)

TEACHER NAME: Sandra Parviz

SCHOOL AND GRADE: Grade 3, North Broadway Elementary

SUBJECT AREA(S): Social Studies / Visual Arts / Language Arts

MATERIALS: Brown construction paper, thin black markers, colored pencils, rulers, pencils, a large picture of a covered wagon in a canyon

DESCRIPTION: Have students use a ruler and pencils to make a 1½-inch margin around their paper. Discuss the picture and shapes included in the picture, and begin a directed drawing. Define and discuss the terms *foreground, background,* and *perspective.* Direct students to draw the wagon in the foreground first and then finish the remainder of the foreground. Have them complete the background last. Have children go over the pencil in black marker, and then complete the art portion by coloring anything in the picture that's not brown in colored pencil.

Brainstorm sights and sounds that people might have encountered when traveling west. Have children put these words together to make a poem. Have them write their poem around the border of their artwork.

This type of activity could be done with most any subject matter. Some kids need a lot of guidance when creating an original poem.

SUAVE Curriculum and Project Description

PROJECT TITLE: Mosaics of 6 Geographical Regions

TEACHER NAME: Jennifer Murphy Nelson

SCHOOL AND GRADE: Grade 3, North Broadway Elementary

SUBJECT AREA(S):   Social Studies / Visual Arts

MATERIALS:

- Large pieces of black butcher paper
- 2″ strips of various colors of construction paper
- Ellison letter cutouts for region names

DESCRIPTION: Six $2\frac{1}{2} \times 3\frac{1}{2}$ mosaics of sea coasts, rivers, lakes, mountains, deserts, forests, and prairies

1. **What happened in class?**
   Students outlined six geographical regions and a 2″ border. These were lightly sketched in soft pencil. Students then worked in groups, cutting strips into triangles, rectangles, and squares and laying them out and gluing them within the sketched lines.

2. **What skills, elements, vocabulary were taught?**
   Vocabulary: *Mosaic, geometry, triangle, squares, rectangles,* and various geographical terms

   Art: Color, contrast

3. **How did you assess the children's understanding?**
   I checked to see that they included the geographical elements that they had learned about as they studied the regions.

4. **Where could you go from here?**
   Begin with a smaller project on black construction paper, so students get the idea of what it will look like before doing the larger piece. This project took three sessions with my art coach and one final session to finish up.

5. **Comments for others trying this project.**
   This project could be used with vocabulary-building words, story settings, underwater scenes, etc.

SUAVE Curriculum and Project Description

PROJECT TITLE: Community Puppets

TEACHER: Sheri O'Campo

SCHOOL AND GRADE: Grade 1, Richland, San Marcos

SUBJECT AREA(S):   Social Studies / Visual Arts / Drama

DESCRIPTION: Students were introduced to the concept of *community*. Discussion topics included specific jobs and occupations as well as roles and responsibilities.

Our first task was to match each student with an occupation. Children were given choices. Then we discussed how most occupations required clothes or tools that would be specific to the job. An example is a mail carrier. Kids decided that a mail carrier would have a bag, letters, uniform, cap, and name tag.

Each child was given a template of a human shape. It was traced on tag board. We used construction paper to design the clothes, props, hair, etc. for each puppet. The back of the puppet had to be dressed as well as the front. We used the puppet as the template for the clothes (like making clothes for a paper doll) as well as the props.

After dressing the puppets we had a directed lesson on drawing a human face. We used colored pencils to finish the skin areas.

The puppets were finished when they were laminated and glued to sticks.

The next step was to build a stage. The stage needed to be light and portable as well as inexpensive. We used cardboard for a backdrop. We used a flat strip of cardboard to be the front stage. This allowed us to place the front stage on a table and put the students between the stages.

The next directed lesson was on dimensions. The backdrop needed one-dimensional props while the front stage needed three-dimensional props. The props were created out of construction paper and glued onto the cardboard. This

was a difficult concept for first graders but they were able to be successful with the construction of the backdrop.

The next step was to write scripts for the puppets. Children were put into small groups and were responsible for creating a script that would include details of the community workers. This served as an assessment tool.

SUAVE Curriculum and Project Description

PROJECT TITLE: Ancestor Quilt

NAME: Nancy Swan

SCHOOL AND GRADE: Grade 2, Rock Springs

SUBJECT AREA(S): Social Studies / Visual Arts

MATERIALS:

> 8″ square piece of white paper (for practice)
> 8″ square piece of muslin
> Crayons
> Fabric paint/brushes
> 2″-wide strips of red cotton fabric (for joining fabric squares)

DESCRIPTION: The second-grade social studies book has a unit on ancestors, so Berta (my art coach) and I decided to make an ancestor quilt. We first had students think of something they had learned from their ancestors (i.e., how to make tortillas, how to fish, how to play piano, etc.) Then we had them pantomine the activity while the others tried to guess what it was. During our next lesson, we had the students draw the outline of a picture showing what their ancestors had taught them on the white paper. We emphasized not using too much detail, as it would be hard to paint on the fabric square. Then they colored these. At the next class lesson, we used the practice as a guide and drew the design on to the muslin. Then we painted the picture with fabric paint. The dry squares could then be joined together with the strips of red fabric either by sewing or gluing with a glue gun.

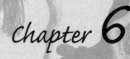

Chapter 6

The Wonder of Discovery: Science and the Arts

THE LIFE OF A WAVE

I envy the life of ever-pounding waves.
The huge steep hill of water coming
steadily, surely towards me at an alarming rate
Seeming like they are swallowing me, though never brushing my skin.
my human friends, a mere ten feet away
seems like infinite space impossible to travel,
getting longer every whole second, while the waves seem to be getting closer
bigger every half
the sensation of getting crushed,
alone yet contentful and cool.
cold and bleak
but together
together with others the same
I wish my life was one of a wave.
the mere secret of the truth and meaning of life.
overall the purpose of wishing and wondering
excitement,
fun and
survival.

Michael Sieble, fifth grader

The work of scientists and artists could be seen as very closely aligned. Each is engaged in a process of discovery as they experiment and search for new connections in and to their world. Each experiences a sense of urgency, wonderment, and perhaps magic as a

121

new connection is pondered or an intriguing questioned is pursued. Sue Halpern (2001) gets to the crux of passion and wonderment by asking, "How do people know what they know?" She writes of science and continues, "The world presents itself: the sky is blue, the birds are singing. Our senses are an open window. . . . Science, like any belief, starts with wonder, and wonder starts with a question." She relates wonder to passion and the irrational in a thought-provoking excerpt:

> . . . All these years later, I hardly remembered the difference between an igneous and a metamorphic rock. What I did remember was the single-mindedness with which I had picked through the woods behind my house, and the pure joy of finding something valuable enough to hold on to. It seemed reasonable to call this *passion,* and to think of myself—and everyone else—as a collection of passions. What this suggests is that it is not simply our ability to think, to be rational, that distinguishes humans from other species, but our ability to be *irrational*—to put stones in our pockets because we think they are beautiful.

What I love about Halpern's excerpt is her thinking of humans as "a collection of passions." I think this is a wonderful way to approach children in our classrooms. Each and every child holds his or her own collection of passions. If as teachers we can tap into and find out what those passions are, we will be better able to reach out to and connect with each child. Of course, with English language learners this becomes a bit more of a challenge because students might not be able to "tell" us about their passions. In this case, art can be an important tool for both teachers (in uncovering passions) and for students (in expressing passions).

"All of us are born with an interest in the world around us," writes Gerald Durrell (1983). He continues:

> Watch a human baby or any other young animal crawling about. It is investigating and learning things with all its senses of sight, hearing, taste, touch, and smell. From the moment we are born we are explorers in a complex and fascinating world. With some people this may fade with time or with the pressures of life, but others are lucky enough to keep this interest stimulated throughout their lives. (p. 9)

If we accept Durrell's notion of the human as explorer, then we can say that scientists and artists live parallel lives, although they express themselves through different media. They share a curiosity about the world, a desire to reflect upon it, and a need to express or communicate their understandings. They are investigators on a mission to explore or answer questions; in so doing, both tend to create new questions in addition to uncovering "findings." According to Kimberly Tolley (1993), the differences between scientists and artists are evident in how each reflects upon her or his relationship to their environment: "The scientist asks questions about the working of the natural world. The artist asks questions about the ways in which the world can be interpreted and re-created" (p. v.). Though both are essentially concerned with questioning the world and its inhabitants—be they animate or inanimate—each relies on a distinct way of thinking about and reflecting upon her or his "findings."

Now let's examine the methods of the scientist and artist and their commonalities and differences. The scientific process, according to Bass, Contant, and Carin (2009, p. 30), involves observing, classifying, inferring, measuring, communicating, predicting, hypothesizing, and experimenting—all of which are components of controlled investigation. The artist, according Tolley (1993, p. v), "uses the processes of perception, creation, and evaluation." Consider the example of a visual artist and a naturalist as they study a seashell. In order to create a painting of the seashell, the artist observes it closely, looking for colors, shapes, lines, inconsistencies. The artist takes the context and environment into account. The scientist looks at the shell from a different perspective. She seeks an understanding of the object, but utilizes a different form of observation through which she classifies the lines, colors, and context of the shell. Her representation might be in the form of field notes rather than a pictorial representation. To illustrate this point further, let's compare the attributes of a naturalist and an artist.[1]

A naturalist could be described as someone who:

- Questions his/her world and the things in it
- Learns to be silent and patient
- Uses all the senses to develop his/her power of observation
- Keeps an open mind
- Has an inquiring mind and poses questions
- Takes copious, detailed notes and sketches
- Develops a deep reverence for the world around him/her
- Is disciplined and reflective about his/her findings
- Interprets findings in relation to other scientific findings
- Expresses his/her findings in words and drawings

An artist could be described as someone who:

- Questions his/her world and seeks to explore it
- Learns to utilize solitude
- Uses many senses in observing the world around him/her
- Sees things in new and often interesting ways
- Poses questions and ponders
- Carefully records and interprets the world in sounds, colors, shapes, words, and movement
- Develops an understanding of the world around him/her
- Is disciplined and reflective about his/her work
- Expresses his/her understandings through a variety of media

The characteristics associated with the naturalist and the artist can be remarkably similar. A fundamental difference between their work and thinking lies in (1) the expression and communication of their "findings," and (2) the objects (or issues) of their questioning upon reflection. Their reflections are what take them on different journeys.

---

[1] The attributes are adapted from the writing of Durrell (1983).

The artist reflects upon nature, considering its relation to the everyday and human experience. Moreover, the artist generally has a broader range of expressive media than does the scientist, who relies heavily on the written word. The scientist usually reflects upon findings in order to place the work in the realm of other scientific data and to further uncover mysteries of the natural world.

Although the ways in which the scientist and artist consider the natural world can differ, each offers the other an opportunity to expand the exploration. In fact, Bass et al. (2009) suggest that in communicating scientific findings, students "draw pictures." The overlap between the work of the scientist and artist is strikingly compatible, and learning the processes involved with each discipline will strengthen the work of each. As well, scientists and artists often share a fundamental curiosity and desire to understand the wonders of nature.

The remainder of this chapter is devoted to science/art connections in teaching and learning. Beginning with ways in which science can be introduced *with* the arts, the reader will find examples of activities and exercises that serve as an idea bank.

LEARNING WITH THE ARTS

Painting

If you and your students have access to an art museum, you might find this an interesting exercise. Choose a gallery that features landscapes. Examine the paintings, using the following questions as a springboard for a discussion about the natural world: How would you describe the weather in the different paintings? Can you predict the weather? What are your clues? What kinds of clouds are depicted? What elements of nature are shown in each painting? How authentic is an animal in a drawing? How would you describe the light and shadows in the work? (If you do not have access to a gallery or museum, you might replicate this activity by introducing posters of paintings to your class.)

Another use of paintings involves the study of color. What is color? How does the artist create colors? What combinations of colors might an artist have used in order to create a particular scene? You might even move into mathematics by estimating the proportions of colors mixed to achieve an effect.

Music

Many people have introduced the study of acoustics through musical instrument demonstrations. For example, study the sounds of drums as they vibrate. Perhaps a more familiar activity that involves music and science has to do with listening. I have often gone on "musical" listening field trips, where the students and I document the songs and sounds of nature. After completing this exercise, I draw upon the works of musicians who have incorporated or imitated the sounds of nature in their compositions. When we listen as a class to a selection, we discuss the ways in which the music expresses an aspect of nature—what instruments are played, what tempos, feelings, or moods are created, and so on.

A fifth grader sketches plants at the Bataquitos
Lagoon in Carlsbad, California.

Thousands of musicians and composers have recorded pieces on the theme of nature. There are many American Indian song collections, such as *Songs of Earth, Water, Fire and Sky* (New World Records), that relate specifically to earth and nature. Likewise, there are many songs in popular song collections about nature and science. To get you thinking further on this topic, I include a brief sampling of composers and their music as they relate to issues in science.

- Kronos Quartet: *Cadenza on the Night Plain*
- John McLaughlin: *The Mediterranean*
- Steve Reich: *The Desert Music*

- Claude Debussy: *La Mer*
- Ferde Grofe: *Grand Canyon Suite:* "On the Trail"
- Gustav Holst: *The Planets*
- Rimsky-Korsakov: *Flight of the Bumblebee*
- Igor Stravinsky: *The Rite of Spring*
- Antonio Vivaldi: *The Four Seasons*
- Paul Winter: Recordings on whales and the Grand Canyon

Poetry

Poems on the topic of nature and science can be integrated into the science curriculum as a way to generate student interest. *The Random House Book of Poetry for Children* (Prelutsky, 1983) contains many appropriate poems, including "Nature Is . . . ," "The Four Seasons," and "The Ways of Living Things." A poem might be as simple as the one following. Although it is not particularly profound or informative, this anonymous poem has stirred many a young child's imagination during scientific investigation of the life of a bug:

> Curious fly,
> Vinegar jug,
> Slippery edge,
> Pickled bug.

Perspectives related through poetry provide opportunities to view science in an expanded manner. This particular poem might give children insight into the world from the bug's perspective. Students might be inclined to consider the "inner life" of a bug in addition to the more objective description of what it does, how it moves, what it eats, and so on.

LEARNING THROUGH THE ARTS

There are numerous ways to learn about science through the arts. In this discussion, I will highlight the activities of drawing and poetry. But first, a few ideas drawing from movement and drama.

Singing

This next section on singing as a way to learn science and attain language skills was originally published in another book of mine, *Teaching English Language Learners Through the Arts.* This section was written by Eduardo Garcia, an arts coach in southern California schools helping teachers find ways to teach their curriculum through the arts.

Singing is a great way to invite people into a new language. In singing, everyone acquires words, phrases, and concepts of the song. With this idea in mind, the first-grade bilingual class of Mrs. Z embarked on a lesson about sea life. The kids read and learned what kinds of animals and plants live in the sea. I then introduced the song "Yellow

Submarine" by The Beatles. They learned the melody. I then asked them to change the words to suit our needs; they were to show me what they knew about sea life. I modeled the first line and guided them to write the new words together. Every time a child gave an idea we would sing it together to hear if it fit in the melody. Pretty soon they got the idea; they started to count syllables and fit the words to the melody. We thought of hand movements to go with the singing, rehearsed it several times, and presented in class. The students were very proud of themselves and of their "new" song. Here are some of the words:

> Octopus and jellyfish
> shells and sharks, whales and squids
> Hammerheads, electric eels
> Seahorses and schools of fish
> Coral reefs and seaweed
> Live together not so deep
> So we see so many crabs
> Let's all of us dive so deep
> We all live in a Yellow Submarine

Singing is also a way to question the concept of "limited English" and to discover the English language talents of all students. Sometimes, classrooms are not even equipped to make such discoveries, as was the case in Mr. D's classroom. When I arrived to teach a music lesson, I found out there was not a working CD player in the room—obviously not an art-rich environment. However, when I guided the class in composing lyrics about whales to a melody I provided them with, two girls who up to that point hadn't said a word because of their purportedly limited English, contributed twenty lines following the seven syllables per line formula the melody required. We then proceeded to croon to a Whale of a Song:

> Whales are the biggest mammals
> Whales do migrate in winter
> Whales have babies like people
> Whales breathe through their spiracle

Some fifth-grade (ELL) students were studying desert environments with their resource teacher, and to help them assimilate the information we sang the following facts, which they fit to the melody "I've Been Working on the Railroad." They included terms such as *arid, desert, dunes, snakes, lizards,* and *reptiles.* Third graders enjoyed putting together their version of George Harrison's "Here Comes the Sun" and learned a food chain: sun feeds plankton plants feed tiny animals feed small-size fish feed middle-size fish feed the bigger-size fish. Second graders worked on bringing the book *Swimmy* to life. They made big colored fish, seaweed, and the other creatures in the story. After that, they put the words Swimmy pronounces as he organizes the other fish to scare the big fish, to the music of the Beatles's "All Together Now."

As these examples show, music and the arts in general can help students in language acquisition. From personal experience, I know this works. I grew up in the city of

Juárez, across the border from El Paso, Texas. Nobody spoke English in my household as I was growing up. But my older brothers listened to radio stations from the other side of the border. We also watched television without really understanding the words. The number of hours a week I heard English probably did not exceed five or six. Nevertheless, this was of immense help in my own language acquisition, for it allowed me to acquire the phonetic aspect of the language before I ever studied grammar and syntax. So, by the time I learned English in college, I had a good part of the work done already and that made matters easier (Goldberg, 2004, pp. 45–46).

Dance

Dance can enhance lessons in anatomy and physics. Look at the movements of a dancer, perhaps a student in your class. What muscles are being utilized? How does the dancer relate to and create motion and energy? How can the dancer defy motion by being still? What is the dancer's relation to gravity? To momentum? To centrifugal force? To time and space? To contraction and expansion?

To explore chaos, a teacher might have students move throughout a room without touching each other. Make the space bigger or smaller, the tempo faster or slower. To explore the motion of atoms, centipedes, or blood moving through a vein, have students re-create the motion through movement. To explore life cycles, have them dramatize the events of a metamorphosis. Have them act out the life of a butterfly from pupa to full-grown butterfly, or the life cycle of a tornado. The national standards in the arts—dance area—as well as your state standards can be very helpful in creating lessons that integrate dance and the curriculum. These standards provide several examples of such lessons: In one social studies unit that integrates the arts with history, Harriet Tubman and the Underground Railroad are the focus. Students use a variety of resources to research Harriet Tubman's life and accomplishments, then use this information to create a collage and choreograph a movement piece. "Dancing Winds," according to the description of an integrated science/dance unit posted on the Web, "introduces the expanding and condensing properties of air masses and the unequal heating of Earth as the force behind the wind. Working with principles of choreography, participants use movement skills to learn and communicate information about the structure and attributes of the atmosphere." Educational standards at both the state and national levels can be accessed on the Web and include many examples and detailed lesson plans. They are good springboards for exploring ways to teach about the arts as well as to integrate subject areas.

Learning About Animals and Their Environments Through Origami and Storytelling

This fifth-grade example originally started out as a math lesson using the ancient art form of paper folding, origami. Students became extremely engaged as they learned how to create origami animals. Very quickly, they were creating not only a specific creature, but families of creatures. Making the creatures proved so motivating that the teacher decided to extend the lesson to science as a review of previous work on understanding animals and their environments. She explained to her students, "You can't just create a creature and have no life form . . . every person, every living thing has a story to tell." Each student was then invited to tell a story about his or her creature. The teacher reflected on this activity:

> We didn't sit there and discuss . . . you need to include this and you need to include that. I just said it had to be from the animal kingdom and you had to be aware of their environment and somehow put that into your story. But they were real creative. . . . Some of them used personification. Some of them were very scientific and factual, and I thought, well, that's neat they can be so creative. And I had so many kids participate in that. I was just figuring that one or two people would get up there but they all wanted to get up! (Jacobs, Goldberg, & Bennett, 1999).

Ecology: Drawing from Nature

Drawing and sketching are the tools of the naturalist. They are also tools for students as they begin to explore and understand their surroundings. Especially for second language learners, learners who are more visual, and learners who enjoy the visual arts, drawing can be a fantastic tool for building scientific understanding. In this manner, the activity addresses Principles 1 and 2 of equitable education and the arts (see pp. 23–24), which speak to expanding the expressive outlets available to learners and enabling freedom of expression for second language learners. Karen Gallas (1994) relates a conversation to this effect between Juan and David, first graders who were sketching their way toward understandings in science.

DAVID: I'd heard people talk about this thing. I think it was a praying mantis, but I didn't know what it was. So I looked at a book, and then I drew it, and then I knew what it was.

JUAN: Or if you don't know what a wing is and how it's made, you can draw it and then you know. (p. 134)

In teaching a unit on ecology, most teachers want their students to become familiar with objects in nature and make connections to the larger context of their environment. An effective use of the arts in studying nature is to draw nature: sketch leaves, shells, flowers, seaweed, and so on. As a student carefully sketches nature, she becomes an active observer of an object and may become interested in asking questions about the object she is drawing. Margot Grallert, an arts specialist in Massachusetts, works closely with classroom teachers. She sets up "graphic observation centers" where children can illustrate "something they were looking at, or ideas they had that had no concrete form, such as the abstract quality of a weather condition, or of motion" (Grallert, 1991, p. 263).

An interesting technique that Grallert employs is to work from the "inside out." This is both a philosophy about learning and an actual artistic technique. The artistic technique is simple: Pick a place in the middle of the object, and sketch from the inside out. Do not begin with a border; do not outline the object as you draw. For example, if you were on a beach, you might choose a seashell and observe it closely. Then choose a place somewhere in the middle of the shell. Begin your drawing from that middle spot. Draw continuously outward from that spot. You will be surprised with the difference between beginning in the middle and beginning with an outline. As you are drawing you will be observing the shell carefully. You must observe it closely in order to draw it—and re-create its image on paper.

Students sketching from the "inside out" and writing
intently on a path at the Bataquitos Lagoon.

As you are drawing you might become curious about its makeup and history. Most children become curious as they sketch. I often ask students to create two lists while drawing: a list of the things they notice, and a list of questions that arise in their minds as they work. They often note interesting things about their shell, such as the number of lines in its curved shape, the detail in the patterns, and shapes on the shell. They may begin to wonder: What is the shell made of? Does it grow? Did anything live in this shell? Where is it now? How did it get out? How did the shell end up on the beach? Was it out very far in the ocean? Did it travel from somewhere else to get here? Did the waves push it? How far? These and other questions that arise from the graphic exercise form the basis for the science lessons.

The art exercise provides not only the motivation to form scientific questions, but also a method through which students translate a three-dimensional world into a two-dimensional picture. This translation, as I have mentioned previously, is one of the keys to unlocking and stimulating intellectual development. Curiosity inspired through the exercise, coupled with attentive guidance from the teacher, will set students searching for answers to their questions.

Tara deArrieta, a kindergarten teacher in the Reno area of Nevada, tried a plant drawing and question activity with her students. "After introducing the unit with a garden story," writes Tara, "I had the students draw a fresh chrysanthemum flower with the leaves intact using the [inside out] method. The pictures were remarkable and the questions very sophisticated." Following are examples from the students' list of questions.

- Why are leaves in different shapes?
- Why do flowers have leaves?
- What kind of flower did we draw?
- Why are stems green?
- Why do flowers smell?
- What do plants make for us?
- How do plants make their food?
- Why do some plants have thorns?
- Why are there so many different plants?
- Why are they all colors?
- Who names flowers?
- How do you know what flower it is?
- Why do they need soil, water, and air?

Tara reports that in order to answer some of the questions, her class is continuing to learn through the arts:

> We started a movement activity demonstrating the metamorphosis of a seed. We are using art to make paper models of our plants as they grow under grow lights to record the changes from seeds to roots, etc. We are writing a poem about the life cycle of a plant that we are putting into a pop-up book. And, we are using metaphors to connect the needs of plants to our own needs.

The children remained engaged for the better part of the year, following through on their study. Tara also encouraged their explorations through the arts in other areas of the curriculum.

In considering "working from the inside out" as a philosophy as well as a practice, Grallert writes, "[it] is an individually directed thought process, an unpremeditated search for an unknown reality. It is a way of figuring out something that is your own" (1991, p. 260). According to Grallert, working from the inside out can be characterized by the following three conditions:

- a belief that every person has an inner sense of self that can and must provide direction for learning;

- an environment that encourages and stimulates the individual to find his or her personal direction;
- a conviction that there are no final answers. (p. 260)

The third condition might interest readers who consider science a field that is in search of final answers. Unfortunately, there exist very few (if any) truths or final answers. Instead, there are webs of complexities. If we examine the history of science, we find that "truths" or "theories" change as more is discovered about the world. There was a time, for example, when it was common "knowledge" that the world was flat. As scientists sought to understand more about the world and developed tools to interpret it, their theories and knowledge of science evolved and changed. The same is true for geocentric theory, plate tectonics, and the ongoing search to understand the extinction of the dinosaurs. Science is a study of complexities. Our search for understanding never ends; it only evolves as we gather more and more experience.

The Nature of Poetry: Working with Ideas

The first time I approached the study of science through poetry was with a fourth-grade transitional language (Spanish–English) class in southern California. Because of a time-sharing arrangement, a teacher other than the regular classroom teacher taught science. This science teacher worried that children were not retaining the science lessons and she asked us if there was a way to explore science topics at another point in the day. Thus the science poetry project began. Our first strategy was to engage students in brainstorming words related to science while we wrote the words on the blackboard. Within minutes the board filled up, yet children were still offering words and phrases.

As they were brainstorming, another interesting phenomenon occurred. Different students began revisiting the ideas related to certain words. They started asking questions dealing with concepts they had studied; their curiosity about science topics was rekindled. One example that I especially remember involved "nickel." The class was studying the elements, and many element names appeared on the brainstorm list on the blackboard. When one child said "Nickel" another child questioned, "Do you remember how much nickel is in a nickel?" Others thought, then they decided to look it up—without prompting from their teacher. The brainstorming alone gave them inspiration to revisit the properties of a five-cent piece.

Following the brainstorm, we asked the children to choose words from the board and apply them to a poem. We encouraged them over a two-session period to edit and revise their poems. Here are a few examples that evolved from the activity.

Kevin is a special needs student who is in this class for language arts. He is reticent about writing, although excited about the poetry class. He surprised us with this wonderfully descriptive and imaginative science poem.

> There was a night
> I thought I had a dream
> but I woke up

I looked outside and I looked up in the sky
but there was nothing there
but, I saw a star
but, I saw another star
It was a shooting star

Kevin

The next poem, by Alicia Finley, incorporates a number of science topics. Not only does she use science vocabulary, but it is clear to the teacher and me that she knows something about the concept of "chaos." She employs the concept in a way many of us can relate to—our chaotic rooms, or desks, and so on. The poem reminds me of my own room when I was 10 years old!

My room is like science because there is
volume,
liquids,
mass,
experiments,
products,
and different kinds of chaos
and, maybe my sister too.

Alicia Finley

I find the next poem particularly intriguing because Adriana Rosales not only writes a "science" poem, but she incorporates one of the most fundamental aspects of science into her poem: the notion of asking questions. How better to capture science in a poem than to ask questions?

Why is the sky
so blue tell me
why
oh why
do I have
brown hair
Why do I
see with
my eyes
Oh please tell me
why

Adriana Rosales

An interesting way to build on the children's "question poems" might be to write another poem that includes some "answers" to their questions. Students could exchange poems during the questioning and answering.

For the last example from this initial brainstorm and editing activity, I have included the first, second, and final drafts of Susanne Chea's poem about the ocean. Susanne was in an after-school science group that focused on oceanography; one can see through her poem and illustration (Figure 6.1) how much of the topic was integrated into her thinking.

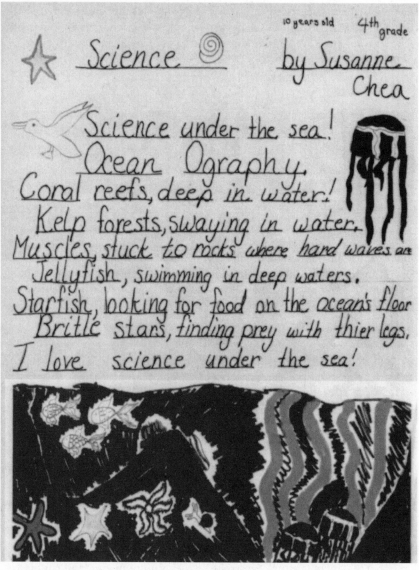

Figure 6.1 Susanne's final poem and illustration.

FIRST DRAFT:

> Science
> Science Under the Sea!
> Sea hair [sic], wet rocky places.
> Coral reefs, Deep in water,
> Kelp forest, swaying in water!

SECOND DRAFT:

> Science
> Science under the sea!
> Sea hair, wet rocky places.
> Coral reefs Deep in water.
> Kelp forest swaying in water
> muscles, stuck to rocks where hard waves are
> I love science under the sea!
>
> *Susanne Chea*

In addition to working with children, I often have my college students write poems and raps about science. Inspired by a child's poem about photosynthesis, one of my graduate students composed the following poem about the food chain. It was written by Paul Montell, a science teacher in the Las Vegas, Nevada, area. I have "rapped" this poem to my fourth and fifth graders to great applause and appreciation.

> I see you twitch
> You caught my eye
> You freeze with fear
> Now prepare to die
> Your mousy scent
> so sweet to smell
> your slender body
> slides down so well
> I'm part of the food chain
> and you're next in line
> It is upon you
> which I must dine
> Symbol of evil
> or so you say
> Hey, I'm just a predator
> in search of prey
> So sorry to kill
> But it's just me
> It's my makeup
> genetically
> So there's my tale

for all to see
I've left nothing back
quite honestly
At least I admit
Everything I do
Can the same be said
for all of you?
So now don't bother to flinch
because my aim is true
Now I must do
what snakes just do.

Paul Montell

Lagoon Poems.   In keeping with the theme of ecology, we will next look at the role poetry can play in studying nature. The first group of poems below were written after a session at a local lagoon that is currently under restoration. The restoration project is a huge undertaking, involving dredging and pumping in order to re-open the lagoon to the ocean. To do so, a large waterway must be dredged and a tremendous amount of sand displaced. While they were at the lagoon, each student took notes or made sketches in a sketchbook. At the start of the exercise, the teacher had them look in all directions—up, down, left, and right. Students then observed, in silence, as they wandered along the perimeter of the lagoon, which was open to school groups. Prior to the trip the teacher had engaged the children in extensive discussions about the lagoon and nature; they also had practiced observation sessions. Because the lagoon is located very close to the school and the children's homes, it is something with which each child had some familiarity.

Once back in the classroom, children were asked to take their notes and organize them into poems. In the first poetry session, we asked them to simply write a poem based on their notes and sketches. In the second session, we asked them to compose a poem from the perspective of the lagoon. What was the lagoon's perspective on the restoration process? If it could speak, what would it say? By asking students to go this extra step, we hoped they would delve more deeply into the issues concerning restoration. At the same time, we were conscious of placing students in a position where they could exercise their imaginations. Both sessions are reflected in the following poems.

The poem in Figure 6.2 was written by Carson Wise, who wrote in his journal, "I can't write what I'm thinking." It is remarkable to see what he created in light of (or in spite of) this statement. Note the careful visual design of his words and all the symbols that accompany them.

"I'm the Lagoon (After)" is Carson's poem from the perspective of the lagoon. It is quite different from his first poem. Many children, including Carson, found writing from the lagoon's perspective easier. It was as if the freedom to write from a perspective other than one's own was an inspiring source.

Alicia finishes her poem and is ready to read it out loud.

Susanne working on her final draft of "Science."

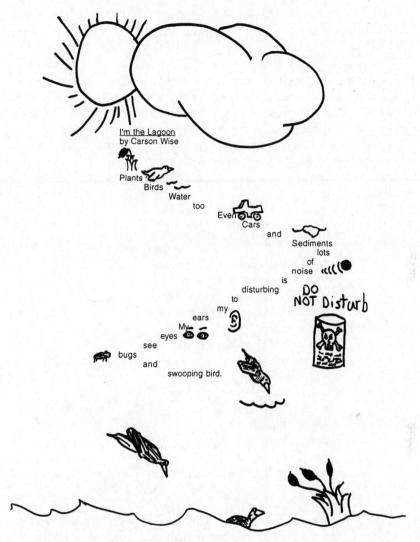

Figure 6.2   Carson's lagoon poem.

I'M THE LAGOON (AFTER)

I have eyes all around
I listen quietly
there is no sound
out of nowhere
a brown pelican
dives into my water

breaking the silence
that was there before.
Carson Wise

The next poem is by Casey Dandeneau, a student who likes to write poetry but is challenged in many other academic areas throughout the day. Like most of us, when he is interested he becomes engaged. When he is not interested, however, he can be a challenge. Fortunately, with expanded avenues of expression and work available to him, Casey has many moments throughout the day when he is actively engaged in learning and even enjoying himself. His poem addresses a number of aspects of the lagoon project. He refers to the sand displacement, the algae, and how once the lagoon is restored its life will return.

JUDGING THE LAGOON

When the pumps first start it starts my heart
To hear the sound of leaving sand
it's like the greatest music band.
When the algae is gone and the fish are near
it makes even more life come near
Life's so great
it's something no one can hate
to help me survive
That's a life so great
it's something no one can hate
No matter what it did
not even if you tried.
When they're all done
and the trouble is gone
that life will return again.

Casey Dandeneau

"I See I Feel" was written by the class-identified poet-in-residence, Emily Birnbaum. This child is constantly writing poems, joyful in sharing them with her classmates and teachers. She composed this particular poem for two voices. The lines in the center are meant to be read simultaneously by both readers. Other than that, each reader recites his or her lines according to the alternating order in which they fall. One could also imagine that the spacing of the words on the page looks like the pistons, simulating the dredging action! It is a poem written from the perspective of the lagoon.[1]

---

[1] A wonderful resource for poems with two voices is the book *Joyful Noise: Poems for Two Voices* by Paul Fleishman (1988). It is terrific for your science classes, as the poems revolve around bugs such as grasshoppers, fireflies, book lice, moths, beetles, and honeybees. I've used it from kindergarten through college, always to delight.

I SEE I FEEL

(a poem for two voices)

YES ME THE LAGOON

Dredging

                        Pumping

Dredging

                        Pumping

Take all this sediment off my face
Once again make me a part of your human race

Oh yes, oh yes let this water flow, sediment algae, bacteria go
Life from the rivers, mountains, and seas

Oh yes bring this all to me

                    My face feels refreshed

But oh no, am I doomed?

                    I don't want to end up a

shriveled prune

                    Emily Birnbaum

Finally, here is another poem written from the perspective of the lagoon. What interested me about this poem was its questioning and wonder. Through the science exercise, Jenna Timinsky has captured the wonderment of science. Her questions, set within the context of an imaginative poem, reveal much of her understanding of the lagoon and the issues surrounding the restoration process.

INSIDE OF ME

What is this I hear?
help? scared cries of fleeing birds?
a change? monsters roaring on my surface?
fresh start? what did I do?
What is this I feel?
my skin ripping into painful wounds?
weights holding me in? a breath?
the rush of incoming water? churning and tossing?
stealing my bottom dwellers?
What is this I taste?
salt? danger? future happiness? fresh body?
renewal?
What is this I smell?
rusty lead? no birds? dying plants? algae?

my deathbed? cleanliness? a war?
Will I die or will I live?
Fogginess invades my mind
I express my feelings to a wise blue heron.

Jenna Timinsky

Ocean and Beach Poems.   The next set of poems was written after students did a similar observation exercise on a local beach within walking distance of their school. Again, the students were asked to look in all directions as they began their observations.

Finding a solitary spot at the lagoon, this fifth grader composes her poem.

Each sat on the beach in solitude for 10 minutes as she or he observed, made notes, and sketched (if she or he chose to sketch) something in the environment.

THE BEACH TODAY

The waves crumbling outside
and the shorebreak pounding
on the smooth surface
and exploding like a volcano.
A pelican gliding across the waves
seagulls eating scraps. That's the beach today!

Darrell Goodrum

Note Darrell Goodrum's attention to motion. He has focused on the action of the waves. In applying his observations, he has chosen interesting descriptive words and metaphors. While Darrell mainly focused on the breaking of the waves and the seabirds in the vicinity, Jenna Timinsky, his classmate, honed in on one rock she found intriguing. It was a speckled little rock broken in texture by a line of another rock or sediment. In addition to documenting the rock's qualities, she goes a step further and adds an imaginative mystery to the rock.

ROCK

I've found a rock
a light gray rock
a plain rock—with something special
it had a heart—a cracked heart
How did it break? Who was the lad?
Was it the pounding sea and its raging waves?
or was it a beloved companion, a long lost companion?
Who was it who cracked the speckled heart?
as speckled as a bird's egg
The heart is now only a tattered stone.

Jenna Timinsky

The next poem was written by Anain Matias, a Spanish-speaking student who is focusing on developing English skills throughout the day. She generally writes and speaks in her first (and at this time, most comfortable) language—Spanish. It was very interesting to the teacher and me not only that (1) she chose to apply her observations in the poem in the manner that she did, but that (2) she chose to write the poem in English, thereby pushing herself in a language direction where she seldom ventured. This might illustrate how poetry can be a useful and manageable tool for second language learners as they explore subject matter.

why the water is blue clean
water is blue the water is blue

> because we take care of it
> the water needs to be blue
> for the fish could swim
> and the birds could eat fish
> that are not poisoned
>
> *Anain Matias*

Through these poems, we can document students' attention to detail in their observations—a critical scientific skill that is reinforced through the writing exercise. We also see how the students have reflected upon their observations and asked new questions—also critical scientific skills. As teachers we are not only involving the students in an interesting study of nature but are giving them the opportunity to apply and reflect upon the study as it relates to their lives and the things that are important to them. Throughout the poetry projects, I have found that most students become actively engaged in creating imaginative poems. This is in part because they are continually practicing their observation, reflection, and imaginative skills. As in any course of study, some students are more interested in the subject and process than others. I have found that this kind of exercise tends to engage most of the children because they have freedom in choosing an object to observe and freedom in the manner through which they apply their work in the poetry.

Question Poems.   The last set of science-related poems was written after an exercise of guided wonderment. The first part of the exercise involved asking questions about nature. I brought a piece of sea glass to the classroom and asked children to brainstorm questions concerning its origin, its travels, and so on. I encouraged children to be imaginative in their questioning. Among their questions were: How did it get to the beach? What was it a part of originally? Did someone drink from it? Who held it? How did it get smooth? Is it smooth on the inside? How far has it traveled? How does the water carry it to different places? Has a seagull looked at it? After this brainstorming session, the children could choose any object and form their own questions. The teacher then introduced them to a number of poems by Pablo Neruda, who has written and compiled a book of question poems. For our purposes, because this was a bilingual class, Neruda was a wonderful choice: His poems are written in Spanish and translated into English, giving both Spanish and English speakers examples and models for consideration. Students could read, and then write, in either Spanish or English.

QUESTIONS

> What do raindrops do after they hit the ground?
> Do raindrops have a life?
> Why do raindrops go only one way?
> Do raindrops miss the ocean?
> Does the sun make water disappear?
> Why are rocks hard?
>
> *Matt Motter*

QUESTIONS

What does the ocean laugh about?
Does a tornado ever get dizzy?
Why do the waves slap the sand?
Does the ocean ever sleep?
Does the sun ever drown?
Is the night afraid of the dark?
How cold is death's hand?
Does death fly or does it walk?
Does solitude talk with silence?
Does solitude ever get lonely?

Megan Riel-Mehan

CLOUDS

Are you friends with the wind?
Why are your tears so wet?
Do you and the sun have fights?
Why do you make your home so high in the sky?
What do you observe about mankind?
If you could talk, what would you say?
How big is the sky?
Do you and the sky understand each other?
Does the wind control you?
Are you and the birds friends, and do you talk with them?
How big are you?
Why do you hide the sun?
How long is your life-span?
How old are you?

Nicole Laperdon

While this book focuses K–8 students, I want to note that there are some incredible opportunities to mesh science and the arts at the college level, too. At my university, professor Judit Hersko, a visual arts professor, worked with Dr. Karno Ng (Department of Chemistry) on developing a learning module based on a chemical equilibrium system that illustrates Le-Chatelier's Principle. Here's what Hersko wrote about the experience.

A student majoring in chemistry and a student majoring in visual art carried out the module during one semester. The science student worked out the details of the experiment and its mechanism and the art student incorporated the experiment into an installation art piece. The constantly shifting chemical equilibrium visualized through the color changes in the experiment (from yellow to orange and back to yellow) became a metaphor in the artwork for shifting emotional states in humans. In addition to the physical product of the artwork, this teaching module provided the students involved with a new type of interdisciplinary learning experience. Previously both students were unfamiliar with each other's field. The art student was uninterested in and intimidated by chemistry. However, after this project she expressed a strong interest and said she will actually study chemistry now. The science student was not interested in art. However, after this project, he started to appreciate art. In addition, he recognized the real application of the chemical theories and was enthusiastic about the project. This shows that creative engagement with science helps students connect to scientific information. The interactive and emotional involvement in art allows students to connect to the facts of science in a personal way and reaches many who are otherwise difficult to engage in science. This model is useful on all levels of education.

SUMMARY

Combining science and the arts creates an exciting and explosive arena for understanding the natural world. The possibilities for exploring science with and through the arts is just about as limitless as science itself. When used as a methodology for learning about science concepts and gaining scientific skills, the arts can lend complexity and inspire further questioning. When children begin to draw an object in nature, they begin to observe it closely—a fundamental skill for any scientist. When children begin to reflect on their experiences through writing (such as poetry), they participate in the work of a scientist seriously contemplating the mystery of the natural world. Thus, the natural bridge between the arts and science engages not only the child's mind but his or her imagination as well.

TECH CONNECT
Technology, Arts, and Science

- Have students create public service announcements or commercials for preserving nature and the environment. Videotape their "spots" and present them to other classes or tape record them as radio announcements. Even simple equipment like a Flip video camera can make this project come alive.

- Have students collect sounds and photographs from nature and present a dance based on nature (for example, the ocean and study of waves). Encourage students to use the sounds and photographs as background.

- Have students write science question poems and e-mail them to another class in another school. Invite that class to write "answer" poems.

- Have students use the computer to create science books with illustrations. Publish students' work and donate it to your school library.

QUESTIONS TO PONDER

1. Think about a person who makes something, perhaps pottery, a musical instrument, or even fireworks (!). What relationships to science are involved in each creation?

2. Would you consider the potter, the instrument maker, or the fireworks developer to be a "scientist"? If yes, how? If no, why not?

3. Can you think of instances when a scientist might also be considered an "artist"?

 ## EXPLORATIONS TO TRY

1. What are three ways in which you can explore some topic in science *with* the arts?

2. What are three ways in which you can explore the same topic *through* the arts?

   To help you with Explorations 1 and 2, consider the following topics (or choose one of your own topics): oceanography, chaos, mammals, energy, astronomy, magnetism, light and prisms, botany, insects, food chains, photosynthesis, the planets.

3. Try drawing a flower or seashell from the inside out. Keep a list of (1) what you notice about the object, and (2) what you wonder about the object.

REFERENCES

Bass, J. E., Contant, T. L., & Carin, A. A. (2009). *Teaching science as inquiry* (11th ed.). Boston: Allyn and Bacon, Pearson.

Durrell, G. (1983). *The amateur naturalist.* New York: Knopf.

Fleishman, P. (1988). *Joyful noise: Poems for two voices.* New York: Harper and Row.

Gallas, K. (1994). *The languages of learning: How children talk, write, dance, draw, and sing their understanding of the world.* New York: Teachers College Press.

Goldberg, M. (2004). *Teaching English language learners through the arts: A SUAVE experience.* New York: Allyn and Bacon, Pearson.

Grallert, M. (1991). Working from the inside out: A practical approach to expression. *Harvard Educational Review, 61*(3).

Halpern, S. (2001). *Four wings and a prayer: Caught in the mystery of the monarch butterfly.* New York: Pantheon Books.

Jacobs, V., Goldberg, M., & Bennett, T. (1999, April). Teaching core curriculum through the arts. Paper delivered at the American Educational Association Meeting (AERA). Montreal, Canada.

Prelutsky, J. (Ed.). (1983). *The Random House book of poetry for children.* New York: Random House.

Tolley, K. (1993). *The art and science connection: Hands-on activities for primary students.* Menlo Park, CA: Addison-Wesley.

SAMPLE LESSON PLANS

Science

For this section, I decided to highlight the solar system from three different perspectives. Featured are "Planet Books" by David Clemesha, a three-dimensional mural of the solar system by Theresa Hathaway, and "Sonic Solar System: A Musical Sculpture" by Nancy Narron. I also include a delightful art/poetry/nature activity, "A Poem Is a Picture," developed by Diana Brown.

SUAVE Curriculum and Project Description

ACTIVITY TITLE: Planet Books

NAME: David Clemesha

SCHOOL AND GRADE: Grade 3, Juniper

SUBJECT AREA(S): Science / Visual Arts / Language Arts

MATERIALS: Watercolors, lettering templates, black ballpoint pens, white and colored construction paper

PROCEDURE:

1. We painted each of the planets from photos provided by the Jet Propulsion Lab in Pasadena, California.
2. We used templates to label each planet page.
3. We ordered the planets in relationship to their distance from the sun and bound them in a book.

    The book each student made gave a clear evaluation of their thought and effort.

    The project was involving and time-consuming but rewarding.

    For future projects, books could be made with information concerning individual planets.

SUAVE Curriculum and Project Description

LESSON: 3-D Mural of Solar System

TEACHER: Theresa Hathaway

SCHOOL AND GRADE: Grade 3, North Broadway School

SUBJECT AREA(S):   Science / Visual Arts

DESCRIPTION: As an extension of our third-grade study of *The System in the Sky* (the sun, earth, and the moon), we enjoy learning about our solar system. This year I suggested to my art coach, Kim Emerson, that I would like to do a mural, and together we brainstormed possible projects. The final result was something the students were proud to share with parents at Open House.

First, we talked about the different planets and size relationships. Using balloons, we made papier-mâché models of the nine planets. These were designed to just be one-half of each planet so that when they were attached to the mural, they would "pop-out" from the paper. We let these dry for a week, and the next week we applied a base layer of tempera paint in the color of the planet. The third week we added the features that make each planet unique, such as clouds, red spots, rings, moons. At the same time, we had the students using toothbrushes to splatter paint "stars" on a long piece of black butcher paper. Some of the stars turned into meteors and/or comets if the paint was too heavy. Our sun was made at the edge of the paper by adding various paints to yellow paper and then stuffing it so it popped out from the wall.

In our Science class we researched the planets with a partner using both books and the Internet. The students listed important facts they had learned about the planet on a 3 × 5 card. The mural was put together by using t-pins to attach the papier-mâché models to the wall, and the labels and information were glued under the models. Moons were either painted on or made from cardboard or half a Styrofoam ball.

We also looked at what the actual scale would be and knew that our model would be more detailed if we did not try to make it to scale. We hung in the room a string with paper circles the appropriate sizes and distances of the planets to show the real scale of the solar system.

COMMENTS FOR OTHERS TRYING THIS PROJECT: The project is time-consuming but well worth the end result. Be prepared to get messy. The models should have at least three layers of paper so they stand up to the paint and don't collapse. Papier-mâché is one part flour, one part white glue, and water to make consistency of thin pancake batter. Use torn up brown (school) paper towels for the paper.

SUAVE Curriculum and Project Description

ACTIVITY TITLE: Sonic Solar System: A Musical Sculpture

NAME: Nancy Narron

SCHOOL AND GRADE: Grade 4, Lincoln

SUBJECT AREAS: Math / Science / Music / Collaborative Skills

MATERIALS: A variety (nine is ideal) of percussive or tonal musical instruments

DESCRIPTION: Students move desks to the sides of the room to create a working space for the lesson. Students are seated on the floor. Students close their eyes and imagine themselves as an individual planet spinning in space. The lesson begins with a review of the order of the planets in our solar system. Students are told that they are going to be able to make a musical model of the solar system based on the orbital values of each planet—that is to say, the students will experience planetary movement based on how long it takes each planet to make one rotation around the sun. Students discuss the distance each planet is away from the sun and use a table that relates each planet's complete rotation (that planet's year) to a complete earth year (one complete orbit around the sun). Using mental math, the students convert these numbers into gross orbital ratios.

Mercury, closest to the sun, circles four times as fast as Earth, and is 4 quarter notes.

Venus, further from the sun, is considered 2 half notes.

Earth's rotation is considered a whole note.

Mars fully rotates every two whole notes.

Jupiter rotates one time for every five rotations of Mars.

Saturn rotates one time for every two rotations of Jupiter.

Uranus rotates once for every three rotations of Saturn.

Neptune rotates for every two rotations of Uranus.

Pluto would rotate every 15 rotations of Uranus, but we made it more frequent 1:3 because this child would have to wait forever to participate in the event.

A child is picked for every planet and given a percussion instrument. They are then placed in their proper orbital position in relation to the sun. There is a visual aspect to the experience, but more important to the success of the project is that each child is next to the planet that his or her musical relationship is based on.

Students are told that all music starts with silence. Just as in visual art, silence and emptiness are as important as sound or form. Pattern is the key to this piece. What we are creating was once described as "the music of the spheres."

Each student is instructed to play his or her instrument only at the point when his or her planet has completed its orbit and has returned to its point of origin. The rest is silence. As the students wait for their rotations to complete, the silence emphasizes the vast distances and varying lengths of time that cannot be conceived by long strings of numbers. Several students in the class assisted musicians with their counting, so for some, one instrument was "played" by two students. This "acoustic sculpture" demanded extreme concentration on the part of the students. Mistakes were discussed and several performances were done so that most students were able to participate.

SKILLS DEVELOPED: Mental math, listening skills, patterning, working cooperatively, self-restraint and patience, knowledge of musical notation, spacial knowledge is extended

ASSESSMENT: Students could be assessed in their ability to round and to mentally manipulate numbers.

Listening skills could be assessed.

The success of this project depended on the understanding of musical notation and ratios—when the piece was produced without error, then understanding is seen as classwide.

Students were assessed on their ability to work as a group toward a common goal.

WHERE TO GO FROM HERE: group mobiles, more patterning, xylophones, rounds, studying patterns in poems, making group poems with pre-established restrictions or structures, mosaics, exploring "noise" as music, looking at Fibonacci numbers. . . . Who knows?

COMMENTS FOR OTHERS TRYING THIS PROJECT: Information used for the orbital chart is found in *The Eyewitness Visual Dictionary of the Universe.* This book is an excellent resource and also has the best illustrations that I have found to really convey the vastness of space.

SUAVE Curriculum and Project Description

ACTIVITY TITLE: A Poem Is a Picture!

Science Vocabulary Development Through Shape Poetry

NAME: Diana Case Brown

SCHOOL AND GRADE: Grade 5, Alvin Dunn Elementary

SUBJECT AREAS: Science / Language Arts / Visual Arts

MATERIALS: Drawing paper, crayons, markers, colored pencils, science resource materials

DESCRIPTION: "When is a poem more than a poem? When it is also a picture! Picture poems are called 'concrete' because they create an actual picture or form on the page. The poem's message comes not only from the meaning of the words, but also from the arrangement of the words or letters."[1] I used this technique to develop vocabulary in a science unit on animal classification. The phylum names were unfamiliar to the students, as well as to me, so we used animal shapes and words to make them more fun and familiar. First, we read about each class of animal and wrote down descriptive words and phrases that sounded "musical" to our ears. Second, we arranged the words in a logical but interesting order. Finally, students drew a representative outline shape of the animal. At any point on the outline of their drawing, they began with the title (vocabulary word/name) in capital letters, then, the words of the poem flowed around to form the shape. All students were enthusiastic about this project, and it was an especially effective tool for sheltered instruction.

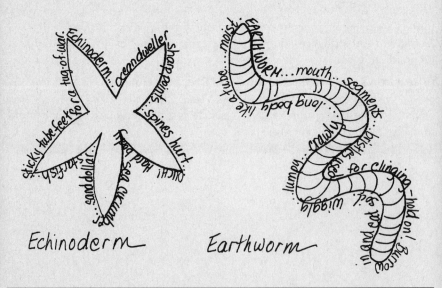

Echinoderm   Earthworm

---

1 Jones, Charla. (1992). *Poetry patterns*. O'Fallon, MO: Books Lures, Inc.

Chapter 7

Puzzles of the Mind and Soul: Mathematics and the Arts

Nature is relationships in space.
Geometry defines relationships in space.
Art creates relationships in space.

Newman and Boles (1992a)

ANSWERS COME TO ME

Soaring high overhead
I become that bird up there,
flowing through the silent roads of nature,
I realize what life really is
it is me
what I like to do,
it is nature

those silent paths I've walked are the paths of life
I feel it, and slowly become myself again
I climb, into the sturdy branches of the tree
opening itself up for any being to sit in, or live in
and I know these are the real virtues of living,
the real reasons that I'm here.

Katrina White, fifth grader

Mathematics and the arts. At first glance they might appear to be distant cousins. But on closer examination we will see that there are so many connections between the two, describing them as fraternal twins might be more apropos. In almost every way the two are interrelated, yet have their own lives. At times they can even be dependent on each other. Consider the painter who at the moment of conceiving a watercolor is also dealing with lines, points, shapes, and space; or the musician who acts as a mathematician working in patterns, time, and rhythms. A dancer is a geometrist moving within the dimensions of a stage or performance area while exploring the possibilities of space.

Leonard Bernstein wrote about the relationship of music to math in one of his Harvard Norton Lectures in 1973: "The fact is that music is not only a mysterious and metaphorical art, it is also born of science. It is made of mathematically measurable elements: frequencies, durations, decibels, intervals, And so any explanation of music must combine mathematics and aesthetics" (p. 9). A common misconception is that mathematics is dedicated to finding answers. This is only a small part of the work. The mathematician is an inventor creating and finding ways to understand relationships among time, space, plane, point, and line. Like the artist, the mathematician seeks the adventure of solving or creating problems. Each does work that demands imagination. Each follows a language of action and reflection moving toward greater understanding.

Consider what each might bring to the understanding of nature. Nature is continually inventing new and complex patterns for the mathematician and the artist: the branching of a river after a great winter melt, or the billowing of cumulus clouds steadily propelled by a forceful wind. While nature gives the mathematician infinite patterns and shapes to consider, at the same time it gives the artist beauty and natural wonder to contemplate. Put together, a greater—or, one might argue, more balanced—perception of nature is possible. "Despite the essential difficulties in understanding the whole of Nature," write Rochelle Newman and Martha Boles (1992a), "both Mathematics and Art reflect a human desire to comprehend [nature] . . . each never fully explains her, but in their complementarity they work to give wholeness" (p. xiii).

Cathy Bullock, a fifth-grade teacher in Encinitas, California, regularly has her students explore mathematical concepts in nature. She brings her students into nature, both around the school and at a local botanical garden, where they sketch flowers and leaves. The students apply their mathematical knowledge to the sketching by describing aspects of nature in mathematical terms. The following examples taken from one child's sketchbook illustrate this point. For the first sketch in Figure 7.1, the child has considered a daylily. She has identified Fibonacci numbers ("13 lines" and "three petals"), something that can be found throughout structures created by nature such as the petals on a sunflower or the scales on a pine cone.

For the second sketch in Figure 7.1, the student has drawn a scarlet pimpernel. The mathematical relationships she identified included the number of petals on each flower, the numbers of flowers in a group, and the number of groups on the stem. For the last sketch in Figure 7.1, the student has drawn millet. She recognized that the "plant is not a Fibonacci, it is a fractal." The student is onto an important discovery as she learns that nature offers infinite fractal and Fibonacci patterns to consider, observe, and understand.

Another relationship between art and mathematics articulated by Newman and Boles relates to games, or constructs of the mind. Games, or constructs of the mind, are

Figure 7.1   Nature sketches.

basic to each discipline, and "both disciplines look for the relationships among the game pieces" (p. xiii). In each case the game pieces, or constructs, build on each other and are related to each other. In music there is often a development of themes, recapitulations, even improvisations. No single note or timbre is enough to create a melody. Even after a melody is established, it is often brought to life with the addition of rhythm, harmonies, countermelodies, and the like. In algebra we find formulas, properties, and proofs. Concepts and/or numbers come to life as they are connected in relationships with other concepts, numbers, measurements, and perceptions. In both cases, the "game" pieces work in harmony toward a greater end, or solution. In both cases, there are endless avenues to explore.

One could argue that the arts are in the realm of metaphor, whereas mathematics is in the realm of logic. If this is true, then the combination of the two provides a unique balance. I would argue that on the surface, this characterization might have some validity. On closer examination, we may find even greater complexities in this relationship. For example, the visual artist is concerned with mathematical relationships among points, lines, and spaces. The concepts are fundamental to the artist's ability to depict a scene or create a design. The mathematician must be able to think beyond the concrete level, as the artist does—in other words, stretch his or her imagination to solve mathematical problems. In this way the mathematician works on a level usually associated with the artist.

Take another example, the geometrist who seeks to understand relationships among shapes reacts to something interesting or worthy of reflection. More often than not, the reaction is an aesthetic awareness. In response to that awareness, the individual seeks greater understanding. As with the artist, the geometrist is guided by a creative force. He or she engages in the same creative process as the artist in seeking to interpret relationships found in the natural world. Thus, when the worlds of the mathematician and the artist meet (as opposed to coexisting in parallel universes), a unique and evolving understanding has the opportunity to emerge.

Before reading on, brainstorm a list of ways in which mathematics and the arts (for example, visual art, music, sculpture, dance, and poetry) intersect. Here are some ideas to get you going.

- repetition, patterns: *reggae music:* recurring rhythms and beats
- points and sets: *pointillism:* Impressionist paintings
- symmetry, geometry: *origami:* the Japanese art of paper folding
- counting, shapes: *square dance:* patterns in time and space
- time: *photography:* shutter speeds, and exposure
- addition: *recipes:* the ingredients in a culinary delight; *oil painting:* the mixing of colors on a palette; *songs:* the additive song "Old MacDonald"
- subtraction: *songs:* the song "B-I-N-G-O"
- equivalents: *rounds:* each section of a round ("Kookaburra," "Frère Jacques," "Row, Row, Row Your Boat")
- equilateral triangle: *round* in three parts
- balance: *pottery:* throwing a pot on a wheel

Now, can you brainstorm a list of professions in which mathematics and the arts meet? Consider the work of architects, engineers, sculptors, muralists, quilters, and tailors. All deal with angles, art, and aesthetics. What other professions connect mathematics and the arts?

LEARNING WITH THE ARTS

In this section we will explore the many ways in which the arts relate to areas of mathematics. We will begin in the realm of visual arts.

Visual Arts

Paintings provide a rich source of material for the emerging mathematician. According to Richard Millman and Ramona Speranza (1991), "art can be used to present early concepts of geometry, including the notion of the infinite" (p. 133). To illustrate their point, the authors focus on the work of many artists, including Georges Seurat (1859–1891), a French painter who developed a technique involving lots and lots of points—dots—applied very closely together to create images. This technique was quite innovative in comparison to the more traditional technique of employing brush strokes. Seurat's technique, also utilized by other Impressionist artists including Manet and Monet, became known as *pointillism*.

In considering works of the Impressionist painters, students learn how points are used as "building blocks" to make sets. A tree can be seen as a set of points as well as a tree; the monkey in Seurat's *A Sunday Afternoon on the Island of La Grande Jatte* can be seen as yet another set. The addition of sets to sets creates a whole.

The works of other well-known artists such as Paul Klee, Pablo Picasso, Wassily Kandinsky, Jasper Johns, and M. C. Escher can offer students a lesson in geometry as well. Moreover, no doubt there are local artists within your community who could provide works for your class's consideration. (Not only is it a chance to incorporate works of art, but it gives your students a chance to meet and interact with local artists.) Observe the sketch in Figure 7.2. This is a work by Deb Stern, a local artist in my community. Notice all the mathematical relationships and concepts in her sketch. Make your own list before reading mine.

Figure 7.2 Original artwork by Deb Stern: Geometrical house.

I notice rectangles, squares, and many lines. There is a perimeter. There are lots of parallel lines. There are many angles throughout: right angles in corners, and angles of varying degrees. Note the triangles. What kind of triangles are there? Is there a line of symmetry? Are there symmetrical patterns? Looking more closely, I identify polygons throughout the painting. Is there any part of the sketch that gives you a feeling of infinity? This is an important concept in Euclidean geometry, "where lines are assumed to be 'straight' and never ending" (Millman & Speranza, 1991, p. 136).

In looking through one of the art books in my school library, I was struck by its organization. The art concepts and math concepts are nearly interchangeable! The book is *Latin American Art: An Introduction to the Works of the 20th Century* (Chaplik, 1989). Most of the chapters are organized around a mathematical theme. The first three chapters focus on line, shape, and space. Other chapters focus on pattern, rhythm, contrast, balance, and unity. This is a good source and model for discussing visual art in a mathematical language. Although intended as a structure for the study of twentieth-century Latin American art, the author's format is perfect for the math teacher. If you cannot find other books organized in a similar way, Chaplik's thematic approach to discussing works of art can be easily applied to other paintings or sculptures as well.

John A. Van De Walle and colleagues (2010), in their 7th edition of *Elementary and Middle School Mathematics,* suggest that children's books create many spaces for exploring mathematics. My favorite example is a lesson they describe based on a description of Hagrid from Harry Potter: "Students in grades 2–3 can cut strips of paper (like adding machine paper) that is as tall as they are and as wide as their shoulders are. Then they can figure out how big Hagrid would be if he were twice as tall and five times as wide as they are. In grades 4–5, students can create a table that shows each student's height and width and look for a pattern (it turns out to be 3:1)" (p. 38). The authors continue with more suggestions for grades 6–8, as well as other ideas to utilize fiction to engage children with mathematics.

The teacher does not need an in-depth knowledge of art in order to carry out any of the explorations mentioned so far. In fact, this work might inspire you and your students to become more interested in artists and their works. A good place to start might be your school or community library. Most collections have art books and slides. A nearby art museum or an art teacher in your school might be willing to serve as a consultant. No doubt, with a little help, you can begin to discover the rich resources within your own community.

After studying various artists' paintings, you might have students create original works of art that incorporate mathematical elements they have uncovered. "The insights that students get from this approach," conclude Millman and Speranza, "range from, at the minimum, becoming exposed to some magnificent works of art to getting a visualization of various concepts from both mathematics and art" (1991, p. 138). Students can begin to understand that seemingly different fields are really quite connected.

Dance

In Chapter 6 I mentioned a few relationships between science and dance. Now consider the mathematical possibilities as well. If you have a chance to attend a dance performance, observe the dancers and note the lines and shapes involved in the choreography.

In southern California, many schools have their own folklorico ballet ensembles. The students learn and perform folk dances from the various regions of Mexico. In watching the performances, one can discern mathematical concepts including shape, lines, parallel lines, symmetry, sequence, patterns—both in groups of dancers and in the repetition of individual steps. Counting is important as well. Are the dancers moving consistently to a certain number of beats? What are the counts? How often do they repeat? Can you detect the concept of odd and even by observing the dancers? What else do you notice?

If you are unable to attend a dance performance, find out if any student in your class takes or has taken ballet lessons. Perhaps the student would be willing to demonstrate the various positions, such as those illustrated in Figure 7.3, and go into pliés and grand pliés in each position. What shapes and angles does the body create in each position?

Do any of your students take tap dance lessons? How is a tap dancer different in mathematical terms from a ballet dancer? Consider the sounds as well. Are there regular patterns? Are there additive steps? Are there any shapes in various steps? What other forms of dance do the students know? In what ways do they relate to mathematical concepts?

Of course, one dance genre that is usually part of a physical education program is square dancing. Work with the physical education teacher and relate the mathematical

Figure 7.3   Ballet positions.

concepts to the dances. Square dancing affords an enjoyable opportunity for mathematical discussion and action. Other ethnic dances or dances associated with a particular geographic region can also be richly "connected" to the study of mathematics.

Literature

There is a world of literature concerned with mathematical concepts. And there is another world of literature that I might label "math ready." Donna Burk and her colleagues, in *Math Excursions 1* (1992), present many wonderful examples of an integrated curriculum. One example begins with the book *Where the Wild Things Are* by Maurice Sendak. The book has been selected as a source reading book, yet its potential for investigating math concepts is great. Burk et al. suggest that the teacher ask children, "How many different ways can you think of to sort this group of wild things?" (p. 1). Take a second look at the literature you are using in your classroom. What potential does it have for math lessons?

Literally hundreds of books relate directly to concepts in mathematics, with themes including algebra, mathematicians, discrete mathematics, problem solving, geometry and patterns, logic and language, measurement and mass, capacity, volume, length, temperature, money, size, and time. There are also numerous books relating to numbers and counting, number concepts, number relationships, place value, addition and subtraction, multiplication and division, estimation, fractions, probability, statistics, and graphing. Many can be used in the integrated classroom as an example of great literature as well as a "math book." What do you already have in your classroom that fits this category?

Music

You might begin to think about the relationships between music and math by listening to some music. Take reggae music, for example. Notice the recurring patterns on the part of the instruments. Are the patterns of equal length? Or, sing a familiar folk song such as "O, Susanna," and discuss the mathematical relationship between the verse and the chorus. Are they the same length? If not, how would you describe the difference? Is the chorus the same as, or longer or shorter than, the verse? Is it half as long as the verse? A third longer?[1] How does "Old MacDonald" convey addition and the song "B-I-N-G-O" convey subtraction? Can you think of any other songs that fall into the same categories? Can you make up different categories?

All the activities just described provide students with real-life (and familiar) applications of particular mathematical concepts. Students begin to associate numbers, lines, shapes, patterns, and the like to real situations. They also see how the study of mathematics is interrelated with many other subjects.

---

[1] In this particular song, "O Susanna," the chorus is half as long as the verse.

LEARNING THROUGH THE ARTS

There are myriad art-based activities through which the teacher can introduce and reflect upon mathematical concepts. I hope the following ideas will inspire you to create your own activities. Most of the examples can be adapted to upper- or lower-grade levels.

Distance Estimation

To get his class of third graders interested in estimating distances, Eduardo Parra, an artist-educator in California, brought in a conch shell and blew into it to produce a sound. He posed this question to children: "If you were on a deserted beach, how far do you think you could travel and still be able to hear the sound of the shell?" Students came up with various answers, mostly in the range of 1 mile to 10 miles. The actual answer is closer to 40. After hearing the true estimate, students were challenged to consider other angles and questions. They began by considering what might cause the sound to travel a lesser distance. They also began to wonder what the distance might be in a city versus along the beach, or if nighttime might make a difference.

Because students became interested in the idea of estimation, Eduardo developed related activities. He brought out his collection of tempera paints and showed students an array of unmixed colors. Into each of three cupcake holders he poured 3 tablespoons of red paint. Then, behind a cardboard screen, he measured different amounts of yellow (using the tablespoon as his guide) and added a different amount to each cupcake holder. The students then estimated the amount of yellow added to each holder. Later that same day, the students mixed their own colors and painted sunset scenes.

Permutations

On another occasion when his students were studying permutations, Eduardo brought in his hand flute made of pottery. The flute has four holes altogether, all on the top section of the instrument. He posed this question: "How many different sounds can I make with this flute by changing the combinations I make with my fingers?" (This is an interesting twist on permutations because, in addition to all the combinations, the flute can sound without any fingers covering any holes.) Although students did not arrive at any definitive answers in this case, they thought deeply about the question and—perhaps more important—were interested in pursuing the answer.

Fractions

Music is a terrific motivator for exploring fractions. If there is a music teacher in your school, consider joining forces with that person in this endeavor. The following examples, however, are easy enough to get you and your students going. Begin with simple "sound fractions" or "sound ratios." In the example that follows, each "x" is a symbol for a beat. The beat may be on a drum or a tabletop; it could be a hand clap or a stomp. You need two players (or divide the class in half—another fraction!) to play this piece, which highlights the fraction ⅓ or the ratio 1:3. Together, one person or group plays the top line while the other person or group plays the bottom line. The vertical lines in between the *x*'s serve to guide us visually but have no sound attached to them. In musical terms, they signify measures. In mathematical terms, they indicate the base of the fraction.

```
x       |x      |x        |
x  x  x |x  x  x |x  x  x |
```

Test yourself. Can you identify the next sound fractions?

```
x    |x    |x    |x    |x
x  x |x  x |x  x |x  x |x  x

x  x     |x  x    |x  x     |
x  x  x  |x  x  x |x  x  x |
```

The first one signifies ½. The second one signifies ⅔. Have your students create their own sound fractions. This might serve as an assessment tool as well as a learning tool. The more confident students become, the more inclined they might be to create intricate pieces that mix fractions. As long as the students can identify them, they are onto something important.

Another approach to the fraction idea comes from Marni Respicio, a dancer and artist-educator who integrates movement and fractions. Keeping a steady beat, she has her students create movement patterns to ⅔, ¾, or ¼ time. In this case *o* indicates hands up in the sky and *x* indicates hand clapping. Here are three patterns. Try them yourself and see if they make sense to you.

1.   o   x   o   x   o   x
2.   o   x   x   o   x   x   o   x   x
3.   o   x   x   x   o   x   x   x   o   x   x   x

In all these examples of sound and movement fractions, students are exploring not only fractions, but also the fundamentals of musical composition. By creating their fractions, they are putting sound or movement to symbols, creating original compositions, and arranging the "instrumentation." These are the same tools used by the composer and arranger. The composer places sounds together to form musical pieces. The arranger decides which instruments should work together and when. For example, when blues singer Bonnie Raitt plays with the Boston Pops, an arrangement has to be created so that her songs—originally written only for guitar, bass, and drums—can be played by violins, trumpets, trombones, and so on. The arranger takes the original material and rearranges it for a full orchestra. Sometimes a composer and arranger are the same person; sometimes arrangers take the compositions of others and arrange them in another way. Our "fraction composers and arrangers" are beginning musical composers and arrangers.

Should some of your students prefer a more visual exercise, consider one presented by Cathy Bullock: "fraction collage." Students are given six rectangles of equal size but different colors. The first one is a whole. The second one must be cut in two halves; the third one in thirds; the fourth in fourths; the fifth in fifths; and the sixth in sixths. The students then create a collage using all or some of their pieces. What was interesting about one student's picture was her attention to symmetry and design. She cut the rectangles in such a way that she created interesting shapes, including polygons.

Shapes, Symmetry, Angles, and Geometry

Students can create shapes with their bodies. In small groups, students might be challenged to create parallel lines, right angles, perpendicular lines, squares, triangles, and circles. Have students move around the perimeter of a figure, or walk in a diagonal line through a square. Individually, can they form shapes with their arms, fingers, or legs only? Can they form symmetrical shapes with their two hands? Can they create symmetrical figures with a partner? How about an asymmetrical shape? Have the students choreograph a short movement piece that includes three shapes (various triangles, square, circle, rectangle, polygon) and/or concepts (parallel lines, symmetry, perpendicular) to present to the class. Encourage the class to identify the shapes/concepts.

More advanced students might even add sounds to their performance. In addition to presenting the shapes, they might present them in time that can be described in terms of fractions. For example, student one taps the desk once to every three claps of student two (⅓), who moves into various positions. The positions/shapes change at specific times, or last for specific times. Give your students this challenge and see how many mathematical concepts any given group can incorporate into their "performance piece."

Origami, the ancient Japanese art of paper folding, can provide students with magical lessons in line, symmetry, angles, and function. Students apply concepts of geometry as they create swans, fish, or the wings of a dragonfly. Because many of the shapes come from nature, this can also be part of an integrated unit on nature. According to Peter Engel in *Folding the Universe: Origami from Angelfish to Zen* (1989), one of the wonders of both nature and origami is that "simple elements make complex patterns" (p. 46).

Cathy Bullock and Karen Burke (another teacher in the San Diego area) both use art extensively to teach geometric concepts. In exploring bilateral symmetry, each teacher gives her students half a photograph, which the students must complete by mirroring the image. Burke indicates that she has the greatest success when she asks them to work on the images upside down. This forces them to carefully mirror the lines and shapes; otherwise some students tend to draw to make it "look good." Following are examples from the fifth grade and second grade. Can you tell which side was the original photograph in Figure 7.4?

Of course, students can create their own original symmetrical paintings as well. Karen Burke has used an exercise she adapted from a workshop to create symmetrical castles. Students begin by folding a paper in half to create and identify a symmetrical reference line. Then, by carefully measuring the shapes they place on one half of the paper, they create a symmetrical castle. The teacher may want to place an example on an overhead for reference. Both teachers expand on this concept by

Figure 7.4   An example of bilateral symmetry by a second grader.

adding the notion of positive and negative space. This concept can be easily introduced through symmetrical cutouts. In the examples in Figure 7.5, students have explored positive and negative space and symmetry.

Single-Digit Addition and Subtraction

I have had young students create "secret codes" in addition and subtraction through sound. An easy way to begin is with hand clapping simple problems such

Figure 7.5 Symmetrical cutouts.

as 2 + 3. Student A claps twice, and student B claps three times. Student C must clap the answer:

$$// + /// = /////$$
$$/// - / = //$$

The secret codes can become more complex for older students as they invent sounds to represent things other than single digits. One group of students working collaboratively presented the class with the following problem. (The / represents a handclap. The * represents a foot stomp.)

/ * / + / * = 7 Can you guess what number * represents?

A group of fifth graders working with Eduardo Garcia, SUAVE arts coach, invented another twist in the secret code game. They wanted to do multiplication problems in sound, but realized it was too difficult to clap the answer to 8 × 7. Rather than clap all 56 beats, they substituted a stomp for units of ten. So the answer was: stomp stomp stomp stomp stomp clap clap clap clap clap clap. When they got into even bigger numbers, they decided to do a twist for units of 100. For example, twist stomp stomp clap clap clap represents the number 123. In doing this, the students were inventing a decimal system!

I have challenged my student teachers to create these kinds of problems to present to each other. Admittedly it can be a stretch for many students, but a stretch that has them truly *thinking* about mathematics and representation. I usually provide students with instruments that have multiple tones, such as xylophones and glockenspiels, and send them on their way. I never know what they will come up with, which is part of the fun. Many students have created addition, subtraction, multiplication, and division problems by adding or taking away tones played simultaneously. Students have also found ways to represent permutations and concepts, such as sequence and patterning, through sound.

Points and Coordinates, Parallel Lines

Visual arts lend themselves to mathematical concepts such as graphing. Murals, for example, provide the math student with an opportunity to make use of graphing skills, to study proportion and measurement, and to apply those skills to a real-life setting. In an integrated study, the mural can reflect a curriculum theme in addition to being a mathematical focus for learning. With the help of an art teacher or local artist, you can obtain appropriate paint materials.

In considering this undertaking for the first time, I recommend collaborating with an artist who can guide students in design and implementation. You can take charge in terms of theme and mathematical connections. If you are unable to collaborate with an art teacher or artist, start small and work yourself up to larger murals. Schools often have ample wall spaces for this kind of project. Some classes have even created murals on moveable walls and large boards so they could be displayed rather than remaining permanently in the classroom.

As an entry into the world of mural making, you might consider the option of drawing to scale. Take a cartoon character, such as Luann (drawn by Greg Evans), and place it on a graph with coordinates. Then, on larger paper, have the students re-create the cartoon using the coordinates as their reference. Another idea is to cut up one or more greeting cards into squares or rectangles and hand them out to students without letting them see the whole. Each student enlarges his or her square or rectangle using the same predetermined scale. When the students have completed the task, put both cards back together and see the finished products!

To work with parallel lines, consider the following exercise. Students in Cathy Bullock's class were asked to create a visual art piece using parallel lines. Their tools included a pencil, ruler, and—later on—colored markers, pencils, or pens. Students created a design and completed it by using parallel lines only. Figure 7.6 is an example of one student's work. In reflecting on this math-art project, Anabel Contreras, a fifth grader, incorporates mathematical language, indicating not only that she can apply her

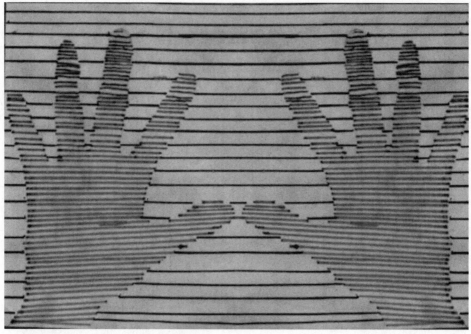

Figure 7.6   Parallel line drawings.

understanding to a project, but that she can also discuss it in mathematical terminology: "If you draw two parallel lines, then you would be using math by making the lines equidistant from each other. For instance, if you drew a road, the two lines for the sides of the road will never meet."

Drama, Story Problems

Students might enjoy the following challenge. Create a story or drama to illustrate $4 + 3 = 7$, or $3 - 2 = 1$. "As students dramatize, tell, write, share, and solve story problems over an extended period of time," write Burk et al. (1992), "they begin to learn about processes, language, and symbols associated with addition and subtraction" (p. 15). Cathy Bullock integrates story problems with language arts. She gives groups of students a newspaper headline: for example, "$3 - 2 = 1$." Students then write a story to go along with it, paying attention to who, what, where, when, and why.

SUMMARY

The possibilities of integrating art and mathematics are numerous, if not infinite. Interrelationships among the two offer creative and enjoyable activities that will no doubt interest your students and inspire them to work seriously with mathematical concepts. As I have shown throughout this chapter, activities in the arts can offer many avenues to students as they become open to the wonders of the natural world and the connections to mathematics within their own world. As students begin to comprehend that much of their world revolves directly or indirectly around mathematical concepts, they may also become interested in the application of those concepts.

 TECH CONNECT

Technology, Arts, and Mathematics

- Have student create math stories on the computer, illustrate them, and publish them for the class or other classes. Here are a few titles to get you thinking: "The Adventures of Sir Ican Add and Lady Minús," "Captain Multiplication Seeks a Dividing Line," and "Mrs. Ratio and the Point Guard."

- Have students create visual or rhythmic patterns on the computer to study patterning.

- Have students create geometric collages on the computer based on geometry skills.

- Have students access information (including pictures of paintings) on the artist Mondrian and use his work as a way to discuss parallel lines and shapes.

 QUESTIONS TO PONDER

1. What math/art connections can you find in the poem by Katrina White, fifth-grade student, at the opening of this chapter? Can you identify any other connections between this poem and the chapter (philosophical, theoretical)?

2. What connections can you think of between math and arts in your own life?

3. Brainstorm a list of professions. Now consider the ways in which math and the arts relate to each profession. Is one more important than the other? Is it different in other cultures?

4. Consider quilting and weaving. In what ways do they directly relate to mathematical concepts? How could you infuse them into your curriculum, both learning *with* and learning *through?*

5. Consider the work of M. C. Escher and its relationship to mathematics. How about tessellations?

 EXPLORATIONS TO TRY

1. With a friend, create a sound piece that represents a mathematical problem or concept. Now add movement to make it even more complex. In what ways does the movement add to the original concept? What new mathematical ideas can be derived from the *addition* (hint) of the movement?

2. Create a project that demonstrates ways in which you can learn specific mathematical concepts *with* music.

3. Brainstorm a way to learn multiplication *through* visual art.

4. Create a way to represent subtraction *through* movement.

5. Go into your kitchen. What are all the connections you can make to math with things found in the kitchen? What are all the connections you can make to art with things found in the kitchen? How many of the connections incorporate both math and art? Can any of them exist without one or the other?

6. Look at a painting in your house or local museum. How many shapes, patterns, and concepts can you identify? Do you think that all paintings would be good for this exercise? How would you begin to differentiate?

7. Create a geometrical collage by using an arts program on the computer. Use a minimum of five geometric shapes.

REFERENCES

Bernstein, L. (1976). *The unanswered question: Six talks at Harvard.* Cambridge, MA: Harvard Unviersity Press.

Burk, D., Snider, A., Symonds, P. (1992). *Math excursions 1: Project-based mathematics for first graders.* Portsmouth, NH: Heinemann.

Chaplik, D. (1989). *Latin American art: An introduction to the works of the 20th century.* Jefferson, NC: McFarland & Company.

Engel, P. (1989). *Folding the universe: Origami from angelfish to zen.* New York: Vintage Books.

Millman, R. S., & Speranza, R. R. (1991, February). The artist's view of points and lines. *Mathematics Teacher,* (Vol. 84).

Newman, R., & Boles, M. (1992a). *The golden relationship: Art, math & nature* (Book 1, 2nd rev. ed.). Bradford, MA: Pythagorean Press.

———. (1992b). *The golden relationship: Art, math & nature* (Book 2, 2nd rev. ed.). Bradford, MA: Pythagorean Press.

Van De Walle, J., Karp, K. S., & Bay-Williams, J. M. (2010). *Elementary and middle school mathematics: Teaching developmentally* (7th ed.). Boston: Allyn & Bacon.

SAMPLE LESSON PLANS

Mathematics

The lessons included here are "Animal Division" by Camille Armstrong and three math-literature plays: "Math Menagerie," by Sandy Thorne; "Fraction-Action Colonial Style," which includes quilting, by Dale Murphy; and "Playing Detective: Using Mathematical Language to Describe Art," developed by Laura Wendling.

SUAVE Curriculum and Project Description

PROJECT TITLE: Animal Division Game

TEACHER: Camille Armstrong

SCHOOL AND GRADE: Grade 4, Valley Center Upper

DISCIPLINE AREA(S):   Math / Science / Dance

PROJECT GOAL(S):   Teach students division using dance and science

PROCESS AND STEPS:

1. Explain that we're going to learn about division through science and dance. One child will suggest a type of animal to move in the space (no bumping).

2. Count total number of students (animals) present. Students move like animals.

3. When teacher blows whistle, students form equal groups according to a number held (i.e., 5 = five animals in a group). Animals left over go to the remaining area (designated with yarn or marker)

4. When students divide up, discuss the results with the whole class. Construct a chart to show results. Continue as many times as you want.

MATERIALS NEEDED:

1. Large space to move; gym, outdoor area with rectangle

2. Yarn to make circle for remaining animals

3. Large number cards with 1–9 on each card

ESSENTIAL QUESTIONS:

1. **What skills, elements, vocabulary were taught?**
   Division, fair share, reminder, move like the animal

2. **How did you assess the children's understanding?**
   Review the results with the whole class

3. **Where could you go from here?**
   Repeat the activity. Make a handout that uses the idea of animals divided into groups.

4. **Other comments?**
   This is a very fun activity and the students understand the idea of dividing a fair share and remainder. They enjoy choosing animals and moving like them.

SUAVE Curriculum and Project Description

PROJECT TITLE:　Math-Literature Plays—"Math Menagerie"

TEACHER:　Sandy Thorne

SCHOOL AND GRADE:　Grade 5, **Miller School**

DISCIPLINE AREA(s):　Math / Language Arts / Drama

PROJECT GOAL(s):　To have students write, produce, and put on plays using literature about mathematics

PROCESS AND STEPS:

1. Pick 10 students to pair up and read the books and *write their own version* in play format.
2. Classmates pick which play they want to be in. All students have a part in one of the plays.
3. Backdrops are done by all students.
4. Performance for school and parents—videotape.
5. View videotape of self—self-evaluation on performance skills.

MATERIALS NEEDED:　Five books—*Baker's Dozen, Grandfather Tang's Story, The Doorbell Rang, Gator Pie, How Big Is a Foot?*

ESSENTIAL QUESTIONS:　How can I get students to have stronger oral language skills—eye contact—voice—stage presence?

1. **What skills, elements, vocabulary were taught?**
   Play production—performance skills
   Math concepts—writing skills—art skills
2. **How did you assess the children's understanding?**
   Final performance—watching videotape of the performance—discussing what was learned
3. **Where could you go from here?**
   Went to a "professional" play—compared our experience with what we saw them doing
4. **Other comments?**
   This was done during April, National Mathematics Month

SUAVE Curriculum and Project Description

PROJECT TITLE: "Fraction-Action Colonial Style"

TEACHER: Dale Murphy

SCHOOL AND GRADE: Grade 5, Felicita

DISCIPLINE AREA(S): Math / Social Science / Visual Arts

PROJECT GOAL(S): Teach students about quilting, which was a major activity for the colonists, and have them get a better understanding of what fractions are and how they work

PROCESS AND STEPS:

1. Divide class into groups of 4.
2. Give each child a 10×10 square (of graph paper) so they each have 100 small squares.
3. Tell students that as a team they will be making a *block* to later be used for a class quilt. Explain that each person in the group will be responsible for ¼ of the block. Also explain that they will have to work together to come up with a theme or picture for their block.
4. Let the students know that they have to use exactly ½ of their square. Try to get them to "discover" that ½ of 100 is 50. Further explain that they *can't* use more or less than ½ of the squares. As they experiment with the squares, they will discover that this may actually lead to using more than 50 small squares (they may use ½ or ⅓ of 2 or 3 smaller squares to equal 1 whole square).
5. Give plenty of time for brainstorming and experimenting. Once they have their ideas, let them go to work. Tell them to be sure to color with bright colors.
6. Put the 4 pieces of each block together, mat onto a bigger, bright square, then "sew" or tie all blocks together to form a beautiful class quilt. Display and enjoy.

MATERIALS NEEDED: Graph paper (10×10 squares), bright crayons or markers, larger squares of construction paper (for matting), yarn and hole puncher (to "sew" or tie blocks together)

ESSENTIAL QUESTIONS:

1. **What skills, elements, vocabulary were taught?**
   Fractions (½, ¼), quilting, blocking, colonial living
2. **How did you assess the children's understanding?**
   Checked to see if each child used 50 squares (exactly) and if ¼ pieces created a smooth block
3. **Where could you go from here?**
4. **Other comments?**
   This is a great cooperative learning group or team project! It's also a great way to combine math and social science together in a nontraditional way.

SUAVE Workshop
Presented by Laura Wendling

PLAYING DETECTIVE: USING MATHEMATICAL LANGUAGE TO DESCRIBE ART

Upon entering the museum with a partner, immediately go into different galleries. Select one work of art and, in the space below, write a description of the work using mathematical language.

Try to find clever ways to describe details of the work so that your partner will have to carefully examine many works of art in your gallery.

Then, at an agreed-upon time, meet together and take turns reading the descriptions to each other!

Following are examples of mathematical language that could be used to provide your partner with clues about the work of art you have selected.

- There are two small lines that form right angles in the upper left (or northwest) corner of this work . . .
- There is a bright concave shape about 3 inches above the middle . . .
- There is a repeated pattern that takes up about 1/8 the total space . . .
- There is an object touching the bottom of the work that in real life would be approximately six feet tall . . .

Have fun using your imagination!

_____

_____

_____

_____

_____

_____

_____

_____

_____

_____

Chapter 8

Visual Literacy, Aesthetics, and How Subject Matter Informs Art Making

ODE TO A CLUSTER OF VIOLETS

Crisp cluster
plunged in a shadow.
Drops of violet water
and raw sunlight
floated up with your scent.
A fresh
subterranean beauty
climbed up from your buds,
thrilling my eyes and my life.

One at a time, flowers
that stretched forward
silvery stalks,
creeping closer to an obscure light
shoot by shoot in the shadows,
till they crowned
the mysterious mass
with an intense weight of perfume
and together
formed a single star
with a far-off scent and purple center.

ODA A UN RAMO DE VIOLETAS

Crespo ramo en la sombra
sumergido:
gotas de agua violeta
y luz salvaje
subieron con tu aroma
una fresca hermosura
subterránea
trepó con tus capullos
y estremeció mis ojos y mi vida.

Una por una, flores
que alargaron
metálicos pedúnculos,
acercando en la sombra
rayo tras rayo de una luz oscura
hasta que coronaron
el misterio
con su masa profunda de perfume,
y unidas
fueron una sola estrilla
de olor remoto y corazón morado.

Poignant cluster,	Ramo profundo,
intimate	intimo
scent	olor
of nature,	de la naturaleza,
you resemble	pareces
a wave, or a head of hair,	la ouda, la cabellera,
or the gaze	la mirada
of a ruined water nymph	de una náyade rota
sunk in the depths.	y submarina,
But up close,	pero de cerca,
in your fragrance's	en plena
blue brazenness,	temeridad azul de tu fragancia,
you exhale the earth,	tierra, flor de la tierra,
an earthly flower, an earthen	olor terrestre
smell and your ultraviolet	desprendes, y tu rayo
gleam	ultravioleta
is volcanoes' faraway fires.	es combustión lejana de volcanes.
Into your loveliness I sink	Sumerjo en tu hermosura
a weathered face,	mi viejo rostro tantas
a face that dust has often abused.	veces hostilizado por el polvo
You deliver	y algo desde la tierra
something out of the soil.	me transmites,
It isn't simply perfume,	y no es sólo un perfume,
nor simply the perfect cry	no es sólo el grito puro
of your entire color, no: it's	de tu color total, es más bien
a word sprinkled with dew,	una palabra con rocio,
a flowering wetness with roots.	una humedad florida con raices.
Fragile cluster of starry	Frágil haz de violetas
violets,	estrelladas,
tiny, mysterious	pequeño, misterioso
planet	planetario
of marine phosphorescence,	de fósforo marino,
nocturnal bouquet nestled in green leaves:	nocturno ramo entre las hojas verdes,
the truth is	la verdad es
there is no blue word to express you.	que no hay polabra azul para expresarte:
Better than any word	más que toda palabra
is the pulse of your scent.[1]	te describe un latido de tu aroma.

Pablo Neruda, Odes to Common Things (1994)

---

[1] From ODES TO COMMON THINGS by Pablo Neruda, selected and illustrated by Ferris Cook. Odes (English translation) copyright © 1994 by Ken Krabbencroft. By permission Little, Brown and Company.

Imagine! Pablo Neruda could have been out in the field with us using poetry to describe his observations of the violet. His scientific and aesthetic descriptions are not dissimilar to the fifth graders' in Chapter 6, though admittedly he has had a bit more practice in expressing himself through poetry.

Although the bulk of this book focuses on using the arts to teach subject matter, this chapter takes a slightly different viewpoint. Here we will explore four related topics: (1) the aesthetic experience and how it is related to arts in education, (2) how the arts can set the stage for learning, (3) how subject matter informs the arts, and (4) how the arts, in and of themselves, are intrinsically valuable in the school curriculum.

By nature, human beings have an aesthetic sense. We see the world in many colors. We react to sights, smells, sounds, nature, and just about everything and everyone with whom we come into daily contact; and our reactions are integrated according to previous experiences. In other words, each of us does more than merely *exist* in a world; we *perceive* our world. That perception is, in part, an aesthetic perception. Pablo Neruda's poem is an aesthetic expression of his observation of a cluster of common violets. It also includes what one could consider scientific description. It is likely that any of us, upon viewing a cluster of violets, might have an aesthetic reaction. The difference between Pablo Neruda and the rest of us is that he is a practiced poet; he applies his perception to a poem and shares his perception with a public.

There is a tension in Western life, as well as in schools, that pits "aesthetic" experience against "practical" experience. Daily life is seen as a series of practical exercises, including waking up on time, planning for dinner, reporting to work, finishing the report, taking tests (or administering them), and so on. Aesthetic response, on the other hand, "comes when we stop, even briefly, to look, to listen, to *savor* the qualities of experience beyond what is required for fulfilling our practical needs" (Hospers, 1982, p. 335). Everyone has an aesthetic sense. You might exhibit this sense in the way you arrange the furniture in your living room or by the choices you make when you create a bulletin board display in your classroom. Unfortunately, because of the rapid pace of our lives, we risk losing a sense of the aesthetic, even to the point of forgetting it altogether. One could argue that as a result, many of us lead lives that are out of balance.

What is the importance of balance and aesthetics to teaching and learning? At first glance, one could argue for its intrinsic value. We live in a world that is not only objective but rich in experiences. Even practical applications have some element of the aesthetic. One need only look to the most simple and common objects to understand that design is an important element. Consider telephones. Compare the phones in your home, school, and/or office (not to mention your cell phones and their covers). You will note that they come in many colors, sizes, even shapes. Some phones may be more practical, some may be more aesthetically pleasing. Every object falls somewhere on a continuum of practical/aesthetic. However, understanding this dualism is not the most important function that aesthetic awareness plays in the classroom.

Using our aesthetic sense means that we are aware. We stop to look, to listen, to feel, to reflect. By participating in an activity that involves our aesthetic senses, we are in a position to think more deeply about something and reflect upon it. Many would describe this as a goal of teaching and learning: to be intensely engaged in considering subject matter. In this manner the arts, by definition, enable students to stop and reflect deeply upon what they are learning. For some people, acts of awareness are not so separated from the everyday. Instead, they are fundamental to culture and daily life. Consider the words of Tewa Vickie Downey, of the Tesque Pueblo:

> Most people look to the elders as teachers. They are. But we also look at the children, look at them as teachers. We study life. Our life is studying. We study everything, everybody, even the tiniest insect. Like the other day, we noticed that the ants went into the house early. So what does this mean? We study that. We watch the ants or the bees or the trees. Every second of our life we're studying everything around us. The sounds. The music. Outside our culture people don't have that awareness. We have to bring that awareness back. It's just being in tune with the spirit. So what people have to do now is be in that awareness.[2] (qtd. in Wall, 1993, p. 20)

In an earlier chapter I mentioned how practicing my guitar in childhood helped prepare me to be a disciplined and dedicated writer and thinker. It prepared me to take on other areas with the rigor and self-discipline needed to follow through in my studies. When practicing my guitar, I was able to experience varying states of awareness: I was aware of my own abilities, the sounds I could create, the quality of sounds I created. Through my practicing, I was being trained with an aesthetic awareness. That awareness potentially transfers to all other areas of learning, promoting deep reflection and a wholeness of experience.

As teachers, we are in positions to reach students so they may begin to tap into the action of being aesthetically aware. An important distinction to make at this point brings us back to the realm of judgment and personal taste. When I talk of the aesthetic experience, I mean an action that requires each individual to stop and consider aspects of his or her world. This is outside the realm of personal taste. For example, as someone who is not a fish eater, I will never like the taste of fish. Yet I can appreciate its preparation and presentation despite my distaste for it. Therefore, one can be aesthetically aware regardless of personal likes and dislikes.

The arts provide a means and form to express our understanding of the world in an aesthetic as well as objective manner. Just as we can learn subject matter through the arts, the arts can teach us about the world in which we live. Recently, I attended a dance performance that included a piece on homelessness. Through the dancers' movements, expressions, and contact with each other, I felt I was introduced to the emotions and stresses of homelessness. Although I didn't learn facts or figures relating to numbers of people who are homeless, I did walk away with a deeper compassion for what it could feel like to be homeless. That feeling no doubt informs my overall understanding of homelessness.

Even though the arts might not provide an answer to questions of AIDS research, how to curb pollution, or, as Denis Donoghue remarks (Greene, 1991), "cure a toothache," they do provide the tools needed to imagine the solutions and the dedication needed to follow through in pursuing answers. The student who is practiced in seeing things from an aesthetic point of view and in using his or her imagination is more likely to come up

---

[2] Quote from WISDOM'S DAUGHTERS: CONVERSATIONS WITH WOMEN ELDERS OF NATIVE AMERICA by Steve Wall. Copyright © 1993 by Steve Wall. Reprinted by permission of HarperCollins Publishers, Inc.

with solutions to problems. The more practice one has in working imaginatively and reflectively, the more likely one will be able to apply those skills while discovering, say, cures in medical research or solutions for promoting a clean environment. So, while I wouldn't want an artist giving me medical advice, I surely want my doctor to have practiced the arts.

I do not mean to imply that a student who thinks aesthetically is necessarily going to think with clarity. In fact, one of the most wonderful things about the arts is their ability to let us, in the famous composer and conductor Leonard Bernstein's words (1976), live in "the beauty of ambiguity," which underlies how many musical passages can be so expressive. When we contemplate things deeply, ambiguity or confusion

Katrina White, a fifth grader, finds a moment of awareness as she writes a poem reflecting on the sturdy branches of a tree and the virtues of living.

often arises before clarity. However, confusion is as normal a state of being (in learning) as is clarity. Confusion implies thinking—if I am confused about something, I am certainly thinking about it. When my thinking becomes clear, I can then move on to an even deeper understanding. Confusion often leads to curiosity, and curiosity paves the way to learning. When I stop to contemplate the design of the chair in my kitchen or the colors of a flower in my patio garden, I usually come up with questions in addition to logging an observation. Why doesn't the weight from the back of the chair knock it over? Where do the colors come from to make such vibrant flower petals? These questions may emerge from an ability to stop and ponder objects in an aesthetic manner, forming the genesis of what could evolve to be more objective or scientific, pursuits.

Aesthetic experiences lend themselves to teaching and learning in at least five ways: (1) *perception:* an awareness of one's surroundings and actions; (2) *concentration:* a tool for exploration through actively stopping, listening, seeing, and feeling; (3) *imagination:* a journey of the mind to new places; (4) *contemplation:* an opportunity to question and search; and (5) *action:* our questions and searches are pursued.

ARTS SETTING THE STAGE FOR LEARNING

One use of the arts that we have not addressed so far is in setting the stage for learning. In the next section we will explore ways in which a teacher can utilize art forms to create a learning atmosphere and prepare students for serious reflection. Drawing on our discussion of the aesthetic, the arts can promote or awaken perceptions and imagination while at the same time providing a tool for concentration and contemplation as students begin a study.

An example can be drawn from one of the elementary classes I visit weekly. Once I showed up on a cloudy spring day. The children had been on the verge of acting up for a few weeks now, and it seemed like a lot of class time was spent dealing with discipline issues. On the spot, the teacher and I decided to try something new. I always carry my penny whistle in my backpack and have played it for the class on numerous occasions. The penny whistle is a small Irish flute, familiar to those who listen to Irish folk music. It has a high and delicate sound, and the kids love to listen to me play. When I arrive it is not unusual to hear, "Do you have your penny whistle today?!"

We sat the children in the front of the room where we usually sit for class discussions. I explained to them that we would try an experiment today, and that I wasn't sure if it would work or not but wanted their participation nonetheless. The experiment was that I would play the penny whistle and the students would write poetry at the same time—on the subject of nature. The students readily agreed and went back to their seats, where they pulled out their poetry journals. I began to play an improvisation on an Irish tune, the "Swallowtail Jig."

As I played, each student began to write. The only sound in the class was of my penny whistle. When I stopped to rest for a moment the silence seemed almost strange, unwanted. The children were extremely engaged, writing with ease; so I continued my improvisation. After a few moments I would stop, but the children wanted me to continue. Before all was said and done, I improvised for half an hour as the class composed their poems. Even the most boisterous students seemed calmed by the magic of the flute and engaged in reflective writing. We stopped only because the art teacher arrived, ready to continue her lesson from the previous week—a watercolor work to accompany the nature poetry. As we shifted into the art lesson, we were surprised at the concentration and attention students continued to exhibit. What was going on?

It was clear to me that the music had set the stage for students. For many, it was a calming mechanism, and for others it was an inspiration as well. Students were concentrating on their writing and were serious in their contemplation of nature. Their imaginations were freed and their ability to perceive—their awareness—was heightened. Although I have experienced the effects of music in other circumstances, this experience was a reminder of the power such a simple musical melody can have in a teaching and learning situation. Others have noticed this as well. Research has shown that music can reduce anxiety and increase attentiveness in classroom settings (Blanchard, 1979; Russell, 1992). Listening to music can even improve test scores (Black, 1993; Giles, 1991).

Creating illustrations and artwork may improve a child's ability to write, according to Beth Olshansky (1994): "When art becomes truly integrated throughout every stage of the writing process, both children's creative processes and their finished products share a quality of richness previously unequaled" (p. 351). Olshansky argues that when children have the opportunity to express themselves both visually and verbally, they are in a better position to work with ideas and unleash their creative juices. Illustrations give rise to words as words give rise to illustrations, offering students pathways to understandings. This speaks to learning styles as well. For the student who likes to draw pictures first, the pictures help with describing words for a poem or story. For the student who prefers to start with words, the words lend shape to pictures.

In both cases, we have examples of how empowering children through the arts serves many purposes. Music might calm and center students as they return from recess or lunch. It might refocus them as the teacher prepares to switch lesson gears. Further, it might inspire students to visualize images or stories, formulas or methods, as they work seriously on the subject matter at hand. Similarly, having the opportunity to draw while working on subject matter such as writing can further thinking and inspire original thought. Of course, other art forms can do the same. Photographs might inspire a historical essay, and movement might clear up a mathematical problem. In sum, use of the arts in the curriculum may set the stage for reflective, creative, and serious contemplation.

SUBJECT MATTER INFORMING ART

In this section we will consider how subject matter knowledge informs art, rather than how art informs subject matter. It is a bit of a twist, but an interesting twist nonetheless. This brings me back to balance in learning. If the arts inform subject matter, then subject matter should inform the arts.

We will begin by thinking about mathematical knowledge. I learned how important mathematical skills were to a group of university students as they prepared to paint a mural on one of the walls outside our school. Like all muralists, the students were faced with re-creating a design on a wall that was much larger than their original design on construction paper. The math majors began graphing and calculating, creating grids to facilitate the painting. Without a math background, the students might have labored long and hard and ended up with a lopsided or out-of-proportion product.

Now let's imagine that we are visiting a museum with a mathematician. We are in a gallery hosting a special exhibition of work by Diego Rivera and Frida Kahlo. Imagine the perspectives that you and the mathematician bring to your viewing of the paintings. Whereas you might be interested in the colors and representational figures, the mathematician is drawn to the geometry, symmetry, and patterns in various paintings. Knowing something of mathematics, in this case, informs our viewing of the painting. Indeed, knowing something of mathematics directly informed the artists Braque and Picasso as they created their works. Once you begin to view paintings, murals, and sculptures mathematically, a whole new view of the art will be opened to you. This is an example of how math helps you better observe and appreciate the visual arts. Walking through a gallery with a mathematician, you might be more likely to pay attention to aspects of artwork you would not notice otherwise. The mathematical perspective opens routes to understanding something more about the painting. Mathematical knowledge informs our viewing of the painting.

Now, in addition to looking at the hidden figures in paintings, we are looking at the geometric shapes creating and surrounding them. As we follow a rectangular figure, we notice other shapes in the painting and how they connect. Our initial reaction to a painting begins to change as we notice the intricate and detailed lines and points and how they work to highlight a representational figure similar to a guitar. As we look even closer, we notice the figure is composed of a series of polygons; the "guitar" begins to appeal to our math sense as well our aesthetic sense. Our viewing of the painting is now more complex. We have a greater appreciation of the mathematical knowledge communicated through the painting, as well as the aesthetic appeal.

It is time to leave the mathematician with the artworks and move next door into the natural history museum, where we will view a gallery dedicated to prehistoric rock art. Here we will be joined by Juanita, an archeologist in town on a grant spending a year at the local university. Juanita's expertise happens to be in the area of animal rock art. Lucky for us, much of the exhibit is dedicated to exactly that!

We enter into the gallery and are confronted with an exhibit titled "Roadrunner Tracks in Southwestern Petroglyphs." What we notice immediately is the rawness of the shapes embedded in rock: tracks, bird shapes, faces, and interesting geometrical patterns. Admittedly, we haven't a clue as to what they represent. We walk around in wonder, contemplating the figures created by the Mongollon peoples of the lower desert of southern New Mexico between roughly A.D. 1050 and 1400. The figures, we read on the exhibit wall, are in the "Jornada style." We are impressed by what is before us. The figures appeal to our aesthetic sense and are interesting works of art in and of themselves.

Juanita at this point cannot contain her excitement. Her knowledge of archeology gives her a very different perspective of the rock art. She and we are looking at the figures in the rocks, but are seeing very different things. She begins to tell us that "the mere presence of the roadrunner track in prehistoric rock art was strongly indicative that the roadrunner and/or its track had religious significance in the prehistoric southwest." Barely taking a breath, she continues, "The whole animal may be signified by a track, although in certain cases the track, or paw—in the case of bears—is imbued with specific ritual powers"

(Morphy, 1989, p. 261).[3] We are speechless, for our newfound understanding of the figures is deeply enhanced by the ethnographic information Juanita so excitedly shares.

What we are experiencing is the way in which the work of an anthropologist or archeologist can inform our overall understanding of, and experience with, specific rock art. Although we can enjoy the artwork on its own, the subject matter background lends a context and foundation for interpreting the art in addition to reacting to it.

In contemplating this notion, I can make a connection to a similar experience during my forays into bird watching with fifth graders. Though I often go bird watching at the lagoons in southern California, when I go out with a real "birder," I become even more excited as I find that not only am I looking at a beautiful bird, but my sighting is rare because the bird is endangered and a highly infrequent visitor to this particular lagoon.

On one of our class trips to the lagoon we were accompanied by Barbara Moore, an experienced naturalist and bird expert. Through a grant the school had acquired enough binoculars and bird cards so that each child had a pair of binoculars and an Audubon bird reference card identifying local birds most common to southern California. Bird watching came alive for us as Barbara identified a certain bird and told us about it (e.g., it was an adolescent or it was nesting). We spent two hours at the lagoon with her, absorbing valuable information.

When we returned to the classroom, we settled into our writing and sketching routine as a way to think about our experience. What interested me in reading students' poems and journal entries that day was how much of the information Barbara had relayed was incorporated into their work. Her knowledge of birds, offered to the students, made many of the poems more detailed in a scientific manner than previous poems. Here, subject matter had given the students more options as they reflected on their experiences through an art form. As a result, their poems were richer and more interesting.

A related example comes from a dance class at the university. A group of students was choreographing a new piece based on environmental issues. As a way to develop their piece, they met with several environmentalists. As they met with the environmentalists, the students became more and more invested in the issue for its own sake in addition to its being a topic for a dance piece. When they finally performed their dance, it was clear that the work was far beyond a show of technique. Their understanding of the environmental issues informed their dance and performance. How wonderful!

ART AS SUBJECT MATTER

In this section we will consider the arts in and of themselves as a matter for study. First I will argue for their inclusion in the daily curriculum; then, following the formula of learning *with* and *through,* I will show how to use the arts to teach *about* the arts. So far we have examined the arts in relation to methods for learning. Now we explore their intrinsic value in and of themselves.

The arts serve to ground many students as well as allow them to experience accomplishment. By participating in artistic activities, students engage in transformative thinking. By studying works of art, students are introduced to a fundamental aspect of

---

[3] Juanita's information is taken from the book *Animals into Art,* edited by H. Morphy, London: Unwin Hyman.

humanity and the history of humankind. The arts can set the stage for learning. They remind us that we are whole beings who can "experience" through multiple perspectives and lenses. As subject matter in and of themselves, the arts provide lifelong learning opportunities. They intersect with our lives every day, from music on the radio on the way to work, to literature we read when we have returned home, to movies we watch on the weekends, to murals we pass when we venture into the city. We cannot escape the arts in our daily lives. Thank goodness!

Cultures have built monuments to artists. Consider the number of art museums and concert halls throughout the country. Where I live in southern California, the county has just opened up an $81 million arts facility with two concert halls, an art museum, four studios, and a conference center. Go into any city and visit the galleries or music shops; no doubt they are active places. Consider the parks in your city—many are sculpted with flowers and trees—or walk past the city hall and notice the sculpture by the entrance. As I have argued in earlier chapters, the arts are intimately connected to people and cultures, defining who we are to others and serving as self-expression within our own lives. Thus, as a topic of study the arts present a rich, if not overwhelming, source of knowledge and documentation.

Shaping the teaching of arts in schools, national and state standards offer by far the most detailed information on implementing an arts curriculum. In addition, an older, but still relevant initiative in arts education is the Getty Center for Education in the Arts, Discipline-Based Arts Education (DBAE). DBAE focuses on four areas of art: creating art, art history, art criticism, and aesthetics. "Why discipline-based arts education?" one might ask. The following quote from Getty explains the philosophy:

> We increase our understanding of the meaning of an artwork if we have worked with the materials and processes that artists use to create art. We also broaden our understanding if we know when and where a work was made, something about its creator, the function it served in society, and what art experts have said about it.
>
> Artists, art historians, art critics, and aestheticians contribute different perspectives about an artwork. These perspectives are instructive and useful because each one deepens our understanding and our appreciation of the various levels of meaning the work of art conveys. (Getty Report, 1985, p. 13)

Two important premises guide the Getty philosophy (Getty Report, 1985): (1) Art is a repository of culture, and (2) the study of art is a principal means of understanding human experience and transmitting cultural values. If a significant change is to occur in the way art is perceived and taught in the schools, we need to better understand how art should and can be taught. I think the Getty initiatives have broadened and structured the role the arts can play in schools, especially with regard to history, criticism, and aesthetics. The arts provide such an overwhelming landscape of opportunity that it can be difficult to identify what to do in specific instances. Getty begins to give us a direction, and it can be seen in how our National Standards for Arts in Education have been authored.

It is my experience that when students are empowered to utilize the arts as a teaching and learning mechanism (learning *with* and learning *through*), they are in a better position to appreciate and understand the arts as subject matter themselves. My student-poets are interested in reading the work of poets. My math students who use paintings to study geometry are more likely to appreciate artworks outside of math class. Children who have used movement to depict the story of the Raven are more likely to be drawn into the ballet's performance of *Swan Lake* and appreciate it. Thus, broadening the classroom to encompass the arts on various levels also engenders an appreciation and understanding of the arts as a source of knowledge in and of themselves.

LEARNING ABOUT ARTS WITH ARTS

I would like to point out a few ways in which one might teach about subject matter—in this case, the arts themselves—with and through other art forms.

Numerous works of art are concerned with artists. I would like to highlight a few to illustrate my point. Georges Seurat was an artist of considerable importance and notoriety. There is a musical based on him and one of his more famous works. The musical is called "Sunday in the Park with George"; it was performed on Broadway and later produced for PBS. It is widely available on DVD. The musical presents aspects of Seurat's life, personality, and the sentiments of the era. Throughout the work, various figures in his painting come alive and reflect upon the action of the tale. It is a delightful introduction through music and drama to the Impressionist period and to the painter himself.

Music can often provide lessons for understanding and identifying musical concepts. The music of *Peter and the Wolf* provides the listener with a delightful introduction to musical instruments. Throughout the story, each character is depicted by a specific instrument. Not only is the story delightful in and of itself, but the music deepens our awareness of musical instruments.

Literature is a rich source for learning about artists and arts. So many books are available in this realm that the few I highlight in this chapter should be taken as merely the tip of the iceberg. Readers interested in this area should turn to Nancy Lee Cecil and Phyllis Lauritzen's *Literacy and the Arts* (1994), for it includes a comprehensive bibliography of children's literature about the arts.

Not only are there numerous picture books concerning the arts written for young children, but many novels with artist themes are written for adolescents as well. We will begin our discussion with a book that itself serves as an introduction to the art of picture books. Sylvia Marantz's *Picture Books for Looking and Learning: Awakening Visual Perceptions Through the Art of Children's Books* (1992) lends insight into approaching picture books that recognize the importance of the arts and artists. Her aim is to give teachers the confidence "to deal with the art aspects of [children's] books as well as . . . the literary aspects" (p. 5). She shows teachers how they can pay attention to art while introducing literature.

Since the previous edition of this book, I have found many more wonderful children's books about the arts. One of my most favorite authors has become Susan Goldman Rubin. She has written numerous books about arts and artists, including *Degas and the Dance* (2002), *Vincent van Gogh and Paul Gauguin Side by Side: The Yellow House* (2001), *Art Against the Odds: From Slave Quilts to Prison Paintings* (2004), and *Fireflies in the Dark: The Story of Friedl Dicker-Brandeis and the Children of Terezin* (2000), to name a few. I have been lucky enough to meet with Susan and have her come to my university.

What a treat! I've also come across an original Laurent de Brunhoff book published much later than his others, *Babar's Museum of Art* (2003). Those of you who grew up reading Babar are in for a really big treat, as this book features Babar's art museum. In the world of music there are numerous books: *Strange Mr. Satie* by M. T. Anderson (2003) and *Ella Fitzgerald: A Tale of a Vocal Virtuosa* by Andrea Davis Pinkney (2002), for example.

Your reading texts can also be a rich source of stories with arts themes that can be used not only for the reading curriculum, but also to teach about arts. In California, the Houghton Mifflin Reading series (2003) for third grade features a beautiful story written by Mary Brigid Barrett and illustrated by Sandra Speidel titled "Sing to the Stars." The story is about a young boy in Harlem who plays the violin. Through a series of interactions with Mr. Washington, a blind man he passes every day, the boy finds out that Mr. Washington used to be an amazing jazz pianist who, because of personal tragedy, stopped playing the piano. It is a sweet and poignant story that offers children not only a great read, but an opportunity to learn something about music.

In terms of children's books themselves, let me highlight a few categories. First, some books are concerned with the lives of artists. For young children, *Diego* by Jeanette Winter (1991), text by Jonah Winter, is about the painter Diego Rivera. A bilingual book (English and Spanish), it is a celebration of the powerful art of Rivera and his home, Mexico. *Pish, Posh, Said Hieronymus Bosch* by Nancy Willard (1991) is a fanciful tale based on paintings and creatures of the imaginative (and even bizarre) Hieronymus Bosch. *The Painter and the Wild Swans* by Claude Clement (1986) is the story of Teiji, a renowned Japanese painter whose work is so connected to experience that he ultimately embarks on a magical search toward capturing nature on canvas. Christina Bjork and Lena Anderson's *Linnea in Monet's Garden* (1987) is a novel for adolescents that combines illustrations, reprints of paintings, and photographs. The reader joins Linnea on her adventure into Claude Monet's garden, where she learns about Monet the person and what it means to be an Impressionist artist.

There are even books about children as artists. *The Young Artist* by Thomas Locker (1989) tells the story of a 12-year-old apprentice to a painting master. *Ben's Trumpet* by Rachel Isadora (1979), one of my favorite books, is about a child who learns to play the jazz trumpet. *Rondo in C* by Paul Fleischman (1988) concerns itself with a young girl who plays Beethoven's Rondo in C on the piano while inspiring others to imagine all sorts of scenes. *I Am an Artist* by Pat Lowery Collins (1992) is a fanciful adventure of a child who, like all children, is opening up to the life of an artist by detecting patterns in the sand, seeing colors inside a shell, and noticing the feathers on a bird and feeling them as the bird does. Finally, *Cherries and Cherry Pits* by Vera B. Williams (1986) is about Bidemmi, an African-American girl who illustrates her own story.

Many children's books focus on artistic activities while incorporating wonderful artistic forms in their presentation. Gerald McDermott's (1975) *The Stone Cutter*, a Japanese folk tale about Tasaku, a lowly but happy stonecutter, is one such example. McDermott hand colored and then cut out design forms to create the collages on each page. *Voices of the Heart* by Ed Young (1997) is a beautiful book that offers an interpretation of many Chinese characters; and *Kites* by Demi (1999) is a wonderfully illustrated book of magic wishes "that fly to the sky" based on Chinese folk tales and traditions. Wendy Ewald is a wonderful photographer who has spent much energy on getting cameras

Second graders in Escondido, California, show the covers of books they have created to be given as presents to their dads.

into the hands of children. Her work is a terrific model for what can be done with photography and education. A book I find especially intriguing is *I Dreamed I Had a Girl in My Pocket* (1996), with pictures and stories of, and by, children in a village in India. A somewhat different take on this genre comes from Judy Collins and Jane Dyer (1989) in the book *My Father*. This book is an illustrated version of Judy Collins's song by the same title. It also includes the musical notation written for piano and/or guitar.

More recently, graphic novels have made their way into schools and especially into children's hands! My own daughter got hooked on reading because of graphic novels. This category of art-integrated reading is highly engaging to many readers. Finally, in the realm of the graphic novel, I would be remiss if I didn't mention Pulitzer Prize–winning *Maus* by Art Spiegelman (1986), a comic-book depiction of the author's family struggling to survive the death camps of World War II. Appropriate at the high school level, this book is a compelling work of art that captures the experiences of a family in a way that readers will not forget.

Visual Literacy: Using Illustrations to Engage Readers

A way to engage students as they read is to encourage them to utilize illustrations as supplementary, complementary, and contrasting information to the text. Students must be taught the skills of visual literacy if they are to become educated consumers of goods, services, and information. The following are questions that my colleague, Laurie Stowell, a reading specialist and professor of literacy, developed for a teacher training institute called DREAM (Developing Reading Education Through Arts Methods).

1. Why did the artist make the choices she or he did?

2. What additional information do the illustrations add to the text? What do we learn in the illustrations that we don't know from the text?

3. Are there details in the illustration that are not mentioned in the text? What are they? Are there details in the text left out of the illustration?

4. Do the illustrations provide any conflicting information? What? Why?

5. What is the perspective of the illustration? Do we see the scene from the point of view of someone in the text? Which character? You, the reader?

6. Who is in the foreground? Who is in the background? Why?

7. What do the positions of the characters convey about their relative importance (main, secondary, tertiary?) Does the writer/illustrator want us to identify with a particular character and her or his story?

8. Who is in the illustration? Everyone mentioned in the text? Who's in and who's out? Who is looking at whom? Why?

9. How are the relationships of the characters depicted? Who is standing close? Who is far away? What do the expressions on their faces convey?

10. Where are the characters looking? At the action? At each other?

11. What do we the reader see that the characters do not? What do we know that they do not? Why?

12. What do the characters know that we (the reader) do not know?

13. What do we learn about the setting from the illustration? Are we looking straight on? Airplane view? Why?

14. Is the reader intended to be part of the scene or an onlooker?

15. Did the illustrator zoom in or zoom out? Why? Was the illustrator drawing our attention to something in particular? Why is a close up or wide angle used for this particular part of the text?

16. What medium is used? Why do you think the illustrator made this choice? How does the choice of medium contribute to (or detract from) the reader's understanding? How does it contribute to the mood or tone of the text?

17. How are the illustrations arranged on the page? How is the text arranged? Why?

18. What font is used? How do font size and style add to or detract from the text?

19. What is the size of the illustrations? One picture per page? Two-page spread? Are there multiple pictures on a page? What does this convey?

20. What kinds of lines are used? Thick and heavy? Light? No lines? How does this contribute to the story, information, and mood?

21. What color palette is used? How do color choices contribute to the story? To the mood?

22. How is action depicted? How is stillness depicted? What kinds of lines are used? Is the action fast or slow? How do you know?

23. Do the illustrations appeal to more than our visual sensibilities? Do they help us smell or touch or taste or hear some part of the text? In what way(s)?

LEARNING ABOUT ARTS THROUGH ARTS

In teaching about music, I actively listen to music with my students. I generally begin class with simply listening to music. Sometimes I choose the music; at other times students do. At the middle school and high school levels, I establish a few rules—for example, profane lyrics are not appropriate. As we listen we identify instruments, rhythms, and sounds that are new to us. We discuss what the music seems to express and what in the music creates that expression. For example, after listening to Stravinsky's *Rite of Spring* (my choice), many students noted that the beginning created an uncomfortable feeling. We then examined what aspect of the music gave that impression. Students discussed the uneven beats and harsh accents on certain beats. The rhythm, especially, created an uneasy feeling, they reasoned. They also had questions about specific sounds. The piece begins, for example, with a bassoon solo. Many students were not familiar with the bassoon or its sound. Here was a perfect opportunity to learn, through Stravinsky, about the bassoon.

Even the untrained listener can begin in this manner. You might not choose Stravinsky as I did, but you can begin with music that you listen to at home. Perhaps you like jazz or hiphop. The next time you listen, pay special attention to the instruments. Can you identify any of them? The CD liner notes will help if you are stumped. Try to listen to a song and follow the bass throughout, or the violin. We can start training ourselves to be more active listeners simply by listening. Having in-class listening parties provides a wonderful atmosphere to become more acquainted with new and familiar music.

Throughout just one semester my students and I listened to a variety of music, including (1) reggae, from which we learned about the role of the bass; (2) klezmer, in which we focused on the sounds of the clarinet; (3) an excerpt from a Tchaikovsky ballet, after which we discussed with delight how we could imagine dancers twisting and floating; (4) music from Senegal, gamelan music from Malaysia, and gospel music, from which we began a historical discussion of the role of music in culture and a musical discussion of acapella singing, melody, harmony, and call and response in the African-American tradition. With each piece of music, students learned more and more. They began to use musical terms. They became comfortable identifying musical instruments and concepts. They could express whether the music appealed to them or not. Their musical landscape was broadened.

Many people use visual arts to understand music. I remember the following exercise from my own early education and many of my student teachers have done the same with their students: draw while listening to music. The activity of drawing helps focus the child on listening; the drawing provides a structure through which the child engages with a piece of music. Later, in talking about their drawings, children can make connections to the sounds, emotions, and images the music evoked. The teacher can pursue the connections even further. What in the music inspired the picture? What aspect of the sounds evoked anger or pleasure? What aspect of the music gave the impression of a country setting? And so on.

An interesting idea about the introduction of paintings came up on a recent visit to the local gallery. A group of teachers on an afterschool field trip was exploring ways to relate the gallery to teaching about the arts in their classrooms. One suggested having students create stories or poems to accompany paintings or sculptures. In this way, students would have to closely observe the paintings. Movement would work as well, they concluded: Have students create a movement that describes a particular painting. "You might even create a game," mused one of the teachers. "Students could be presented with four or five reproductions and be asked to determine which reproduction a given small group has represented through movement [or story]. In this way students have a concrete way [through the arts] to connect with specific paintings and think about them."

SUMMARY

I am interested in balance. I enjoy turning concepts on their head or upside down to see if they work in different directions. If ideas can work in reverse, then I generally think I've found something important. Thus, as I worked harder and harder on my notion of the arts informing subject matter, I stepped back and contemplated a twist: How does subject matter inform the arts? This led me to consider *awareness* manifesting itself in a reflection on aesthetic experience in education and its role in teaching and learning.

The arts are intrinsically valuable and basic. Like other academic subjects, they can be approached in a reflective and harmonious manner by creating active learning situations. Just as the arts can enhance other subject matter, subject matter can inform our understanding of the arts—both in creating art and in appreciating arts. Arts can set the stage for learning by creating conducive learning atmospheres. They can be inspiring, a thinking tool. Finally, by understanding and incorporating the aesthetic, students can become more aware. That awareness can lead to further wonder, inquiry, and discovery.

TECH CONNECT
Technology and Arts

- There are many ways to learn *about* the arts using technology. DVDs are abundant and available through libraries highlighting the work of artists, musicians, dancers, writers, sculptors, and photographers. Take advantage of them.

- Create a Web site for displaying student artwork, digital or otherwise. If creating your own Web site seems daunting, search for Web sites that accept submissions of student artwork.

QUESTIONS TO PONDER

1. In what ways do you (or will you) incorporate teaching *about* the arts in your classroom?

2. How can math help inform an appreciation for dance, music, and visual arts?

3. Brainstorm ways to teach about dance through visual arts.

4. Brainstorm ways to teach about visual arts through movement or music.

5. What books do you have in your own collection with artistic themes? What sites have you visited on the Web that relate to artists?

 ## EXPLORATIONS TO TRY

1. *Learning through the arts:* Music. Choose a short musical selection from your collection. For your first try, choose a piece without lyrics.

   a. Listen to the selection carefully. Identify as many of the instruments as you can. What feelings does the piece communicate? How might it do that? Does it create an image? What aspect of the music gives you that image, as opposed to some other image?

   b. Now listen to your selection again. What else do you notice about the piece? Jot down your ideas.

   c. Invite a friend to listen to the same musical piece and then identify the instruments she or he hears. Also have your friend note the feelings and images evoked in her or him by the selection. Invite your friend to listen a second time to the piece and to record any other observations about it that come to mind. Compare your friend's responses to your own. How are they similar? How are they different? Now try the same process with your class. You or your students might become interested in other aspects of the music. Who is the composer? When was it written? Where was it written? How long did it take to write? Is it written down or is it improvised? Can you name all the instruments you hear?

2. *Learning about the arts:* Visual art. Choose a painting, poster, or reproduction of a piece of visual art.

   a. Write down your initial reaction to the piece.

   b. Now look at the piece more closely. List twenty things about the work that you notice.

   c. List ten mathematical qualities or concepts you see incorporated into the work.

   d. Create a story to go with the piece.

   e. Reread your initial reaction to the work and consider how your thoughts about it have changed. You might become interested in other aspects of the work. Who created it? When? Where? How long did it take? What media were used? How did the artist produce a certain effect? Try this activity with students. Do their perceptions match yours?

3. *Setting the stage for learning.* See if you can "set the stage" for your own learning. Choose one of the questions above to ponder. Before writing a response, listen to folk or classical music (harp or guitar music work well). Did the music set the stage for you? Try drawing to the music as well. How does this strategy impact your thinking?

4. *Aesthetic awareness.* Look closely at an object on your desk or in your kitchen. List several things you notice about it. Then list several questions you have about the object. What is your level of awareness? How many things are you noticing about the object that you didn't notice before? Do the same as you walk outside of your school or front door at home.

REFERENCES

Anderson M. T. (2003). *Strange Mr. Satie.* New York: Viking.

Bernstein, Leonard. (1976). *The unanswered question: Six talks at Harvard.* Cambridge, MA: Harvard University Press.

Bjork, C., & Anderson, L.(1987). *Linnea in Monet's garden.* New York: R&S Books.

Black, J. (1993). *The effects of auditory and visual stimuli on tenth graders' descriptive writing.* Jurupa, CA: Jurupa Unified School District.

Blanchard, B. E. (1979). The effect of music on pulse-rate, blood-pressure and final exam scores of university students. *Journal of Sports Medicine and Physical Fitness, 19,* 305–308.

Cecil, N. L., & Lauritzen, P. (1994). *Literacy and the arts for the integrated classroom.* New York: Longman.

Clement, C. (1986). *The painter and the wild swans.* New York: Dial Books.

———. (1993). *The voice of the wood.* New York: A Puffin Pied Piper book.

Collins, J., & Dyer, J. (1989). *My father.* Boston: Little, Brown.

Collins, P. L. (1992). *I am an artist.* Brookfield, CT: Millbrook Press.

de Brunhoff, L. (2003). *Babar's museum of art.* New York: Abrams.

Demi. (1999). *Kites.* New York: Crown Publishers Inc.

Ewald, W. (1996). *I dreamed I had a girl in my pocket.* New York: DoubleTake Books/ W.W. Norton & Co.

Fleischman, P. (1988). *Rondo in C.* New York: Harper and Row.

Getty Report. (1985). *Beyond creating: The place for art in America's schools.* Los Angeles: J. Paul Getty Trust.

Giles, M. M. (1991). A little background music, please. *Principal, 71,* 141–167.

Greene, M. (1991). Texts and margins. *Harvard Educational Review, 61.*

Hospers, J. (1982). *Understanding the arts.* Englewood Cliffs, NJ: Prentice-Hall.

Isadora, R. (1979). *Ben's trumpet.* New York: Greenwillow Books.

Locker, T. (1989). *The young artist.* New York: Dial Books.

Marantz, S. (1992). *Picture books for looking and learning: Awakening visual perceptions through the art of children's books.* Phoenix, AZ: Oryx Press.

McDermott, G. (1975). *The stone cutter: A Japanese folk tale.* New York: Puffin Books.

Morphy, H. (Ed.). (1989). *Animals into art.* London: Unwin Hyman.

Neruda, P. (1994). *Odes to common things.* Boston: Little, Brown.

Olshansky, B. (1994). Making writing a work of art: Image-making within the writing process. *Language Arts, 71.*

Pinkney, A. D., & Pinkney, B. (2002). *Ella Fitzgerald: A tale of a vocal virtuosa.* New York: Hyperion.

Rubin, S. G. (2000). *Fireflies in the dark: The story of Friedl Dicker-Brandeis and the children of Terezin.* New York: Holiday House.

———. (2001). *Vincent van Gogh and Paul Gauguin side by side: The yellow house.* New York: Abrams.

———. (2002). *Degas and the dance.* New York: Abrams.

———. (2004). *Art against the odds: From slave quilts to prison paintings.* New York: Crown.

Russell, L. A. (1992). Comparisons of cognitive, music, and imagery techniques on anxiety reduction with university students. *Journal of College Student Development, 33,* 516–523.

Spiegelman, A. (1986). *Maus.* New York: Pantheon Books.

Wall, S. (1993). *Wisdom's daughters: Conversations with women elders of native America.* New York: HarperCollins Publishers.

Whipple, L. (1994). *Celebrating America: A collection of poems and images of the American spirit.* New York: Philomel Books in Association with the Art Institute of Chicago.

Willard, N. (1991). *Pish, posh, said Hieronymus Bosch.* New York: Harcourt Brace Jovanovich.

Williams, V. B. (1986). *Cherries and cherry pits.* New York: Greenwillow Books.

Winter, J. (1991). *Diego.* New York: Alfred A. Knopf.

Wolkstein, D. (1992). *Little Mouse's painting.* New York: Morrow Junior Books.

Young, E. (1997). *Voices of the heart.* New York: Scholastic Press.

SAMPLE LESSON PLANS

Arts

The lessons in this section focus on *Flowers* by Georgia O'Keeffe, developed by Ana Hernandez; Animal Sun Dials, a project by Linda Bohn; a study of music and primary colors by Pat Saville; and a torn-paper art project on animals of the rainforest developed by Karen Sleichter.

SUAVE Curriculum and Project Description

PROJECT TITLE: *Flowers* by Georgia O'Keeffe

TEACHER: Ana Hernandez

SCHOOL AND GRADE: Grade 4, Valley Center Upper Elementary

DISCIPLINE AREA(S):   Science / Visual Arts

PROJECT GOAL(S):   Creative expression of artist's flowers

PROCESS AND STEPS: Students learned about the life of Georgia O'Keeffe and her interest in nature. Samples of O'Keeffe's work were shown to students while discussing characteristics of her work with flowers (large flowers, details, colors, use of paper, etc.) Students were given silk flowers to study flower structures. Then they were given the materials to create tissue/starch flowers on construction paper by tearing tissue.

MATERIALS NEEDED:

- variety of tissue paper (students rip pieces to starch on construction paper)
- white construction paper for background
- starch and brushes

ESSENTIAL QUESTIONS: What was the artist trying to convey in her paintings? How are you looking at nature differently?

1. **What skills, elements, vocabulary were taught?**
   Structure of flower; diagrams in science; how to use materials; modeling

2. **How did you assess the children's understanding?**
   Following directions, using materials properly, and taking risks on creative expression

3. **Where could you go from here?**
   Explore other modern artists or artists who also have painted flowers

4. **Other comments:**
   Entire construction paper needs to be covered with torn pieces of tissue paper.
   Flatten art piece before matting with a complementary color. Option: Outline flower with black marker.

SUAVE Curriculum and Project Description

PROJECT TITLE: Animal Sun Dials

TEACHER NAME: Linda Bohn

SCHOOL AND GRADE: Grade 2, Lincoln

SUBJECT AREA(S):   Math / Science / Visual Art

MATERIALS:

- black construction paper
- glue
- popsicle sticks

DESCRIPTION: Students learned aspects of time and read literature about day/night animals. Each student was given a 6" by 6" piece of black construction paper. They drew their favorite animal (as big as the paper) and cut it out. They described the characteristics of their animal, then glued it onto the stick. Students predicted what their animal shadow would look like when placed in a sunny area at a specific time (for example, twelve o'clock noon). The next morning we put the cutouts in the sun and charted the shadows for the rest of the day, checking them several times.

SUAVE Curriculum and Project Description

PROJECT TITLE: Colors

TEACHER NAME: Pat Saville

SCHOOL AND GRADE: Grade 2, Pioneer

SUBJECT AREA(S):   Math / Science / Social Science / Language Arts / Music and Dance

MATERIALS:

- Brubeck's "Blue Rondo"
- 54" chiffon scarves
- *My Many Colored Days* (Seuss)
- *Colors* (Reiss)

How do colors suit our emotions, choices, actions? Why do we choose/relate/ respond + or − to certain colors? What happens physically when we express the range we feel? Can you organize it with others into a pattern?

DESCRIPTION: We had just completed our movement/dance project with Mr. Todd and were most enthusiastic. We made a performance for our Spring Study units that was a creative culmination of the students' ideas and our guidance in a study of color. We were interested in representing feelings and emotions as well as objects in our dance. We had preparation in making shapes and repeating patterns emerging from group exploration and discussion. We attempted to show emotions in our movements and constructed a dance from student-generated ideas. We used 54" chiffon scarves to extend in the space, and tried to make movements that would be clear and contrasting. The theory that color permeates all our daily lives and relationships to one another was explored. The dance that emerged needed editing and polishing, just like any other work we do. The process and product amazed us!

1. **What happened in class?**
   I permitted letting go of or loosening the constraints (i.e., sitting, holding still) that usually are required. I let students be responsible.

2. **What skills, elements, vocabulary were taught?**
   Large/small movements in rhythm; timing and memory for images; coordinating with others; evaluating; changing (editing, adding)

3. **How did you assess the children's understanding?**
Although they might not articulate it readily, children do feel a range of emotions. They need movement skills awareness.

4. **Where could you go from here?**
Extend to art, language, other images, drama

5. **Comments for others trying this project?**
It was a visual treat, took a lot of risk acceptance to develop the performance, varied, needed strong community feeling to pull together, was exciting in ways other learning isn't—kids who are kinesthetic were able to develop—show strength—make a video—did performance for Spring.

SUAVE Curriculum and Project Description

ACTIVITY TITLE: Torn-Paper Art (Rainforest Animals)

NAME: Karen Sleichter

SCHOOL AND GRADE: Kindergarten, Felicita

SUBJECT AREA(S):   Science / Visual Art

MATERIALS: A variety of colored construction paper, glue crayons, tempera paint in a spray bottle, literature about the rainforest

DESCRIPTION: Pictures created by tearing paper offer a unique opportunity for children to use their fingers rather than a scissors in an art form. This technique should be demonstrated before children do it themselves. Have children select an animal and then close their eyes and imagine how that animal looks. What are the animal's special characteristics? What kind of habitat does the animal live in? Start with a 16" × 10" piece of white construction paper. Fill spray bottles with blue tempera paint and water and have children spray the mixture on the white background to resemble falling rain. Provide a variety of pre-cut shapes such as squares and rectangles. Demonstrate how to tear an animal from a piece of paper. (I demonstrated how to tear an elephant from a 6" × 7" gray rectangle. I also tore a strip of green paper for grass. Other background features could be trees, flowers, mountains, the sun, etc.) Have children review pictures of the rainforest to get ideas about how the animals they selected and their habitats look. Glue children's finished pictures on a 12" × 18" piece construction paper. Have children glue various pre-cut shapes in a pattern to make an interesting border around the picture. This technique could be used to create other art projects.

Chapter 9

Assessing Students'
Understandings through
the Arts

I am struck with how often my fellow teachers reported that their supposedly lower functioning students came up with the most creative responses when engaging in art activities.

Angela Ennen, teacher, Las Vegas, Nevada

I have seen more of what my kids really are learning because of using the arts, visual and performing arts, as part of assessment. You are seeing a true picture of what they really know.

SUAVE program teacher (in Goldberg, 2006)

[In writing haiku] I found the students who really shined were the ones that were considered "low" . . . the arts lend themselves to showing kids in a whole new light.

Leslie Brinks, teacher, Las Vegas, Nevada

When students create poetry, visual art, dances, music, sculptures, and so on, they are not only exploring and expressing understandings of subject matter, they are also offering original "documents" that provide evidence for assessing their grasp of important concepts in the subject matter areas. Viewing the arts as an assessment tool may broaden the methods available to you as well as challenge some traditional notions of what constitutes a "lower-" or "higher-functioning" student.

The arts can deepen teachers' awareness of children's abilities and provide alternative methods of assessment. "Expanding notions of assessment to incorporate the possibilities offered by the arts can create exciting opportunities for teachers and learners" (Goldberg, 1992, p. 623). The arts are "languages of learning" (Gallas, 1994) that offer a lens into a child's view of the world. Young children's ability to use languages, especially the languages of the arts, provides useful information about their conceptions of the world. By studying children's expressions through the arts, teachers can broaden their knowledge of a child's progress and learn something of a child's inner thoughts and concerns, dreams and hopes.

"Good assessment in arts education requires many of the same things that assessment in any content area requires. . . . Good arts assessment supports and develops teacher instruction and student learning" (Saraniero & Jessee, 2008). Assessment is such a hot-button issue that even the notion of assessment in and through the arts can be intimidating. Therefore, this chapter will start off by debunking four myths related to arts education assessment. These myths were originally published in a guide developed by Patti Saraniero and R. Jessee (for which I was a consultant), and published by the San Diego County Office of Education with funding from the California County Superintendents' Educational Services Association (CCSESA) (Saraniero & Jessee, 2008). I've adapted them slightly for our purposes.

Myth #1: *Success in Arts Is Subjective.*   Achievement in the arts is often thought as highly subjective. We are all familiar with having a personal response to a piece of visual art or music that differs from others' responses. Sometimes this might because of a difference in "taste." In fact, you've probably heard the phrase "There is no accounting for taste," as you've experienced a difference in opinion about a particular work of art. Because of this, there is a prevalent myth that the arts cannot be assessed because they are too subjective. In actuality, however, there are many aspects of the arts that can be assessed! And state and national frameworks in arts education provide guidance in this practice.

a. *Technique:* Each art form employs *technique.* Technique involves specific skills that can measured. For example, it is easy to assess if a musician is playing a scale or a song correctly. If a saxophonist plays "Happy Birthday" and hits a wrong note, everyone will know! That is very easy to assess: The wrong note sticks out. In ballet, one can assess whether or not the student dancer is in the proper positions. The same is true for other art forms as well. In visual arts we can assess the use of line, the mixing of colors, and knowledge of foreground, middle ground, and background. Technique is readily assessable.

b. *Content:* Each art form has *content.* Traditions, history, vocabulary—all are assessable knowledge included in each art form. In classical music from the Baroque era, there are certain forms, uses of melodies, and uses of harmony that are identifiable even without theoretical knowledge. The historical context of the period has bearing on the music. All of this is easily assessable. The same is true of Baroque art forms such as paintings. The vocabulary used to describe the artwork and the history and context of its creation are concrete ways to assess knowledge of the artwork and the era.

c. *Intellectual behavior:* Creating art utilizes several identifiable *behaviors.* Carmen Armstrong, in her book *Designing Assessment in Art* (1994), identifies the following seven behaviors developed through engaging in art making: *know, perceive, organize, inquire, value, manipulate,* and *cooperate.* These behaviors can become part of a rubric to assess students' abilities throughout a project or unit. For example, Armstrong illustrates how a student's ability to *inquire* can be measured across a continuum from low to high.

Myth #2: *It Is All About the End Product.*   If you are a professional musican, dancer, sculptor, or artist, then yes! It is all about the end product. However, in arts education, the *process* of making art is as valuable and as important as the resulting end product. The end product is only a slice of the student's learning and experience. Arts education entails both attention to the process and to the end product and should be assessed accordingly. An example that might resonate with some of you is the middle school band performance. When I was a music teacher, my students would do remarkably well in rehearsals. They made music. On the day of the concert the kids didn't have enough practice in performance skills to pull off a wonderful performance—though it was clear they were capable. If I were to grade their performance, they would only merit a "C." However, it was clear to me that they merited an "A" in playing music! So, I tried an experiment. I planned only half a concert and had my band play their pieces twice. Predictably, the second performance of the piece was much better than the first. The audience loved it, too.

Rather than only assess students' ability and achievements according to an end product, there is an opportunity to assess their progress and growth over time. Measuring growth is at least as important as measuring the quality of the product a student produces. In a study published by the National Art Education Association, Dorn, Madeja, and Sabol (2004) listed several criteria arts teachers used to assess their students' learning in the art classroom. They identified effort, problem-solving ability, improvement or growth, classroom behavior, and self-motivation and initiative as areas they could adapt to a scale and assess accordingly.

Myth #3: *Teachers Can Just Tack on Assessment to Their Arts Instruction.*   Many teachers have little experience in the arts themselves, much less in assessing arts education! Don't worry if it doesn't feel right to simply apply methods of assessing other areas of the curriculum to arts education. You're probably not going to find a fit! Hopefully this chapter will give you some confidence in and insight into how to use appropriate tools to assess both students' understanding of subject matter through the arts and the art making in and of itself.

Myth #4: *Assessment Is Contradictory to the Artistic Process.*   Nothing could be farther from the truth! As one engages in creating art, one also engages in self-reflection and continuous assessment! This is an essential aspect of art making that is built into the process. Here are a few examples. A visual artist generally develops several sketches before moving to canvas, Photoshop, or another medium. The sketch provides a starting point and is used as a way to reflect upon what is working and what is not, what should be added, changed, deleted, and so on. Performers in a band will gather to learn a new tune. As one musician introduces the tune, another listens and suggests a different harmony or rhythm. The group begins to play and tweak the new tune. This is because they are engaged in an assessment of their work in order to make it better! I've also seen this process of assessment in full gear at tapings for television. I happen to be very lucky to have a dear friend who is a successful writer in Los Angeles, Larry Reitzer. He worked himself into the business having started in theater; he then moved on to TV and ascended the professional ladder all the way up to lead script writer for several shows, including some he has been asked to develop and create! I wrote about attending one of the tapings with Larry on a blog I write for Americans for the Arts. Here is a small excerpt from that posting that underscores the importance of assessment as part of the artistic process.

> A typical taping begins at 5:00 and can easily go until 10:00 or later—all for a show that lasts approximately 22 minutes! Scenes are acted out several times—perhaps even four or five times—each time with slightly different actions, lines, or stage directions. Actors continually accept multiple directions and literally act upon them. Egos, to a certain extent, must be left at the door, as part of the process of the taping is engaging with the different points of view taken from the director and producers. And this process is what makes the art of acting—or, in fact, any of the performing arts—come alive. Throughout this process leading to and including the performance itself there is constant attention to making the art the best as it can be.
>
> A parallel artistic process has played itself out much earlier in the week via the writing process. Earlier in the development of the show, the writers develop and pitch story lines, after which scripts are developed and written to prepare for individual episodes. On the week of each new episode, the new script is presented to the actors. On Monday the actors and writers engage in a read-through and the process of adapting, tweaking, and change begins. This process lasts right up until the taping, when it is not uncommon to tape scenes trying out a few different punch lines. Though there is a lead writer for each episode, the entire team has contributed to each script. Here again, the lead writer must have the ability to listen and take suggestions and watch as his or her script evolves in many ways, including some that might not be the writer's choosing.
>
> This artistic process is fundamentally important to the creation of a great show. It is also a process that truly teaches one to listen to and ultimately be accepting of varying points of view and changes to one's work as the team moves forward. This process—involving the writers and then the actors, director, and producers—plays itself out on a weekly basis. Isn't this a process that one should learn to do well in life?! Gosh, if there ever were a great reason to have kids engage in the arts, never mind the intrinsic value of the arts in and of themselves, the process of art as a tool to teach listening, adapting, and accepting different points of view and being able to give up enough ego to be part of a successful team (but keep enough ego to contribute to the conversation) is key to engaging with society no matter what field one enters as an adult. All of this emphasizes the reason to engage in the artistic process in schools on a daily basis.

Now that we have identified and debunked a few myths, what assessments can you employ when the arts are integrated into your curriculum? I've tried to narrow the list down to a few areas.

1. *Content and Concept Assessment:* Art can serve as evidence in the assessment of children's understandings of concepts in the content areas. In this case, the teacher uses children's artwork to determine the degree to which they understand a particular concept in one of the subject areas.

2. *Incidental Assessment:* Artistic events can provide a powerful understanding of children. Incidental assessment occurs when a child exhibits something through the arts that leads toward a fuller understanding of the child and his or her general abilities. For example, in assessing a child's poem to ascertain understanding of a science concept, the teacher might also gain understanding of the child's ability to create metaphors, apply language, or empathize with another living creature. In all cases, the artwork offers a way to assess the child.

3. *Artistic Assessment:* One may assess a child's ability to play a violin, write a poem, or paint a watercolor. This assessment can be specific to the child's knowledge of arts vocabulary or art techniques, such as how to create perspective in a line drawing or how to play a musical instrument in tune.

4. *Formative and Summative Assessment:* You've probably heard these terms already, so here is a quick review. Good assessment of student learning involves looking at both the students' process in learning as well as the resulting outcome or end product. If you could take in what I wrote earlier about art as being both process and product, then formative and summative assessment should make parallel sense! Formative strategies, such as observation checklists, rubrics, and reflections, allow both teacher and students to guide learning. Summative strategies look at outcomes and assess the extent to which students learned something or were able to accomplish what they set out to do.

THE NEED FOR ASSESSMENT

There are many ways to approach each assessment. I will address how to identify evidence of learning, how to set assessment parameters, and how to create strategies to collect evidence, including portfolio assessment, performance-based assessment, and effective ways to listen to children and interpret their responses.

In considering the arts as evidence of learning—and perhaps more importantly as documents of a child's world—the teacher gains an accumulating and evolving picture of her or his students. But there are many reasons to assess students' abilities. They range from obligatory classroom grading for report cards to the district's desire to be competitive in terms of state standards. A question to consider is: Who is the assessment for? Is it for teachers, parents, students themselves, districts, or states? Who does the assessment? The teacher? The student? I suggest that in the spirit of a democratic classroom, *both* should be involved in the assessment process. Enabling students to enter into self-assessment trains them to be reflective of their own work. It is also a lesson in self-reliance. It can build confidence rather than creating a state of dependence whereby the student relies on the judgment of others for gratification.

Other questions emerge. What constitutes evidence of learning? What criteria should be used to judge competence, or learning? What is the role of a culminating activity in assessment? Can students apply what they are learning to another situation? Does the student understand what he or she is learning? What is the student's interest level in the subject activity, and how does that relate to assessment?

One of the wonders of the arts is that they can either be integrated in teaching and learning as curriculum events and strategies or stand on their own as independent artistic learning activities. When you begin to incorporate art activities into your lessons, then, it is important to remind yourself of teaching and learning goals. Consider these questions:

- What are the children learning by engaging in this activity?
- Is this a project/activity or does it have more long-range implications? Projects or activities can be fine, fun, and appropriate, but in an integrated thematic unit, how does the artistic event fit into the bigger picture?

- In what ways does the artistic event fit into students' lives? How does it reach the interests of the child?

- Where can you go from here?

- In what way does the curriculum encourage children to want to learn? In other words, does this curriculum *create learners* as opposed to focusing on *what to teach?* (I consider this one of the most important questions in teaching and learning.)

- How will you determine if children are actually learning?

- How does this activity meet the visual and performing arts standards mandated by your state?

I believe that assessment is most important to the teacher and student in the class and the student's parents or guardians. Debates over standardized local, district, and national testing are another story altogether, which I will address later in the chapter. There are numerous ways to document and assess a student's learning through her or his artwork. I will highlight a number of ways as they relate to the art-based activities reported throughout this book.

EVIDENCE OF LEARNING

The arts provide a unique forum for assessment because they constitute evidence of students' work and thoughts. As children work through the arts, they engage with ideas and create representations that express their understandings. Because creating art involves translating ideas into another form, children's representations are especially instructive windows into their thinking. Their artworks form a body of evidence that can be assessed and even compared—both to the student's individual progress over time and to others in the class.

In working with teachers and student teachers on integrating the arts as a methodology for learning, it is not unusual to hear comments like the ones at the very beginning of this chapter: that the "lower-ability" student seems to shine when activities turn to the arts, or that students who consistently test poorly seem to have the most creative insights in the artistic media of poetry, painting, dance, music, rap, and so on. Comments of surprise at once excite and sadden me. It excites me that the arts provide a venue for students who often test "low" to shine in another area. It saddens me that, according to traditional assessment tools, many of these same children have been labeled as low achieving.

Left to their own devices, children will naturally express themselves through music, dance, and visual arts. It is more a matter of traditional schooling practice that has limited the expression of knowledge to the spoken and written word. Unfortunately, through that practice we have unwittingly closed doors to many children who, for one reason or another, work better through the languages of the arts than through only the spoken and written word. As I have written elsewhere, "as many teachers seek to reflect our multicultural society in the subject matter they present and in the questions they explore, I believe it is time to embrace the multifaceted ways of knowing and expressing knowledge" (Goldberg, 1992, p. 623). Incorporating the languages of the arts expands the possibilities for all children in the classroom to work with ideas.

Teachers and students have multiple experiences, ways of knowing, and ways of expressing their knowledge. Limiting this knowledge to expression in a logico-mathematical manner (as is dominant in most school settings) prevents many children from demonstrating their abilities and creativity, thus placing them at a disadvantage. Incorporating the arts as a way of working with knowledge and as a standard for assessment levels the playing field for all children. By widening their vision of acceptable expression and ways of knowing, teachers can begin to create a community in which all students have the freedom to learn and be recognized for their contributions and insights.

Valuing the Arts as a Teaching and Assessment Tool

"The arts inherently elicit and support multiple ways of knowing and learning in contrast to the more traditionally limited school approaches," according to Victoria Jacobs, (Jacobs et al., 2004). A teacher in the SUAVE program, Rita, noted that the arts were an effective assessment tool as they often allowed her to gain more accurate pictures of students' understandings than traditional assessments. For example, in a lesson on character evolution, Rita reflected on the importance of the artwork of one student who was getting all D's and F's academically.

> So here was a way—if I had given her a test, she probably would have failed it. If I had asked her to write a paragraph, or five paragraphs, she probably wouldn't have gotten the main idea, but *through her art,* she could give me—that was her way of showing me all the information that she gleaned from that.

A fifth grader discusses his understanding of a poem with the author.

"Using the arts as an alternative form of assessment often has an additional benefit of allowing different groups of students to excel," continues Jacobs. Students who are typically considered academically low, shy, or difficult behaviorally are often the ones who excel in art. Rita, the teacher mentioned earlier, valued these surprises, as they "kind of balanced the class out." Rita also valued the arts as an assessment tool because they allowed her to view students more holistically, sometimes revealing talents of students that she (and they) may not have known existed.

> I think that's probably one of the greatest things about art. You find out who your kids really are. I mean, my real quiet ones turn out to be some of my best artists. . . . If we weren't bringing this into the classroom I would never see that side of the child, and I'd always have this view. But now I have a complete picture. . . . It's like little treasure that you don't even know that you're looking for, and then they come out.

Using the arts with English language learners can allow students to express deep understandings without having to rely on words they are just becoming accustomed to using. Often second language learners are at a disadvantage when taking written tests because of their emerging vocabulary. These students' test results are a poor indication of their understandings and more an indication of their confidence with vocabulary. For example, although a student learning English may not be able to write about the life cycle of a butterfly, his dance or drawings might demonstrate his deep and detailed understanding of the concept. Restricting students from languages of learning through the arts, then, potentially prevents them from fully working with, constructing, and communicating knowledge.

Using the arts as tools for understanding and assessment can bolster self-esteem and self-confidence in all learners. Once a child gains confidence that he or she can effectively communicate his or her understandings through means other than traditional forms, he or she becomes willing to do so on a regular basis. As a next step, he or she might attempt more standard exercises, such as writing a paragraph in prose. Most important, the arts may set the stage for both teachers and students to reassess labels and prior conceptions of abilities and intelligence.

CONTENT AND CONCEPT ASSESSMENT

There are numerous ways in which to consider children's artwork so that it reveals their understanding of subject matter. Most simply, paying close attention to the artwork will give many clues about how children conceptualize a subject and the degree to which they are interested in details. In Chapter 7 I discussed sound and movement fractions. One method of testing a student's understanding might be to give him or her a written test. Other options, however, would be to have him or her perform the fractions in sound or movement. The following vignette demonstrates what I mean.

> "Tess," asks the teacher, "What might ⅓ sound like?" Or, "What could it look like?" Tess considers this for a moment (needless to say, it is also good to create situations in which children are challenged in their thinking) and then performs a piece in which she moves and makes a sound, jumping three times and whistling once per every three jumps (on the first jump). Other children come up with creative ideas inspired by Tess's performance. Playing off of their excitement, the teacher suggests that students

perform a fraction while the rest of the class tries to identify which fraction it could be. One student demonstrates ½ by walking two steps and clapping every other one. Another student stamps his feet three times while clapping his hands to the first and second stamp (an amazing act of coordination!), demonstrating ⅔.

Through this artistic "game" the teacher can observe children's demonstration of their understanding of fractions. She can assess their understanding by observing their performances, noting each child's identification of the fractions (if it matched what she was seeing and hearing), and asking occasional questions for clarification.

Consider another math example. If your class is studying groups, patterns, or sets, ask children to create the patterns in sound, movement, or a work of visual art. If a child creates a sound piece that clearly has a repetitive three-note pattern, she or he is demonstrating an understanding of repetition and sets of threes. If a child creates a visually consistent repeating pattern, she or he is applying and demonstrating an understanding of the concept of patterning. Successful (or unsuccessful) application in the art forms can be easily recognized and utilized as a measurement of understanding. In the end, the measurement of understanding in art is not only an adequate tool but usually an enjoyable activity as well.

INCIDENTAL ASSESSMENT

Children's art can provide a teacher with information that may go undiscovered through traditional testing mechanisms. Leslie Brinks, a second-grade teacher in the Las Vegas area, describes how through writing haiku with her students she was able to learn more about the students themselves and their ability to use words. The following are some of her favorite poems from the class, accompanied by comments about the children.[1] In order to write their haikus, students took inspiration from the outdoors, where they sat in the schoolyard observing their environment.

The first poem was written by Marta, an ESL (English as a second language) student who is considered "the shyest girl in our class." Because she is quiet and reticent, it is easy to overlook her abilities. This poem is a sweet reminder to offer her opportunities to express herself outside of traditional writing and speaking exercises.

> I see bumble bees
> buzzing in the summer sky,
> Stay away from me!

"Shadows on the grass" was written by Sean, who goes out of the room for two hours a day for language development. Because Sean is labeled a "resource-room student," it is easy to dismiss his ability to participate in nontraditional activities such as poetry writing often reserved for gifted students. However, we see Sean blossom in this circumstance rather than be confounded by it.

> Shadows on the grass
> The sun shining close to me
> Fresh air around Sean.

---

[1] The children's names have been changed.

"Children playing loud" was written by Karen, an almost nonreader who struggles with second-grade work. It is interesting that she uses so many verbs in her poem. It was striking to her teacher to see how clearly she expressed herself through this minimalist form.

> Children playing loud
> Jumping Screaming, running fast
> I would like to play

The last example, "I see a shadow," was written by Kelly, an ESL student.

> I see a shadow
> I feel my mom hugging me
> I see flowers

Leslie asked Kelly why she wrote the line "I feel my mom hugging me." Kelly answered, "That's just what it felt like when we were outside." Leslie then told me, "I loved that!" It was an opportunity for Leslie to share the magical association her student was capable of creating. Leslie learned something of Kelly's personal thoughts, but in addition she was introduced to Kelly as a poet creating relationships between images and feelings.

SETTING ASSESSMENT PARAMETERS

Content and concept assessment plans must be intimately connected to curriculum goals and standards. In fact, curriculum should ultimately guide assessment plans. Assessment tools must also be contextualized to individual students and situations. In other words, I am advocating assessment plans that can be utilized in the entire class while at the same time addressing the progress of individual students. Admittedly, in my own teaching I am more interested in following the progress of each student than in comparing him or her to a class standard.

The first priority in assessing any student's understanding of subject matter involves collecting evidence and/or data that will in some way indicate the student's progress. Consider the work of the fourth graders in Chapter 4 who were exploring language through writing poetry. The teacher's curriculum goal in the poetry unit was to engage her students in writing and to increase their vocabulary. As evidence of their work, the teacher had each student keep all brainstorming and poetry in a journal. Therefore, a log of work was available when the teacher wanted to check on their progress.

The next step is to establish a way to interpret the evidence. This will vary according to both the activity and the individual student. In our language development poetry activities, the teacher and I established that we were interested in (1) the amount of brainstorming the individual students were doing as evidenced by the amount and complexity of words they brainstormed and the seriousness with which they did this work; (2) the metaphors and similes they created and the degree to which those devices were abstract or concrete as indicated by uniqueness; and (3) the level of success with which they applied their words, metaphors, or similes to a poem as indicated in the drafts and final form of their poem. The curriculum goals and ensuing assessment go hand-in-hand. The following example illustrates how we approached one of the poems referred to in Chapter 4.

Simile: My mom is like a beautiful flower blooming in the spring
Brainstorm: flower beautiful, smell good, bloom, rose, spring, red, bouquet, pollen, bees, garden
Poem

MY MOM

My mom is like a beautiful flower blooming in the spring
she is like the beautiful red rose in a bouquet
you could plant her in your garden and
she smells so good!
Anybody would like to plant her in your garden
she is beautiful!

Heather Mendez

---

1. Heather brainstormed over ten words related to *flower*. In addition, she went to the dictionary to look up *bouquet*. Overall, in relation to her previous poetry work, including other brainstorming exercises, she did above average on this task. Her words were more detailed and sophisticated than in previous sessions and her interest in utilizing the dictionary was new.

2. Heather created two similes in her poem: "My mom is *like a beautiful flower* blooming in the spring" and "she is *like the beautiful red rose* in a bouquet." Both similes include descriptive words and modifiers that further their impact. Compared to her previous work and to other children's, Heather's similes were more extensive and descriptive. As a result, I would judge Heather's effort on this poem as above average.

3. The level of success with which Heather used her words is good. She included all her brainstormed words except *pollen* and *bees*. I imagine that, given another editing session, she might be able to use those words as well. Her word order and usage was good—with the exception of the second to last line, which is grammatically awkward owing to her use of *your* rather than *their*. Overall, however, I would say this is an example of a good application of words and ideas for Heather.

In assessing children's drawings (as opposed to language-based art activities), a similar method may be employed. The nature sketches mentioned in Chapters 6 and 7 constitute a body of evidence demonstrating children's understandings of nature and math topics. The trick is in interpreting the evidence. To begin, you might simply examine the sketch closely and make note of all the parts displayed. Again, I suggest setting up criteria to guide your judgments. This might include the level of detail. For example, if the sketch is of a Fibonacci pattern, then you would want to check how accurately the child has re-created the pattern. Other criteria: Does the child accurately depict the pointiness of the oak leaf? Does the child capture the ridges in the mussel shell?

Students' sketches provide information that can be translated into an assessment tool indicating levels of detail and expressing student understanding. One note of caution, however. It is important to pay attention to the essence and detail of the sketches rather than their "beauty." Some talented student-artists might produce lovely pictures but fail to provide accurate detail of the object. Conversely, some students who lack drawing skills might capture the details of an object more accurately than you think at first glance. Be a careful and close observer of your students' work.

STRATEGIES TO COLLECT EVIDENCE

To collect evidence the teacher can use a number of strategies, some more structured than others. A structured strategy might include checklists. For example, teachers might create conference checklists that guide conference sessions with their students. In keeping with the goals of a particular unit or activity, the teacher lists questions or discussion topics she will ask of each student during a conference. A less formal method involves a journal or log in which to record notes about each child. There are many options in keeping journals and logs: Some teachers prefer journals with a page or so devoted to each child; others keep index cards. I have found this to be a useful classroom method. Often, when I look back at the end of the week at my notes, I am surprised at the amount of or lack of notes about a particular child. This serves as a reminder that I must pay more or less attention to individual children.

Portfolio Assessment

A method of collecting evidence that works quite well is the portfolio. In creating portfolios, students and teachers collect various items to reflect individual progress. Portfolios might include poems, drawings, essays, reports, reflections on included samples, and so on. If the teacher is interested in quantifying collected data from students' portfolios, journals, and logs over time, an easy way to do so is to create a rubric.

In order to assess a portfolio, a simple rubric can be created. In an issue of *Portfolio News* (1994), the editors proposed a scale with five categories to judge the quality of each student's work over time. You will need to fill in each category to match what you want students to learn in a particular subject. I have adapted that scale for our purposes.

4—Outstanding Progress: Portfolio shows consistent progress, and there is a significant difference between early and most recent work. The student's understanding of material has considerably broadened, and the student can reflect upon the changes.

3—A Lot of Progress: The student has expanded his or her notions of subject matter and is able to assess his or her own work. He or she is able to delve more deeply into subject matter as evidenced by his or her work, but has not yet reached skill levels represented by a category 4 portfolio.

2—Some Progress: The student's examples are coherent and easy to understand, but the topics and content have not changed much over time. There is less material than in a category 3 portfolio; artifacts show less application to real-life situations.

1—Minimal Progress: The portfolio contains little material. Little progress has been made over time as exemplified in the samples.

X—Ungradable: The portfolio contains little material, and in that material no progress is evident.

RUBRICS AND PORTFOLIOS

Rubrics are efficient and effective tools to use in assessing projects and activities. What's even better is that they can be developed with the students in your class.

Performance-Based Assessment

Performance-based assessment is highly touted. It often involves a culminating event whereby the student or group of students "perform" in order for the teacher to assess what they have learned. This will likely also fall under the category of "summative assessment," as it "sums up" a student's experience and learning. The activity also gives students an arena to explore and work with their ideas. When I had my fifth-grade students create raps about photosynthesis and then perform them, I was able to assess their understanding of the concepts related to photosynthesis and the vocabulary they used in expressing their understanding. Culminating events might also guide the structure of your everyday class activities.

The following example from Chapter 1 illustrates the possibilities of assessing a performance or culminating event. "The Cliff" was written by Joey Strauss, a fifth grader. It was composed as a culminating event following many class discussions, a visit to the ocean, and a series of note-taking and sketching activities.

THE CLIFF

It stands alone in silence
never losing its strength
except sometimes a wave
will come and dig beneath
the sandstone shell
It cannot lose more than a chip
but slowly it disintegrates from
all the time the tide has come and
all the time the wind has gone

Joey Strauss

In this poem we can find a number of indicators of Joey's understanding of the beach. In terms of vocabulary, he has incorporated words such as *sandstone, disintegrate,* and *tide* and used them appropriately. From the vocabulary, we can see that he understands and applies key elements of the science lesson. Although I don't feel the need to create a rubric to judge Joey's understanding on some scale in this case, in another circumstance I might be inclined to do so. For example, if I were using the poems as a test, a scale would help in terms of grading more formally.

A caution concerning performance-based assessment: Sometimes a performance is a poor indicator of a child's understanding. This happens when a child lacks the "performance skills" necessary to undertake a performance. My dissertation research was in the area of musical performance. I was interested in investigating the relationship between performing and playing music. A question that concerned me was, "Can a person play music but not be a performer?" What became increasingly clear was that performing was a skill *added on* to one's ability to play music. The core activity was playing music. When performing, all sorts of other factors came into play, such as the ability to express oneself in public (which has little to do with one's ability to play an instrument). I found this to be true as a music teacher. During class time my students would play their music unbelievably well, but in front of their parents and peers the music would sometimes evaporate into some other universe. It became clear to me that students could be wonderful musicians yet poor performers.

Performing is a skill added on to a core activity—whether it be playing music, understanding science concepts, or exploring a topic in mathematics. Thus, it is important to tap into the core activity as a measurable indicator of understanding rather than relying solely on a child's performance. I do not mean to imply that performances are not important or that curriculum units should not include culminating events. One of the reasons musicians perform before an audience is to heighten their ability to play the music. In schooling, a performance and/or culminating event might serve as motivation to push students beyond everyday limits. What I do mean to emphasize is that (1) not all students are terrific at performing, and (2) for those students, attention to the core activity itself will provide more reliable information on their understandings than an actual performance event.

The performing notion is also illustrated in the failure of standardized tests to adequately measure students' abilities. There are numerous reasons why a student may fail a standard test—ranging from lack of testing skills, to cultural differences, to lack of vocabulary. For example, the second language learners with whom I work inevitably score quite low on standardized tests. The tests are not designed to reach their ability or general intelligence. When I interact with a 10-year-old who can read and interpret poems by Longfellow but scores miserably on a standardized test for comprehension, I am deeply saddened.

Here is where the arts can give us an alternative, if not a more rounded and authentic assessment of a child's abilities. In the case of the 10-year-old, it was clear that the child could think abstractly and interpret the Longfellow poem—a high-level thinking skill completely unmatched by her performance on the standardized test. If I were to rely on that test as a true measure of her intelligence, I would be doing her a severe disservice. She was an interested and thoughtful student who could demonstrate through her ability to comprehend poetry that she was able to think abstractly. Had it not been for the opportunity to prove her abilities, through the arts, she was at risk of being judged as less competent.

One final criticism of performance-based and culminating activities is that units rarely end with a period. Good curriculum units should end with more question marks than they started with and with enthusiasm for continuing adventure. In that sense, I suggest that a unique and very telling assessment tool would be to inquire of your students what their continuing questions are at the conclusion of any given unit. Recalling Piaget, the test of a children's thoughts and interests often lies in the questions they ask of themselves rather than the information they are willing to give back to us. Betsey Mendenhall and her social studies students, whom I presented in Chapter 5, provide a good example of ending a unit with more questions than it began. Her students became so interested in the conversations the puppet presidents might have that they created discussion topics that could fill a lifetime. Betsey, then, could judge—by the kinds of questions her students asked—the level of their engagement and their ability to conceptualize the role of a historian.

I suggest that students work closely with teachers to create their own assessment rubrics and tools to match curriculum units or activities. They should also be encouraged to critique each other's work after establishing ground rules for discussion. Assigning children these tasks teaches them to be responsible and reflective learners. It is also a lesson that can be applied later in life in situations of judgment. I remember my own graduate work and a class in which I worked very hard. Because my conceptions of the subject matter did not match the instructor's, I was given a lower grade even though my ideas were carefully and thoughtfully constructed. Although disappointed with the grade, I was not disappointed in myself or my work.

Listening to and Observing Children

Listening to and observing children can be an engaging and instructive activity for a teacher. A way to assess students' understandings is to observe their actions and listen to what they say. But how can we know if our observations and conversations truly tell us what children are thinking? To be sure to collect evidence and data while listening to children, the teacher may set up parameters that match curriculum goals. In other words, the teacher (perhaps in consultation with students) decides what is important to record. For example, if the subject is understanding the skills of a naturalist and you are teaching these skills through the arts (i.e., sketching and writing poetry), you might consider the following questions to guide your observations, discussions, and note-taking:

- Can the child identify qualities associated with being a naturalist in conversation or writing (e.g., silence, close observation and identification, sketching objects in nature with detail)?
- To what extent does the child apply these qualities in the field?

When I closely observe children, I am tuned in to their general awareness, interest, and curiosity. If we are in the school garden and children begin to identify plants, I know they can apply some of our classroom work. If they spot a heron (likely where I live!) and become excited at the sighting, I know there is some measurable level of success with encouraging wonder. If, on the other hand, I notice a child who is uninterested or reticent, that is another clue I might consider in terms of my understanding of the child's learning.[2]

---

[2] Like all poets, some children take liberties in utilizing poetic devices whereby they juxtapose seemingly incongruous events or concepts. In these cases, rather than assume the children are missing some point, I ask them to tell me more about their poem and what they were thinking about when they came up with certain phrases.

Jean Piaget outlined a number of interesting guidelines in considering the words and actions of young children. In *The Child's Conception of the World* (1976), Piaget was interested in understanding children's conception of the natural world. He discovered that children's actions and language are not always true indicators of their understanding of particular phenomena. Therefore, he started his investigation in an interesting manner. Rather than asking children about their conception of various phenomena to ascertain what they thought of them—such as what the sun does at night—he began paying attention to the questions children asked on their own without any prompting from inquisitive adults. Thus, by collecting questions that the children themselves asked, he began to understand the issues that concerned them and began to formulate his own course of investigation. The *questions* that children ask provide important insights to their *thought processes*.

Piaget also realized that in assessing children's understanding of phenomena, he could not rely on accepting their answers at face value. He outlined five kinds of responses that children present to adults when they are asked about natural phenomena. I offer my interpretation of Piaget's five responses so that you may begin to consider the complexity of dialoguing with children.

1. Answer at Random.   In this case the child is not particularly interested in the question and says anything to the questioner just to appease him or her. For example, if the questioner is interested in a drawing a child has created during a science lesson, she might ask, "Tell me about your picture." If the child responds, "I like to eat pickles," then the child has probably answered at random. Perhaps the inquiry did not make sense to the child, or the child was simply not interested in the question.

2. Romancing.   Romancing occurs when the child is taken with his or her own ability to tell a story and perseveres at length in the retelling. Many of you with small children are familiar with this creative ability. In responding to the inquiry "Tell me about your picture," the child may begin, "Well, I see the moon and then the tree at the very top of the forest and the dinosaur likes that place and he eats bagels there with little Oreo cookies and then the giant comes to the forest and eats the dinosaur and the . . ." In this case, the child is interested in his own ability to tell the story, but we are not offered a lot of material about his conception of the science lesson as it relates to his picture. The child exhibits a creative flair for storytelling, but the information is not particularly useful in assessing his picture or his understanding of the science lesson.

3. Suggested Conviction.   This occurs when the child answers to please the questioner. In other words, the child answers what she thinks the questioner wants to hear rather than answering what she truly believes. Sometimes this is the result of the way in which the question is asked. A leading question, for example, will often result in a suggested conviction. Therefore, the way in which a question is framed is very important. For example, the questioner might ask, "Is that a picture of the sea grass we were learning about?" Upon hearing that she might be onto something, the child could likely answer "Yes!" to please the questioner. What she was really drawing, however, was a picture of her family at the beach.

4. *Liberated Conviction.* This occurs when the child truly thinks about the question and answers it, having never considered it before. This is an interesting moment because the questioner is able to tap into the child's thinking as it is happening. You might find that the questions you ask inspire the child to think even more.

5. *Spontaneous Conviction.* Sometimes the child has considered the issue under question beforehand and answers right away, without having to think about the answer. If a child is asked to "Tell me about your picture," having already considered and drawn what she set out to do, she will answer without having to reflect on what she has done.

In both liberated and spontaneous convictions, children's responses are true to their thinking and reflect their beliefs. These responses are most valuable in assessing children's thoughts and beliefs. A note of caution, however: The answers need not match convention nor will they in many cases. For example, a young child who has drawn a picture of the moon and is asked what the moon does when the child walks home at night might very well respond with a spontaneous conviction, "It follows me, silly!" Although his answer does not match physical reality, the child no doubt had considered this question before and "knew" the answer already. Thus, whether the answer is "right" or "wrong" is independent of the kind of response the child offers.

STANDARDIZED TESTING AND THE ARTS

I can hear all of you now. Your screams can be heard all the way to my office in southern California. This is especially true of all of you who are already teachers and administrators. Fortunately, Diane Ravitch (2010) published a landmark book just prior to this edition of my book that enables me to take a closer look at where testing—to be more specific, standardized testing—has taken us. Ravitch's book, *The Death and Life of the Great American School System: How Testing and Choice Are Undermining Education,* represents a huge turnaround for Ravitch insomuch as she was one of the most influential educational advisors responsible for much of today's testing mania. Furthermore, another book, this one by James Catterall, *Doing Well and Doing Good by Doing Art* (2009), was released at about the same time. Catterall is the researcher who worked with enormous databases analyzing the links between arts involvement and achievement on SATs. His new book followed the same students twelve years into their careers and found that "intensive involvement in the arts associates with higher levels of achievement and college attainment, also with many pro-social behaviors such as volunteerism and political participation". Both books are important and enlightening when considerng the pros and cons of testing.

"I saw my hopes for a better education turn into a measurement strategy that had no underlying educational vision at all," Ravitch writes. "Eventually I realized that the new reforms had everything to do with the structural changes and accountability, and nothing at all to do with the substance of learning" (p. 16). Sadly, as the movement grew with regard to testing, the arts and other subjects took a backseat in curricula because the only subjects tested were reading and math. However, as Ravitch points out, the overall mission of education has become diluted as a result. "Knowledge and skills are both important, as is learning to think, debate, and question. A well-educated person has a well-furnished mind, shaped by reading and thinking about history, science, literature, the arts, and politics. The well-educated person has learned how to explain ideas and listen respectfully to others" (p. 16).

The major problem is not testing in and of itself. Tests can be designed to measure many important aspects of the learning process. The big problem is using standardized tests to make "high-stakes decisions" concerning education and the curriculum (Ravitch, 2010, p. 152). "Accountability," Ravitch continues, "is not helping our schools. Its measures are too narrow and imprecise, and its consequesnces too severe. NCLB (No Child Left Behind) assumes that accountability based solely on test scores will reform American education. This is a mistake" (p. 163). Ravitch supports efforts to reform education—or to return education to a more well-rounded endeavor by which students' learning results in their being able to think, reflect, and gain knowledge and skills and to apply them in a conscientious and respectful manner. She reminds us that "schools are responsible for shaping character, developing sound minds in healthy bodies (mens sana in corpora sana), and forming citizens for our democracy, not just for teaching basic skills" (p. 167).

The arts—and, I would also argue, sports—are fundamental tools for educating students in character, developing reflective minds, and encouraging healthy bodies. Arts and sports nurture the skills of being a citizen that require imagination, engagement, and participation. As I wrote in a blog posting for Americans for the Arts, "they teach lessons that enable students to look at their world with a more complex lens by building critical thinking skills (Adams, Foutz, Luke, & Stein, 2007; Curva, 2005), and they engage students in learning how to play well together, to be team players, to be responsible, and to take risks (Catterall, 2006; Deasy, 2002; Pollard, 2006)."

SUMMARY

Students' artwork provides a rich arena for assessing their understandings. Their artwork documents students' world of contemplation and exploration. Because it is an original representation of a child's thinking, artwork is an authentic indicator of that child's understanding. Because the child has created representations of his or her ideas through the arts, the teacher gains a source that tests understanding rather than the ability to "give back" information (which essentially tells the teacher nothing about the child's ability to comprehend).

For students who have been labeled "lower functioning" during their years in traditional schooling, the arts may contribute to a more informed view of their general intelligence and abilities. For many creative students, traditional testing as the sole source and measurement of their abilities has failed. Not only do the arts help inform teachers about their students' intelligence, learning styles, and personalities, but they offer a route to success that can heighten students' own sense of their abilities and self-esteem.

 ## QUESTIONS TO PONDER

1. When you assess your students' work, for whom is the assessment meant (yourself, the student, parents, principal)?

2. What role do your students play in assessing their own work?

3. To what extent do you vary the assessment tools in your classroom?

 ## EXPLORATIONS TO TRY

1. List the assessment tools you currently employ in measuring your students' progress. After considering the examples in this chapter, what additional assessment options might you try?

2. Choose an example from one of the subject matter–related chapters in this book, and create a rubric for how you might assess the activity. Check to see if the curriculum goals and assessment rubric match each other.

3. Look at a sketch created by one of your students (or use one of the math/art sketches from Chapter 7). Describe the sketch in detail. How does your description inform you about the child's understanding?

REFERENCES

Adams, M., Foutz, S., Luke, J., & Stein, J. (2007). *Thinking through art: Isabella Stewart Gardner Museum School Partnership Program year 3 research results*. Annapolis, MD: Institute for Learning Innovation.

Armstrong, C. (1994). *Designing assessment in art*. National Art Education Association (NAEA). Reston, VA.

Catterall, J. (2006, Winter). Inside out's school project. *Teaching Theatre*, pp. 3–8.

———. (2009). *Doing Well and Doing Good by Doing Art: A 12-year Longitudinal Study of Arts Education—Effects on the Achievements and Values of Young Adults*. Los Angeles, CA: I-Group Books. (Second Printing, November 2009.)

Curva, F., Milton, S., Wood, S., Palmer, D., Nahmias, C., Radcliffe, B., Forgartie, E., & Youngblood, T. (2005). *Artful citizenship report: Three-year project report*. Miami Beach, FL: The Wolfsonian-FIU.

Deasy, R. (Ed.). (2002). *Critical links—Learning in the arts and student academic and social development*. Washington, DC: Arts Education Partnership.

Dorn, C. Madeja, S, and Sabol, R. (2004). *Assessing Expressive Learning: A practical guide for teacher-directed authentic assessment in K-12 visual arts education,* New Jersey, Lawrence Earlbaum Associates Inc.

Gallas, K. (1994). *The languages of learning*. New York: Teachers College Press.

Goldberg, M. (1992). Expressing and assessing understandings through the arts. *Phi Delta Kappan*.

Jacobs, V., Goldberg, M., & Bennett, T. Uncovering an artistic identity while learning to teach through the arts. In *Passion and pedagogy*. New York: Peter Lang Publishers.

Piaget, J. (1976). *The child's conception of the world*. Totowa, NJ: Littlefield and Adams.

Portfolio News. (1994). Vol. 6, No. 1. San Diego: Portfolio Assessment Clearinghouse, University of California.

Pollard, D. S. (2006). *Evaluation report: Live theater and life skills: Year 2.* Milwaukee, WI: Milwaukee Repertory Theatre.

Ravich, Diane (2010). *The death and life of the great American school system: How testing and choice are undermining education.* New York: Basic books.

Saraniero, P., & Jessee, R. (2008). *CCSESA arts assessment resource guide.* Retrieved from http://www.ccsesaarts.org/content/assessment_guide.asp.

Chapter 10

A Lithograph in the Closet and an Accordion in the Garage: Connecting with the Arts and Artists in Your Community

I'm by a blooming flower
and if you were little
you would look around that flower
and you would think you were in a jungle

I'm by a colorful flower
and if you were little
you would dream
that a bee was really a bear—by its sound—

My mind is by a flower
and if you were little
you would feel the flower
as if it was soft smooth cotton

I'm picturing I'm by a flower
and if you were little
you would picture that smell
as ten jars of honey

Adan Gonsalves, fifth grader

In this chapter I will address getting to know the arts resources in your community as a way to support your efforts to bring arts education directly to your students.

UTILIZING COMMUNITY RESOURCES

Every community has artists and resident "art experts." Although your community might not have an Aretha Franklin, Derek Wolcott, Alvin Ailey, Meryl Streep, or Aaron Copland, no doubt there are many individuals who engage in artistic activities. Perhaps, there is even an arts center close by. Utilizing local arts centers and artists as you begin to conceptualize arts-based activities for your classroom will increase your opportunities for success. Finding creative and artistic individuals requires a little investigative work but can bring many wonderful surprises to your teaching.

To discover artists, creative thinkers, and art activities, you must first be aware of the magic in your surroundings. Often I have found that friends have artistic hobbies I never knew about, or acquaintances that unbeknownst to me have secret talents. Sometimes a relative may surprise you, as my Uncle Bill did when he pulled out of the closet a series of lithographs he had made. I didn't know he knew anything about the craft. But that didn't surprise me as much as my graduate advisor when she pulled out an accordion and started playing Irish folk songs. Indeed, lurking within in your own closets and family may be an accordionist, a mandolin player, a basket weaver, a potter, a watercolor painter. Be especially aware of those closets, garages, and basements for clues!

Almost every town has an art association or gallery. This is a good place to start looking for local painters, sculptors, and other visual artists. You might engage them to help you conceptualize an activity. Or you may simply be interested in inviting them to your classroom. Having artists visit your class introduces the students to people with special talents and provides a connection to people in the arts. Much like inviting a community officer or engineer to your classroom, inviting artists offers students role models in the realm of the arts.

Artists can also be utilized to support ongoing programs. In one school I visited, a local artist who specialized in paintings of the local harbor was invited to show students her work as they studied local history. In another school, a teacher asked a local potter to demonstrate the process of tile making and glazing for a chemistry unit. Another teacher asked a parent who was a painter to help a class design a mural for the school.

Often I have met interesting people at craft fairs, festivals, and even parties! At a powwow in southern California I met a Native American instrument maker who subsequently visited my music class to make drums with students. At a party I met a guitar maker who agreed to visit my class to discuss how he made guitars. Community centers can also be wonderful resources. Many have folk dance clubs, art classes, or singing clubs. At a local Jewish center I was able to find a senior Yiddish folk song club willing to perform for children. Through a local PTA I found out about a folklorico (of Mexico) dance ensemble willing to present school performances. The possibilities within your own community are limitless.

If there is an institution of higher education in your area, you can contact arts instructors to see if their students might be available to visit your class. I've set up multiple programs within my university department student internship programs. One such program is called Jam Control. Jam Control is a student dance organization that

First graders with their teacher stand behind the city they built and assembled with the help of a parent.

specializes in various forms of world dance. As part of a special project, they intern in thirteen local schools, conducting free, mid-day dance sessions with students. Following are some comments teachers have made about this project.

> The dance troupe was simply amazing! They taught the entire fourth grade a dance (all at once in the Multipurpose Room) and ALL students were successful. You should have seen the pride the students portrayed and felt their energy/excitement!
>
> On behalf of the entire fourth grade, thank you so much for arranging this special experience. Please let the dancers know how much we appreciate their efforts and tell them they are fabulous! Thank you for giving Central School's fourth graders a brand new experience and making the students feel proud of themselves.

Internships can also be an integral component of a class. I teach a class titled Musical Activities for Children and Adults. I require all students to give music lessons to children in local schools. Each university student works in an elementary classroom for a total of fifteen hours throughout the semester. My goal is for students to gain practical experience in applying the ideas we discuss (and try) in class. Because none of the local schools have music specialists, my students also perform an important service for schoolchildren. Some of my colleagues have set up similar programs whereby their students in theater and visual arts visit local schools to gain experience working with children. Even if there isn't a class structure as I have at my university, there might be arts majors who would be willing to help you on some project. A simple call to a college or university arts department might result in the establishment of an ongoing relationship between your school and young adult students eager to share their talents and skills.

A few more hints. Art supply stores, music shops, and dance studios are terrific resources for people and classes. Consider asking for their advice and help. Often there are parents who have hidden artistic talents (or know people who do) who might be willing to help on a project. In one class, a child's mother (an architect) helped students construct a small town for a unit that combined history and mathematics. In another class, a mother demonstrated the art of origami. Consider as well the talents of your colleagues at school and in your district. Perhaps the second-grade teacher can teach a few songs from a culture you have been studying. In return, you might read a favorite story of yours to her class. Work out some kind of trade of talents.

Many people in communities are willing to offer their time. This is especially true for parents, senior citizens, and school organizations. If funding for special guests in the classroom is problematic, there are many local organizations (including banks, realtors, supermarkets, and department stores) that might be willing to grant you a stipend for a specific project. Most art centers have funds for scholarships, and local organizations may be willing to negotiate special terms. PTAs might also be encouraged to support art projects or artists in the schools. Many states offer opportunities to apply for artist-in-residence programs. Check at the reference desk in your local library for information concerning funding. All in all, with a little creativity and a willingness to investigate possibilities, you can connect with many artists and arts agencies in your community. Once you do, you will not regret your efforts!

THE INTERNET AND ARTS EDUCATION

A larger community to which you have access is the Internet. By simply searching "arts and education," you will find an arts education news and information network, arts curriculum and teacher training sites, grants and resources, and arts education research and assessment. If you Google "the Kennedy Center," and go under its education tab, you will be connected to many arts education programs and sites. Similarly, if you Google "Americans for the Arts," you will access a wealth of information, advocacy ideas, and an extensive blog that will keep you going for a long time!

In addition to arts education sites (of which you can connect to hundreds, if not thousands), you can access individual artists, musicians, sculptors, photographers, and so on. To access these individuals, simply search according to their name. Many museums also maintain sites on the Internet, offering even more opportunities for enhancing learning and specific subject matter. Recently I accessed museums in Chicago, New York, Florida, and Massachusetts by simply clicking a few buttons!

PARTNERSHIPS IN ARTS EDUCATION

For the rest of this chapter, I will highlight several programs, including DREAM, SUAVE, and AVID for Arts, all programs that I've developed as outreach arts education programs for schools in my community. All of these programs fall under a university-based center that I direct called Center ARTES (www.csusm.edu/centerartes). I highlight these programs in the hope that you might be inspired to create one or more of your own!

THE DREAM PROJECT

Developing Reading Education with Arts Methods

The DREAM project is funded by an approximately $1 million grant from the United States Department of Education Office of Innovation and Improvement: Arts in Education Model Development and Dissemination Grant Program.

The goal of DREAM is to train third- and fourth-grade teachers from schools with 35% or more free or reduced school lunch populations to use visual arts and theater activities in the classroom to improve students' reading and writing skills. The program offers a one-week Summer Institute coupled with in-class coaching by professional artists throughout the year.

The aim of the program is to have a long-term impact through researching and demonstrating the effectiveness of using the arts to improve students' reading and writing skills. This grant follows up on previous studies of Center ARTES's award-winning SUAVE program, which showed clear improvements in language arts test scores among participating children.

SUAVE

SUAVE is a volunteer professional development program for teachers that helps them use the arts to teach the content areas of mathematics, science, language arts, and social studies as well as to develop an appreciation for the arts in and of themselves (Goldberg & Bossenmeyer, 1998). By using the arts as an interdisciplinary teaching technique (versus a discipline to be taught), teachers have found that students both further their subject matter understanding and are also introduced to the arts themselves. The program began as a joint effort of California State University San Marcos (CSUSM), the California Center for the Arts, Escondido (CCAE), and several school districts.[1] The SUAVE program is now the subject of my book, *Teaching English-Language Learners Through the Arts: A SUAVE Experience* (Goldberg, 2004).

SUAVE is an acronym for *Socios Unidos para Artes Via Educación*—United Community for Arts in Education. The word *suave* in English and the word *suave* in Spanish are identical—albeit in Spanish it is a bit more spicy. SUAVE provides multiple learning opportunities and environments for teachers (Bennett, Goldberg, & Jacobs, 1999). The core of SUAVE is its coaching component whereby a professional artist (referred to as a "coach") visits each teacher's classroom once a week for two years. The program is not an add-on and the coach does not provide predetermined art activities, but rather collaborates with each teacher to further that teacher's objectives. SUAVE is designed so that ten teachers per school participate with the same

---

[1] Funding for SUAVE is shared among the partners (CSUSM, CCAE, school districts) as well as grants from the California Arts Council and several local industries.

coach. The coaches rotate yearly so that each teacher has the opportunity to work with two coaches.

When the program began, artists/coaches attended five full-day in-service workshops at the California Center for the Arts, Escondido, with teachers from all participating schools. At these in-services, participants shared curriculum, did arts-based activities, and met with visiting artists who were performing at the Center for the Arts. For example, in one year, the teachers had workshops with the COAD Puppetry Company, the Missoula Children's Theater, The Shakespeare Company, and Marcel Marceau!

Teachers are also invited to attend subsidized performances, have some after-school workshop opportunities, and present their work at the end of the school year at an annual curriculum fair. The goal at the end of two years is that the teacher will have learned strategies to continue teaching through the arts on his or her own. After the two years of training, however, teachers are still provided with limited access to coaches and are invited to attend after-school workshops and in-services.

Teachers have specifically underscored the importance of the following in their overall ability to learn in the program (Jacobs, Goldberg, & Bennett 2004):

- Personalized, sustained coaching in their classrooms
- In-services that provide the opportunity to share with teachers from other schools and engage with professional artists both as learners and as audience members
- Connections between the in-services and classroom coaching
- Communities at their school sites that are active in SUAVE (i.e., each school site includes ten participating teachers and administrative support)

The coach/artists are a wonderful group of people with different backgrounds, both in discipline and in culture. They include a puppeteer, a visual artist, a mosaic artist, a poet, a musician, a dancer, a dramatist, and a mime, and they are an exciting mix of cultures—African American, European American, Native American, Mexican, and Mexican American. The artist/coaches are supported through weekly two-hour meetings with each other and myself (the program director), where we brainstorm ideas concerning specific content and discuss effective strategies for working with individual teachers.

CSUSM students who are focusing on arts integration are placed in SUAVE classrooms for their student teaching or observations. One of the Distinguished Teachers in Residence in the College of Education at CSUSM, David Mackintosh, is a former SUAVE teacher.[2]

---

[2] Distinguished Teachers in Residence (DTiRs) are teachers from local school districts who, through a formal interviewing and selection process, are "loaned" to the university for two years. In those two years the teachers teach courses to credential students on various aspects of teaching and learning. It is a wonderful program that keeps the credential program continually in touch with what is current in school practice from the perspective of local school action and policy.

SUAVE teachers enjoy a movement exercise at an in-service day at the California Center for the Arts, Escondido.

The Coaching Relationship

We call the central piece of the program *coaching*, whereby artists become partners with classroom teachers in developing ways to teach the already-existing curriculum. However, the partnership is not hierarchical, with one or the other partner exercising exclusive power over what is taught and how classroom instruction occurs. Instead, the relationship is a professional-professional model: The artist has expertise and the teacher has expertise—and the intersection of the two can create some incredible opportunities for children (indeed for *all* partners). The teacher has expertise in curriculum and pedagogy, in how children learn, and in the specific needs of the students in her or his classroom.

David Mackintosh, SUAVE teacher, holds up a math/art project he developed with his coach.

The artist has expertise in an art discipline and in the process of art, arts integration, and a passion for arts as a language. Together, they form a powerful team.

The coach's role is multifold and customized to each teacher's needs. Depending on the learning style and needs of each teacher, the coach acts in many ways—and we have found that there is no single recipe for success. The coach can be a resource, a role model, a support person, a motivator, a person to bounce ideas off of, or someone who provides feedback, inspiration, encouragement, temptation, guidance, assistance, ideas, a safe environment for risk taking, and so on. The coach also can provide answers to questions in context and share technical expertise as well as a passion for arts and for learning.

The definitions of the word *coach*, as given in the *Oxford Dictionary*, are (1) "to convey in, seat in, provide with, a coach"; (2) "to ride or drive in a coach or motor coach"; and (3) "to prepare (a candidate) for an examination; to instruct in special subjects; to tutor; also, to train for an athletic contest, as a boat race." The roles of the SUAVE coach resonate these definitions: He or she moves or conveys a teacher from point A to point B; in fact, he or she *is* the vehicle that makes movement possible. The teacher has a voice in where the coach is going and how he or she gets there.

WHAT DOES A SUAVE CLASSROOM LOOK LIKE?

While no two SUAVE classrooms look alike, all have some characteristics in common: active participation by teachers and students, risk taking, expanded methods of assessment, and inclusion of all students. One teacher wrote this about her experience in SUAVE:

> During the year, I have learned many new things about art and teaching. First, I learned that art isn't just something you do on Friday during "art" time. It isn't just drawing, painting, or sculpting. My concept of art was broadened to include dance, mime, story-telling, movement to teach math concepts like symmetry, patterns and number sense, theater, and music as well. I am excited to use movement to teach place value next year, and drama to teach grammar concepts in fresh, creative ways that grab the students' interest; using mosaics to reinforce geography concepts of various regions will be added to my social studies curriculum. Acting out a legend using simple props like pieces of material to simulate water, wind, and sky, as well as instruments for rhythm will be a great way to introduce legends to my students. My students [this year] were able to remember and retell the story to a partner after acting it out, then they wrote beautiful summaries of what they acted out. They went on to create, act, and write their own legends.

As teachers engage in SUAVE, changes in their beliefs and instructional practices occur (Bennett, Goldberg, Jacobs, & Wendling, 1999). This can be seen in classrooms as teachers learn to engage students mentally and physically in the learning process.

> My mind is more open to trying things out through different modalities and presenting it to kids in a different way. So instead of finding out about fairytales by reading, let's find out about fairytales by miming them and then we will compare and contrast fairytales. It is a different way of introducing things . . . it sounds silly but it gets the kids. You always worry as a teacher when you are presenting a lesson, who you are leaving out, who is being excluded because you are presenting it one way. But I think with the arts you have a way of reaching everybody in some way, somehow. No one is excluded.

Movement Poetry

"Hooking a kid is half, if not more than half, the battle of learning," according to a second-grade teacher. "If you can hook them then you can get them to learn." In this example, an art activity enabled students to engage in language arts content (poetry) in a deeper and more effective way. Initially, the teacher was disappointed with students' poems about snowflakes and commented that their poems were very "stale, very dry, very second grade-ish." She then used art to help students "experience" being a snowflake before asking them to write again. For example, while listening to Tchaikovsky's *Nutcracker Suite* (the waltz of the snowflakes), students visualized themselves as snowflakes on an adventure—beginning as a water drop, evaporating, crystallizing, and falling to the ground as a snowflake. After visualization, students repeated the exercise with movement, acting out their adventure. The teacher commented, "We started dancing like snowflakes, we acted it out, we talked about them, and we made snowflakes. And then, what do you know, when we went to write about snowflakes again we got great stuff."

Art and Identity

One teacher made this comment about how arts integration in the classroom helps encourage the emergence of individual identity in the classroom.

> My shy kids have come to life; they feel they are more a part of the community. When they go out there and I look at them and say, 'that cannot be that child, how come she is coming to life?' Otherwise she is sitting there totally quiet, she is never talking to anyone else. (Jacobs et al. 2004, p. 105)

"Wenger's social learning theory provides a useful lens for examining student learning," according to Victoria Jacobs et al. (2004). Wenger conceptualizes all learning as identity development:

> Because learning transforms who we are and what we can do, it is an experience of identity. It is not just an accumulation of skills and information, but a process of becoming. (Wenger, 1998, p. 215).

Wenger views this "process of becoming" as a social process, one that involves participation in the practices of community.

We all have, according to Nel Noddings (1997, p. 35), multiple identities. She argues that we need to give up the notion of an ideal of the educated person and replace it with a multiplicity of models designed to accommodate the multiple capacities and multiple interests of students.

> We need to recognize multiple identities [in our students]. For example, an eleventh grader may be Black, a woman, a teenager, a Smith, an American, a New Yorker, a Methodist, a person who loves math, and so on. As she exercises these identities she may use different languages, adopt different postures, and relate differently to those around her. But whoever she is at any given moment, whatever she is engaged in, she needs— as we all do—to be cared for. (Noddings, p. 35)

In the realm of technology, interactive computer games offer children opportunities to *create identities* or role play. The Internet provides these opportunities as well, creating "worlds for social interaction in virtual space, worlds in which you can present yourself as a 'character,' in which you can be anonymous, in which you can play a role as close or as far away from your 'real self' as you choose" (Turkle, 1995).

Cell Lab and Art

A sixth-grade science teacher wanted his students to study cells. He and his coach decided to introduce drawing into the study by having kids observe and draw cells seen under the microscope. By engaging the class in this activity, the teacher uncovered an identity of one of his students until then unknown. The sixth-grade teacher later wrote about a "magical SUAVE moment," after implementing this activity with his coach in the classroom.

> A very interesting MSM (Magical SUAVE Moment) occurred with a particularly young sixth grader. The student has difficulty turning his assignments in for science class, partly for personal reasons, but mostly language reasons. The student speaks English, but can barely read or write it. The MSM occurred while integrating art and science. The objective was to draw a cell observed through a microscope, label cell parts, and write a reflection, "How the shape of the cell is related to the function of that organism." Well,

it turns out that this student is an extremely talented artist and was able to write a reflection piece of equal quality (of mind) because it was his cell drawing. The student has since turned in all cell labs on time. Art has bridged the language/content gap!

The arts also enable the multiple identities of the teachers and artists to emerge as well. Teachers begin to uncover their own talents or realize that they have the tools to support their students' creativity. An interesting aspect of SUAVE that research has uncovered is its impact on "uncovering an artistic identity" of teachers.[3] When Rita, the teacher whose quote is at the beginning of this section, began SUAVE, she did not consider herself an artist. In fact, she specifically stated she was not an artist, especially in comparison to several family members whom she described as artistically talented. After participating in the program, Rita recognized that she had "learned to think like an artist, take risks like an artist, and believe in herself as an artist" (Jacobs et al. 2004, p. 100). Likewise, through the sharing of ideas at the coaches' meetings, coaches realize identities and talents in disciplines other than their own and begin to apply them in the classroom with their teachers.

Crossing Boundaries—Lessons from Artists Applied to Learning

- Artists thrive on complexity while still being able to understand the beauty or tragedy in simplicity—the simplicity of a musical phrase or a single brush stroke.
- Artists rarely see things as either/or.
- Artists thrive on crossing boundaries and bridges and in jumping walls.

In bringing both teachers and children beyond convention (if that's what we value in education—and I hope we do), the arts enable a way of thinking to emerge. Here is one more delightful example of two teachers and a student going beyond one such wall. The context is a two-way bilingual program in which all native English speakers are learning Spanish and all native Spanish speakers are learning English. The teachers' objective was to use drama as a vehicle for language acquisition. Therefore, while the students were learning language through acting in their second language, the teachers were learning how to introduce drama from their coach.

TEACHER A: I'll never forget the day he [the coach] did the cow. That little girl, she was so worried about her role and all she had to do was just stand there the whole time! And he took about ten minutes to show her what a cow is—and Mrs. B and I are looking at each other, like ten minutes?! On a kid who doesn't even have a speaking part! But after that, this little girl had no more questions on what her role was.

---

[3] For a full discussion of this aspect of our research, I would refer the readers to the book *Passion and Pedagogy,* which includes the chapter "Uncovering Artistic Identity While Learning to Teach Through the Arts," as well as our book, *Teaching English-Language Learners Through the Arts: A SUAVE Experience,* mentioned earlier in this chapter.

TEACHER B: And, she loved her part.

TEACHER A: And she knew how to be a cow. He took the time, he mooed, he ate the grass, he rolled around . . . and the assistant superintendent came in! And [the coach] was on the ground with her at her level and *as teachers we would never have done that.* We would have said, "Don't worry about it," but she really wanted to be coached on how to be a cow—and she felt *so* important—just as important as the kids who had the speaking parts, just because he took the time with her to elaborate and explain. . . . *I think it's teaching us to be free and explore—saying to a teacher it is O.K. to do—it's not a waste of instructional time, it's valuable time the kids need. No one ever taught us that.*

THE ARTS AIN'T FLUFF

Here's another insight from Rita.

> It's kind of a reminder—hey, you know what? Art is here and it's shaped our world in so many ways and it's not going away. And you can take it out of our classroom, but we're going to find a way to bring it back. . . . Because you know other people see art as fluff-fluff or fu-fu, and I'm thinking NO. If you can tie it in with what you're learning, and if you can make this art somehow make it alive and have whatever you're learning come alive in the classroom, then it's not fu-fu and it's not fluffy stuff, it's education. It's learning. It's real, and isn't that the whole point of education? (Jacobs et al. p. 110).

Learning through the arts introduces a whole other role for arts in education—and it's an important role. It can provide teachers and students with effective tools for the study of content in a deep and profound manner. Thus, arts have multiple layers in education—as disciplines in and of themselves and as pedagogy. The process of art can take on numerous functions. As one fifth-grade teacher commented, "to me, art either extends what you're learning, or it ties it all together." It can motivate students or be a vehicle for review. The arts provide ways to engage learners, opportunities to let them "shine," as well as take ownership of the process of learning. The arts provide multiple forms to assess student learning.

Engaging in the arts gives teachers and students something to look forward to—it fosters a sense of *care*—about education, about learning, about each other. Learning to care is a central thesis of educational philosopher Nel Noddings. Through the arts, what I call the "anonymity of learning" is challenged. Teachers have many more opportunities to know their students and their multiple identities and strengths: At the same time—as in the case of the fifth-grade presidential puppeteers mentioned in the social studies chapter, the anonymity drama affords enabled students to ask questions through their characters that they would not have asked as themselves.

Reflections on the Program

What has impressed me most about the SUAVE program is the confidence and open-mindedness the teachers display as they engage in using the arts as a methodology for teaching. Near the end of each year, participating teachers are asked to reflect on a series of questions. I have included a few brief examples of their thoughts.

1. Describe how your thoughts about the role of the arts have changed, evolved, or been enhanced as a result of your SUAVE involvement so far. For example: Do you think about curriculum differently? Has your teaching philosophy changed?

    - It is becoming clearer that none of the disciplines are isolated or separated. On the contrary: They are intimately connected and they interact with each other. The power of the arts is that magic element that binds subjects together. Arts are like the ocean, where all the elements come together.

    - I can now see how you can integrate arts *throughout* the curriculum. I had never thought of using dance in math or in science! I'm excited about that. My philosophy has changed and I feel I can reach more students.

    - I have never thought of myself as "artistic." However, I now feel quite differently. My teaching methods are changing and I'm having more fun—as well as the children! My philosophy, "I teach to learn," has been reinforced.

    - I've found ways to incorporate art into very structured, sequential skill lessons that I would not have thought of before. For example, when I was teaching compound words, two "actors" each acted out a word and then worked as a team to demonstrate the larger word (such as *football*) while the class guessed the word.

    - As we do more art in the classroom, I begin to see children differently because I see them do well when in other areas they did not seem to do so well. I see them more as valuable individuals because I am in contact with the whole person. I feel well-rounded as a teacher.

2. Do you feel the SUAVE experience is making a difference in your students' education? How so?

    - It gives them a different way of seeing things. They feel more confident in presenting their ideas through music, dance, and art. This helps their self-esteem, especially bilingual students.

    - I feel it has offered them a variety of ways to show me their understanding of concepts. I feel a sense of freedom, not that my classroom is totally unstructured chaos, but because I am open to responses in many forms—and consider them all equally valuable.

    - Yes. My children's self-esteem has been boosted in many cases. Other more logical children are being challenged to think/act in different settings.

    - Students develop new skills and expand their perception channels. This directly enables them to integrate new ways of receiving, processing, assimilating, and using information. I have found that the students become more critical and creative thinkers. They also have learned to work as a team and participate more.

    - My students have told me several times that school is "fun." They look forward to SUAVE projects. They are more open to each other, more willing to discuss and debate better ways to learn. Cooperative learning is a daily process.

- It's definitely more fun. Kids are finding talents in areas that they never knew existed. It's amazing how many kids now want to be professional musicians, dancers, or painters. I've never seen this degree of excitement in any group, ever. They want to make these things their life.

Of particular interest to me in reviewing the program and its impact on classroom practice is that the changes in teachers and students are not related entirely to the arts. Teachers are thinking about teaching and learning in general. Students are working cooperatively, tapping into their creative abilities, and feeling good about themselves and others. Students and teachers both are challenged to think in new ways and inspired to pursue interesting questions. Also, through their thoughts and actions they are being artists, musicians, sculptors, writers, poets, and dancers creating unique and often profound works.

AVID FOR ARTS

AVID for Arts is another collaborative initiative between Center ARTES and local school districts. It is an outgrowth of fourteen years of our award-winning Department of Education Model Arts Program, SUAVE, in partnership with internationally renowned AVID.

AVID (Advancement Via Individual Determination) is a national initiative aimed at improving educational opportunities for underserved students by improving their speaking, writing, critical thinking, and study skills. AVID for Arts focuses on using the arts to improve student learning across the curriculum. Students and teachers work directly with a SUAVE coach on a weekly basis throughout the year.

Beyond the immediate student-centered goals of improving communication skills, literacy, and learning across the curriculum, our belief is that the underlying nature of the arts themselves requires the skills of discipline, focus, listening, responding, critiquing, investment, improvisation, and practice. Thus, by engaging students in the study of the arts and in arts activities, AVID goals are achieved and students become even more invested in their own learning while also becoming more engaged, productive members of society.

ARTS VAN

Center ARTES has an actual van that visits schools to bring art activities directly to students. The van was donated and the materials in the van (drums, art prints, and musical instruments) were all purchased with grants. Each year we raise funds to get the van to different sites. It is a truly cost-effective program and enables us to reach several thousand children each year.

SUMMARY

Integrating the arts throughout the curriculum can create magic in the classroom—in the ways individuals approach subject matter and in the ways they view each other. The arts open doors to understanding and paths toward adventure. The arts can create change. Perhaps through those open doors, down those adventurous paths, and in the changes the arts release, students will be able to challenge life as it is and create ways in which it could be otherwise.

Through the arts, children may learn to empathize with others: in so doing, they might have the tools to envision the unexpected or how things can be different. Education that integrates the arts sets the stage for making discoveries a reality. In providing art activities through which students practice their imaginations and creativity, teachers can influence the ways in which children approach their world. At the same time, teachers might be able to see their own world in new ways and with a keener understanding of the complexities that bind us together.

 ## QUESTIONS TO PONDER

1. List all of the potential arts connections (institutions and people) in your community. What sources might you tap in addition to the ones on your initial list?

2. If you had access to an opera singer, what might you ask him or her to do in your classroom? How about a ballet dancer? A rap singer? A graffiti artist? A bluegrass violinist? A potter?

 ## EXPLORATIONS TO TRY

1. Interview a local artist, musician, or dancer. What aspects of her or his work and life are relevant to culture? History? Mathematics? Science? Literacy? Your curriculum?

2. Do an Internet search on the arts and education. Where can you go? What sites can you explore?

3. Write a brief essay outlining five ways in which you imagine integrating the arts in your classroom (or future classroom). Include a rationale of what you hope the students will accomplish as a result.

REFERENCES

Bennett, T., Goldberg, M., Jacobs, V., & Wendling, L. (1999, April). Teacher learning in professional development: The impact of "artist as mentor" relationship. Paper given at the annual meeting of the American Educational Association, Montreal, Canada.

Bennett, T., Jacobs, V., & Goldberg, M. (1999). "The Power of Multiple Learning Environments in Professional Development," Paper presented at the American Educational Research Association (AERA) meeting, April, 1999 in Montreal, Canada.

Goldberg, M. (2004). *Teaching English-language learners through the arts: A SUAVE experience.* New York: Allyn & Bacon.

Goldberg, M. R. & Bossenmeyer, M. (1998). Shifting the role of arts in education. *Principal, 77* (4), 56–58.

Jacobs, V., Goldberg, M., & Bennett, T. (2004). Uncovering an artistic identity while learning to teach through the arts. In M. Goldberg (Ed.), *Teaching English-language learners through the arts: A SUAVE experience.* New York: Allyn & Bacon.

Noddings, N. (1997). A morally defensible mission for schools in the 21st century. In E. Clinchy (Ed.), *Transforming public education* (pp.). New York: Teachers College Press.

Turkle, S., (1995). *Life on the Screen: Identity in the Age of the Internet.* New York: Simon & Schuster.

Wenger, E. (1998). *Communities of practice: Learning meaning and identity.* New York: Cambridge University Press.

SAMPLE LESSON PLANS

SUAVE

The lessons in this section range from the measuring of a dinosaur in the lesson "How Big Was That Dinosaur?" by Kay Willer, to an animal movement and feeding drama for second language learners by Vickie Rosenberg. Also included is a mosaic mural project showing the metamorphosis of a seed by Judy Davis, a transportation mobile project by Ana Hernadez, and a "Knee-Knock Rise" game (making a board game based on a novel) by Dale Murphy.

SUAVE Curriculum and Project Description

LESSON TITLE: How Big Was That Dinosaur?

TEACHER: Kay Willer

SCHOOL AND GRADE: Grade l, Richland Elementary School

SUBJECT OF FOCUS: Measurement (including vocabulary such as length, width, area) / Visual Arts

DESCRIPTION: Before the lesson, students had previous experiences with measurement, both standard and nonstandard. Students had been studying a unit on dinosaurs. This, of course, included information on the sizes of various dinosaurs. Students seemed to have a difficult time visualizing the true size of a dinosaur, prompting this lesson.

Students went out to the playground equipped with their own chalkboard, and a picture of an Apotosaurus. The teachers measured the height and width of the dinosaur on the playground as students dictated the measurements they had learned. A sketch of the dinosaur was made on the ground as students sketched on their individual boards. Then students excitedly filled in the outline of the dinosaur with sidewalk chalk. They also included some other information about the dinosaur and decorated its name for all to see. They were thrilled to see the actual size of the dinosaur, as well as having the opportunity to share it with the rest of the students as they came out to the playground!

As we continued our study of dinosaurs, I was aware that students had a more realistic concept of dinosaurs, and, of course, their skills in measurement were increased.

This lesson led to a study of fossils and footprints, and I was aware that they were more able to compare sizes of fossil footprints to specific dinosaurs.

This same type of lesson could be used to reinforce mapping skills or in a unit on marine life.

I was surprised that such a simple lesson could have such an exciting impact! I'll definitely repeat it again next year!

SUAVE Curriculum and Project Description

LESSON TITLE: Animal Movement and Feeding

TEACHER: Vickie Rosenberg

SCHOOL AND GRADE: Grades 3–5 Transition, Richland Elementary School

SUBJECT AREA: Science / Drama / Visual Arts

BACKGROUND: This activity was used as an assessment of knowledge gained during this unit on animals. We had studied about how animals move and why they move. As part of this lesson we had students do mini-dramas portraying why animals move. Included in the mini-dramas were prairie chickens who do a mating dance, the white-tailed deer who flash their white tails to warn of danger nearby before leaping away, and how birds of prey swoop down to capture unsuspecting prey. We also studied about how an animal's bone structure assists it in movement. We learned about vertebrates and invertebrates as a classification method. We created "x-rays" of the animal's bones. We discussed the need for hollow bones to allow birds to lift their weight in flight. We discussed how backbones allow a snake to slither.

In this unit we also studied animal classifications as eaters: insectivores, carnivores, herbivores, and omnivores. We discussed many kinds of adaptations animals have for eating. Then we did the following activity as a performance-based assessment.

DESCRIPTION OF THE ACTIVITY: Skills, elements, vocabulary taught: classification, invertebrates, vertebrates, omnivore, carnivore, herbivore, insectivore, adaptations

MATERIALS NEEDED:

> tag board
>
> pencils
>
> markers
>
> sample menus from restaurants

DIRECTIONS:

1. Divide the students into working groups (i.e., pairs or groups of 3 or 4). Show the sample menus to give students ideas of what should be included on the menu. Discuss what the menus have in common, for example, the name of the restaurant, its address, and its phone number on the cover; pictures of food items and prices on the menu pages.

2. Each group's job is to create a menu for an animal restaurant, the Critter Cafe. Have students fold the tag board to form a large menu. Have them design a cover and a menu page for herbivores, insectivores, and carnivores. A notation

can be made that omnivores may choose anything from the menu. (Meals at our café included things like "Hot Fly Pie," "Green Grass Quiche," and "Mouse Ribs.")

3. When menus are complete, conduct a role play of going to the restaurant. Give one student the role of waitress and another role of the animal coming to dinner at the restaurant. (We provided an ESL lesson on appropriate things a waitress says and appropriate responses a customer might offer.)

4. Have observers of the role play determine what kind of animal is placing an order at the café: carnivore, herbivore, insectivore, or omnivore. Then have students try to guess which animal the student is "impersonating."

5. Conduct individual evaluations as you observe students working on creating their menus. Listen to students discuss what food items to put in each category for feedback as to their knowledge. Assess again during the role-play.

EXTENSION MATH INTEGRATION: Audience also has to calculate the cost of the customer's meal using the prices on the menu.

COMMENTS FOR OTHERS TRYING THIS PROJECT: If students are accustomed to working in cooperative groups, three or four students can work together with large tag board. However, when I did this activity with my class, there was more time spent on gaining consensus on how to organize the menu than I wanted to spend. I am going to try the lesson again next year because it was so successful and fun. However, I am going to try it using smaller construction paper and having students work in pairs. I hope the changes will allow students to finish the menus more quickly and allow more individual ownership of the product.

REFERENCES

Lesson information drawn from *Pablo Python Looks at Animals* by Wildlife Conservation Society, 1994.

Song "Animal Movement" taken from *101 Science Poems & Songs for Young Learners* by Meish Goldish. Published by Scholastic, Inc., 1996.

SUAVE Curriculum and Project Description

PROJECT TITLE: Mosaic Mural

TEACHER NAME: Judy Davis

SCHOOL AND GRADE: Grade 1, Juniper

SUBJECT AREA(S):   Math / Science / Social Science / Language Arts / Visual Arts

MATERIALS:

- butcher paper
- construction paper
- scissors
- glue

DESCRIPTION: Students created a mosaic to show seeds, sprouts, plants, and plants as part of our "Living Things" science unit.

1. **What happened in class?**
   We assigned shapes and colors to each thing to be represented. For example: brown Δ's soil, blue ○'s rain.

2. **What skills, elements, vocabulary were taught?**
   Geometric shapes, representational expression, mosaic pieces do not touch, science terms

3. **How did you assess the children's understanding?**
   They made labels for a key to show how each term is represented.

4. **Where could you go from here?**
   We saw mosaic sculptures at Balboa Park and could do a mosaic on any theme!

5. **Comments for others trying this project:**
   Organize students so that about half the class is cutting shapes at their seats while the other half is gluing. Also, draw out the design with chalk for guidelines on butcher paper (we used black to contrast with colors).

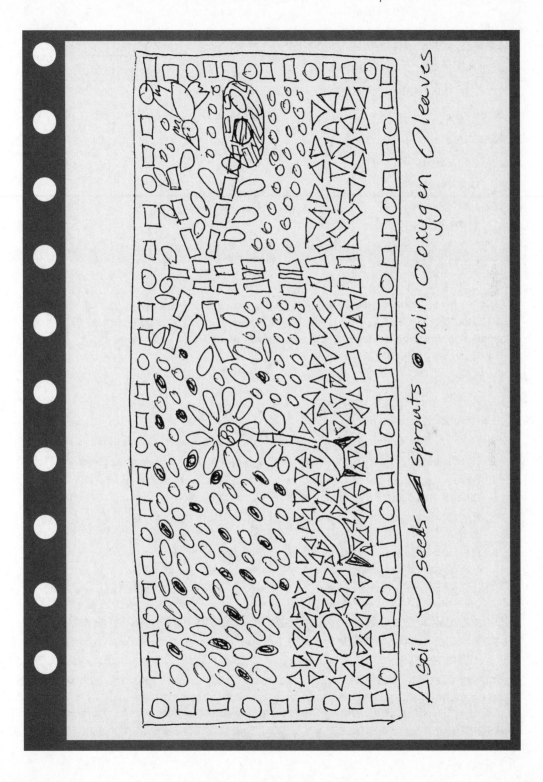

SUAVE Curriculum and Project Description

PROJECT TITLE: Transportation Mobile—Land, Air, Sea

TEACHER NAME: Ana Hernandez

SCHOOL AND GRADE: Grade1/2 (combined class) Lincoln

SUBJECT AREA(S): Science (Grade 1) / Math / Visual Arts / Social Studies

MATERIALS:

- cardboard
- drawing paper
- crayons
- colored pencils
- pictures or boxes of transportation modes, dowels
- nylon fishing line
- construction paper scraps

DESCRIPTION: This is a hanging mobile that shows different modes of transportation used on land and water and in the air. Also featured are different elements that represent land, air, and water environments (train tracks, tree, birds, clouds, octopus and fish, etc.)

PROCESS:

1. Brainstorm modes of transportation (horse, flying carpet, elephant, bicycle).
2. Have students pick one mode.
3. Have students draw, color, cut it out, and glue onto a piece of thin cardboard.
4. Have students cut the piece out and trace it on a second piece of drawing paper.
5. Have students cut out the second piece and place it on the cardboard side of the first piece to see which side of drawing paper needs to be colored.
6. Have students lay the second piece next to the first in order to color it like a mirror image.
7. Have students glue the second piece to the back of the first so that there is one piece with both sides colored and the same exact image.
8. Brainstorm symbols that represent land (roads, grass, flowers . . .), air (birds, sun, stars, wind . . .), and water (fish, whales, seaweed . . .) and have students each make one. Again, they have to complete both sides. Use colored scrap construction paper.
9. String pieces up in mobile form, by forming three branches—one air, one water, one land.

COMMENTS FOR OTHERS TRYING THIS PROJECT: The mirror-image symmetry part is tricky. That is why the second side needs to be traced, cut, and temporarily placed on the first side so that students color the correct side.

SUAVE Curriculum and Project Description

PROJECT TITLE: "Knee-Knock Rise" Game (making a board game based on a novel)

TEACHER NAME: Dale Murphy

SCHOOL AND GRADE: Grade 5, Felicita

SUBJECT AREA(S): Math / Science / Social Science / Language Arts / Visual Arts

MATERIALS:

- crayons
- construction paper
- markers
- graph paper

DESCRIPTION:

1. Read and discuss a novel in class (can also use individual books).

2. Have kids retell the story from start to finish. Be sure to have at least ten to twelve events from the story. I had the kids put the events inside pictures of oysters (that's what we were learning about in science).

3. After they write their events, have them pick six of their favorite events or six events that they feel are not important to the story. Then introduce the vocabulary words *positive* and *negative*. Elicit from the kids what those words mean. From the definitions, they should see that *positive* events are good things and *negative* events are generally bad. Next, have the kids work in pairs and decide which events were positive and which were negative (either to the character or to the reader). For each positive event, place → in the pearl. For each negative, place ←.

4. Pass out one sheet of construction paper to each child. Discuss various types of board game designs. Have kids design their board game, including a place for "Chance" cards (the oysters) and a place for discards. They also need to include the title of the book and an illustration (usually in the center of the board) that goes with the story. All boards must include four ways to show positive things that could happen to the players (e.g., "You got the bigger end of the wishbone. Take a Chance card") and four ways to show negative things that could happen to the players (e.g., "You went to the top of Knee-Knock Rise and got caught in a storm. Lose a turn"). All mini-stories (or ways to get a Chance card or to lose a turn) must somehow relate to the story being studied. This is how you check for comprehension.

5. Extended activities could include making a cube to use as the die (math), planning geography lessons (social studies), weather or earth units (science), etc. The possibilities are endless!

6. Be sure to give kids time to use the board games in class. They could combine oysters to have more Chance cards. ☺

    a. **What skills, elements, vocabulary were taught?**
        Vocabulary → *positive* → *negative;* skills: comprehension.

    b. **How did you assess the children's understanding?**
        By what they wrote on board game squares and which way they placed their arrows.

    c. **Where could you go from here?**
        Anywhere!

    d. **Comments for others trying this project?**
        Be flexible with your time. The more time you give the kids, the more creative their projects turn out to be.

Chapter 11

Beyond Walls: Mural Making and Critical Voices: Collaborative Art Projects

Two times two making four is a pert coxcomb who stands with arms akimbo barring your path and spitting. I admit that two times two making four is an excellent thing, but if we are to give everything its due, two times two making five is sometimes a very charming thing too.

Theodore Michaelovich Dostoievski, 1943

From a place beyond the wall of convention and accepted fact, such as $2 \times 2 = 4$, emerge the most inventive discoveries and ideas—perhaps even that $2 \times 2 = 5$! Dostoievski's character from the underground is unwilling to accept mathematical certainty or scientific law as truth. Instead, he considers such truths and laws as walls, merely stopping points from which all else is judged. Though we travel on daily paths of potential discovery, those journeys, Dostoievski reminds us, often lead only to the walls of convention.

Everyday living hustles people along paths paved by experiences and dominant social practices. In order to "fit into" society, many of us negotiate the paths—even using the dominant practices to secure some position for our own gain. "To resist such tendencies," however, according to Maxine Greene (1991), "is to become aware of the ways in which certain dominant social practices enclose us in molds or frames, define us in accord with extrinsic demands, discourage us from going beyond ourselves, from acting on possibility." "It is unfortunate," writes Sonia Nieto (1992), "that too many young people continue to be disenfranchised, disrespected, and devalued in our schools, and the result is that we lose bright futures, the hope for something better, and even real lives in the process." Creating collaborative art projects, the focus of this

243

chapter, provides an opening through which students can move beyond the walls of such potential acquiescence to find their place in a community—in this case, a community of learners.

As a teacher of teachers in a university that prides itself on cultural diversity, examining issues of whose voice is heard in a classroom is a topic visited in many courses, including my own. Recently, through documenting students' efforts to collaborate on a mural and curriculum project, I was reminded how substantial voice can become when the classroom and community coincide. Both projects served to develop what I will call *critical voice.* In considering the phrase *critical voice,* I am trying to identify the qualities of a student or teacher's voice that is at once reflective, empowered, questioning, informed, and respectful of voices different from itself. Developing a critical voice encourages an individual to explore beyond the walls of convention, opening the possibility to create and recognize her or his own sense of potential while resisting demands of disenfranchisement. Teachers who can create critical voice building in their classroom communities might just stumble on the sense of possibility much as Greene suggests, or as Dostoievski understands when he questions "truths."

Learning and Instruction is a required class for students working toward a teaching credential in the state of California. At California State University San Marcos, where I teach, all credential students are placed in cohorts of approximately twenty-six students and take all their classes together. As part of their coursework, all students are trained in CLAD (Cross-Cultural Language and Development). All of the student teaching placements are in multicultural and multilingual classrooms.

All of the students described in this chapter have chosen to focus on the arts as a theme that runs throughout all their classes. The class was culturally diverse with a wide range of ages (from recent graduates to grandmothers), including European Americans, an African American, Mexican Americans, and Native Americans.

Our semester centered around a unique project—a giant mural project on the theme of educational philosophy to be painted on a long corridor at the university. The mural project was designed to engage the students in creating an educational philosophy, then representing and communicating that philosophy. In documenting the efforts of collaboration and listening to the class discussions, I became acutely aware of how much of the debate related to the issue of accepting as valid the voices that differ from your own. It began with a struggle to create a collaborative vision and design for the mural project. Perhaps one of the biggest challenges was to accept others' ideas. As one student put it, "We have learned to accept the ideas of others as well as give up some of our own." It wasn't easy, though it proved to be extremely powerful.

The mural making highlighted concentrated individual effort and collaboration, which we found to be both challenging and frustrating. There were moments of resistance and epiphany throughout. In the end, however, I believe that students found their own critical voices and learned how to recognize the critical voice (or lack thereof) in others. While this chapter focuses on my students at the university level, I believe that the lessons of collaboration and critical voice apply to students of all ages. The journey begins.

THE MURAL PROJECT

Throughout history, people have created wall paintings to communicate and express culture and beliefs, as well as to decorate their surroundings. From the walls of the dark caves at Altimira Lascaux to ancient Crete and Egypt, on to classical Greece, imperial Rome, medieval England, Renaissance Italy, colonial America, and modern cities all over the world, including San Diego (near our university), wall paintings attest to the lifeblood of societies. According to Meiss (1970), for example, "the Romans of antiquity, like earlier Mediterranean peoples, enjoyed large mural paintings in their palaces and villas. As we know from surviving buildings in Rome and the region of Pompeii, they transformed confining walls into large, fictive spaces. They converted stone, brick and plaster into gardens and fanciful architecture." As Marshall Davidson puts it, "From everywhere in time and place—examples of mural painting have survived that testify to the continuity of this old and entirely human practice" (qtd. in Little, 1952). Thus, our project continues in a long and revered tradition.

I originally planned the mural project as a learning *through* the arts experience for the students of the Credential Arts Cohort, hoping that through the design and production of a mural the students would learn something about educational philosophy as well as techniques related to painting. The project fit in nicely with issues explored in Learning and Instruction, in which the students learn about various pedagogies for teaching and learning. One such strategy that I usually introduce, the reader will not be surprised to find out, involves using the arts as methodology for learning specific content. We study how the creation of artwork can prove to be an effective language for learning—especially in the multilingual classroom, thus pushing the notion of what constitutes a "text" (Gallas, 1994; Goldberg & Bossenmeyer, 1998).

I had also predicted that the project might serve as a way to build bridges among the students in the cohort, for I knew they would need to work as a team and negotiate aspects of the philosophy and painting together. Thus, the project set out to do many things. It served as a method to explore educational philosophy, as an arena to learn something about the arts, and as a forum for experiencing cooperative group work. It was the latter that became so very fundamental to the students and their emerging critical voices throughout the year.

Chronology of Classwork

AUGUST 28

On this day students were introduced to the ideas of educational philosophy and mural making. This was only our second class together at the very beginning of the semester. Students were anxious about the program as well as about getting to know each other. To introduce the notion of educational philosophy, I supplied students with copies of the college and university mission statements. I used the statements in the hope they would serve as a starting point for a philosophical discussion. I asked students to relate the mission statements to what they knew about public schools and their thoughts about their role as future teachers.

The mission statements are an overarching set of beliefs to which the university and college adhere. The college of education, for example, is driven by the following beliefs taken directly from the mission statement.

1. All students can learn not only rote facts, but to reason and use their minds well, and teachers are the primary agents for this learning.

2. In order to meet the considerable challenge that all students will learn, educators must be lifelong learners themselves, professionally empowered and skilled at problem solving and collaboration with peers to design creative, effective learning communities in schools.

After reading of these statements and the university statements, which emphasize diversity and preparedness for a multicultural and global society, students responded by brainstorming words and ideas they believed could relate to an educational philosophy. The following is their initial brainstorm list.

Students' Brainstorming.   (underline signifies relative importance in that the words or ideas were expressed more than once)

- "transfer" <u>knowledge</u>[1]
- <u>responsible</u> citizens
- all children live <u>dreams</u> and can be anything they want
- school <u>equity</u>/nonbiased atmosphere
- <u>inspire creative</u> thinking and desire to learn
- <u>community</u> responsibility
- prepare for society: respect, integrity, honesty, being nice, love toward neighbor, self-esteem, connected to others, understanding, unity–diversity, sense of place, gender equity, global awareness, environmental awareness

August 30

After reviewing the list from the previous class, we continued the discussion, but this time focused on the question "What are important qualities of teaching?" At this stage, students had read many articles and chapters as part of their classwork, including Eleanor Duckworth's *The Having of Wonderful Ideas* (1996), which emphasizes a constructivist point of view, and Karen Gallas's *Languages of Learning* (1994), which focuses on teaching and learning in a diverse and multilingual first-grade classroom.

Brainstorming

- listening to students
- understanding—students' understandings of content and teacher's understanding of how students understand

---

[1] "Transfer" is in quotations because the students disagreed with each other concerning the nature of knowledge. Many students believed that knowledge could be transmitted or transferred to students while others argued that *transfer* was akin to rote and had little value. The compromise was to put the word in quotes.

- art is language for communicating and expressing
- seeing kids as whole beings
- participation—learning as active or action

Other important words/concepts the students wanted to include for consideration were *interactive, universal, explore, constructing new ideas, creative, cultural diversity, actively involved,* and *wonderful ideas.*

September 6

We had our first meeting with artist Alejandro Sanchez. Alex is a twenty-year-old professional artist with extensive mural experience as an apprentice, having worked with several San Diego mural artists. He was introduced to the campus by the Director of Financial Aid, who had previously hired Alex to work with teens in the Upward Bound Program. He was a pre-med student at UCSD. (He now is a doctor in the Los Angeles area and continues to practice arts as well!) I hired Alex particularly because of his reputation for working with non-artists and his ability to bring them to a place where they believe they can create and implement art. I also had in the back of my mind that by working with Alex, students might get the idea of engaging local artists to help shape and implement projects. The project was as much an opportunity for Alex as it was for my students. Alex had never been in charge of his own mural, though he felt quite confident and excited by the opportunity. He was, however, a little worried that he was younger than most of my students. He worried that they might not react positively toward him because of his age.

On his first meeting with the class, Alex introduced himself and offered the students an introduction to the history of wall painting and the activity of painting a mural. We did this at the site of the future mural because Alex wanted to engage students in a discussion concerning site-specific art. Our particular site was in a hallway linking the library courtyard to a major walkway on the campus. Our wall was about fifty feet long and ten feet high, with about ten feet to the opposite wall. In other words, it was a rather long, relatively narrow hallway. The wall was designed such that it already formed five panels outlined by indentations in the concrete. While onsite, we looked at various artists' works, including that of Michelangelo, and discussed the Sistine Chapel. Alex led a discussion that encouraged students to consider the notion of making words and ideas—specifically the ones they had been working with in the last two classes—visual. At the end of class, Alex asked each student to create three sketches that related to ideas they had already discussed. He emphasized that stick figures were just fine; what we were looking for at this point were visual images—not masterpieces. I also asked students to find or create a quote relating to teaching and learning to bring to class, hoping that the visual and written texts together would open up multiple venues for thinking about philosophical content.

September 8

Each student brought in three sketches and a quote. The results were varied and fascinating. Most students indicated that the exercise was a lot easier than they had anticipated.

Many were self-conscious, however, about the quality of their sketches as they shared them and were leery as to how they could possibly transfer their raw ideas and sketches to the mural. After all students had shared their sketches and quotes, we tried as a class to look for common themes, all the while relating the visual images to our previous brainstorming and mission statements. As it happened, certain themes did emerge. They included the following.

- The importance of children's' dreams and wishes
- Links of the past to the present and future
- Embracing the multicultural diversity of our community
- The importance of the environment to learning and culture
- The role of technology in teaching and learning

Alex left the class with all of the sketches, ideas, and notes he had taken and promised to return with draft composite sketches.

September 11

Alex brought in a few preliminary sketches based on students' work. He had tried to combine and blend the students' visual images into five separate panels. We placed students in five small groups and had them refine their ideas and themes by asking these questions:

- How does this relate to the mission statement?
- How will this translate visually? Is it possible to paint?

Students discussed the panels and made suggestions both about content and visual imagery. On hand were many art books with murals to which students could look for help in translating their ideas to visual images. Each group reported their ideas to the class and the artist. Alex took all their suggestions and ideas home to create a second draft of the panels.

September 13

Alex brought in a second set of sketches. In new small groups, students once again refined their ideas and visual imagery. The following general themes emerged as titles for the panels:

Dreams

Tradition

Diversity

Environment

Technology

The students were becoming very eager to paint, though they were still overly concerned about their ability to "draw." Alex tried to put them at ease and explained that we would actually project and trace some of the images onto the wall.

SEPTEMBER 18

Alex brought in four out of five final drafts of sketches (all but the diversity panel, which had not come together quite yet). We discussed the process and students reflected on that process in writing. They focused primarily on two issues: (1) using art in the classroom, and (2) philosophy.

During these past couple of weeks of working on the mural, I have been very excited. I have realized that through doing this mural we are integrating what we are learning to do—learn by using ART. The mural has gotten me to view things and analyze ways of teaching and learning differently. Through looking at our mission statement in the form of art, I think we have all expressed ourselves and our ideas in a "deep" manner. It is neat to put our thoughts into art and actually see it expressed on paper. This has been an awesome experience and I hope to use something like this in the future—with my classroom.

I'm starting to get really excited about this project because we have finally gotten to the point of having solid ideas. Everything seems to be coming together and I am starting to see how art can be integrated into themes within the classroom. It seems very powerful to be able to transfer the knowledge learned in the classroom in an artistic creation. Seeing all the images we have come up with provides an in-depth perspective on what education is all about and how we can use this tool with our own children and in our own classrooms. This is something that I want to be able to give to my children. Being able to create an artistic type of environment will lead to greater insight and deeper understanding—so much more than any textbook ever could.

The mural has really made us focus on our thoughts about what our main points of education are to us. This is something I want to do in my future classroom to get children to think about things and be able to portray their thoughts through art.

Following the reflections on art and philosophy, another issue emerged. Students now began to reflect on their work together and the notion of listening to others. It was at this point that they began to develop a sense of what it means to have and accept critical voices. "We have learned to accept the ideas of others as well as give up some of our own" wrote one student. Another student reflected on the rigor of working together: "When we started out I didn't expect that the process would be so complicated." The following student overtly addressed the nature of collaboration.

I am not used to collaborating with other people on art projects. I am glad to have this opportunity to collaborate because I need this experience and because I want to be a team player. I think it is enjoyable to work with other people because it allows me to recognize other people's thoughts as an integration with my own thoughts. What I mean is if someone gives an idea, I can sometimes add to the idea to refine it, or vice versa. The project has been enjoyable and exciting.

Students were not *moving away from* their own voices, but rather *toward being able to accept and work with* others' voices. The reaction to a peer's voice became an opportunity to examine ideas and place them within a context of many ideas, rather than simply to judge them.

Another issue arose in relation to what students labeled "political correctness." Because the mural was to become a public art piece, debate as to what was appropriate to portray versus what was not became a serious consideration. Together, Alex and I encouraged the debates, while at the same time trying to serve as facilitators of the discussions. The first debate began when an African-American male in the class wanted to put a sign of Black Power in one of the panels—an upright hand with a clenched fist. The second debate occurred when a group of students (including a Latina [Mexican American], a Latino [also Mexican American] married to a Native American woman, a white male, and a white female) wanted to portray a Native American man or woman looking solemnly into an industrial abyss. One student reflected:

> The project lost luster for me when our idea was questioned due to concern over "political correctness." It's something that I have to get used to. I must remember that this is public art and I'm new to this avenue of art. Being new allows me to learn a great deal about it. I just wish that we had no limitations on what we could do but that's not possible with public art. If it were not for that, it would be perfect. On the other hand, there is no such thing as perfection.

The debate was serious. As one of the group members put it, "What a difficult process of refining our ideas—taking bits of everyone's ideas was far from easy." Listening to others and responding critically rather than merely reacting proved powerful. A rich but tenuous discussion emerged as the role of personal, private, and cultural symbols clashed. In the debate concerning Black pride, members of the class argued that if we put up one symbol, then we would need to put up other symbols—where does it end? Others argued that the symbol itself could be a source of pride while others argued it was an attempt at self-promotion. How it would be viewed by the public was another avenue of the discussion, juxtaposed on revisiting the purpose of the mural. A critical question was raised by a member of the class: "What relation and importance does the symbol have to our theme?"

A similar debate ensued with regard to the portrayal of a Native American. Many students argued that the symbol was fundamental to their work on the panel devoted to the theme of the environment. "The Native American with a tear in his eye is a recognizable and powerful symbol," some students argued. Other students argued that it was a stereotype. Still other students argued that we shouldn't include any specific representational symbols concerning culture in the panels. Instead, they proposed, we should take photos of children and adults related to the students in our class and portray them in the panels.

I have to admit that I favored a more neutral design, though with a certain amount of personal angst. I sympathized with various students' desire to express their individual statements though the mural—yet in the end it was a group project. How to bring a group to the point of accepting the importance of its members' views and somehow dealing with them in the final product was a challenging job. I found myself in the tenuous role of facilitator, though I also recognized the power I held as the teacher to make overarching decisions. I found myself constantly questioning my own thoughts about the images as well as my role in keeping some sense of balance among the arguing students.

I continually tried to bring the students back to philosophy and to relating their particular idea or image to their statement of philosophy. I did this because I could sense some arguments getting out of hand and away from the theme as the passion for a particular idea grew. At the same time, Alex was preoccupied with having students continually keep in mind the nature of public art as opposed to art that is not permanently placed. In that light, he asked students to consider the ramifications of the fact that people would not have a choice but to walk past our mural on their way to the library.

As we neared completion of design, the group as a whole displayed various levels of excitement concerning the process and the panels, but all felt a commitment to each other. Some students began to have a sense of pride. One remarked, "It is cool when you think about this mural and how many people will see it. I think after this project is complete there will be a great sense of pride among all of us." Individuals had to give up ideas and designs as they collaborated with others. It was a profound exercise in listening to each other. Not everyone walked away feeling that the mural was representative of what they had wanted or imagined. On the other hand, everyone walked away feeling that their ideas were somehow fundamental to the end product, even if they didn't like everything about the final product—and there were definitely students who didn't like the final product.

During the process of the mural design the students were introduced to another real-world experience. Even though the project had been funded and approved by numerous campus committees, the president of the university decided to shut down the project, explaining (through a representative) that because the campus had no permanent art policy we couldn't do the mural. I suspected, however, that his decision probably had more to do with a controversy at another California state university. A year prior to our project, San Francisco State was involved in a high-profile controversy concerning a mural on its campus. The mural was the subject of a political debate among several factions of students and the community because it depicted figures related to Louis Farrakhan. I suspected that the president and administration of our university were becoming cautious and overly worried about political fallout from the potential mural despite the fact that its themes were based on university and college mission statements.

Naturally, when students heard of the president's decision they were disappointed. They reacted defiantly; they were ready to protest, write petitions, and do whatever it took to get their project completed. Fortunately, their reaction was one of action rather than compliance; inklings of their critical voices emerged. Though angered by the situation in general, they accepted the challenges that accompany innovative initiatives. When we were able to step back a bit, students recognized that being the first group on campus to propose a mural would necessarily create a few challenges. Accepting this, they decided it was better to negotiate than to protest, at least at that moment, and approved of moving forward with a "leasing program" proposal that the dean of our college and I had developed.

The leasing proposal was developed quickly (and in desperation). The dean of the college of education intervened as a mediator and helped with developing alternatives that could be presented both to students and to the president (through the Facilities Committee). In retrospect, perhaps I should have included the students in this conversation. At the time, however, I felt desperate and nearly defeated. My instinct was to seek the advice of the dean, a known advocate of the project. In fact, he was clear-headed, supportive, and helped develop a few alternative plans.

Our first choice was to tackle the question of "permanency" by proposing that the college of education lease the wall in question for a period of three years with an option to renew. We argued that by that time there should be a policy in place. The major problem with the proposal was that it would take the Facilities Committee at least two months to consider the plan; therefore, our painting would have to be postponed. We also devised an alternative plan—to paint the mural on wooden planks and adhere them to the walls of our college over which we had already gained autonomy. However, I hoped we would not have to resort to Plan B.

October and November

The students, Alex, and I were frustrated by the unexpected delay relating to being granted permission. During this time, I had to meet with a number of university committees to describe the project and argue for its viability. Fortunately, with the full support of the college dean, we presented our compromise "leasing plan." If an eventual policy was such that there would be no permanent art on campus, our college would agree to paint over the mural. We never mentioned Plan B.

Beginning of December

Permission was finally granted by the Facilities Committee in agreement with the president. The students were excited, though a little distant from the project as they had just spent the last two months on other projects and the previous five weeks in full-time student teaching. Alex and I ordered all the paints, brushes, and other materials.

December 6–21

The painting began—and everyone showed up for the first day, which entailed painting the entire length of the wall white (with gesso) as a base coat. At this point, students decided that each class member should sign up for a minimum number of required painting hours—and then sign up for shifts for the following two weeks. Even the dean showed up to paint on day one to the delight of students. No doubt his unyielding support for the mural and for the students themselves reaffirmed their commitment to the project. During the next two weeks, Alex guided students and taught them various techniques for both preparing and painting the panels (including finding the midpoints of the sections, outlining spaces, etc.). Students painted images and then repainted the ones that didn't quite work or look right. Fortunately, the paint dried quickly enough to repaint any image, so mistakes were not a problem.

Our biggest challenge emerged during this time. Alex decided to take a day off from painting but encouraged students to keep working. He left them with the instruction to imitate some of the images in an art book he had left on a specific panel. A number of students attempted to do so and were somewhat satisfied with their work. When Alex returned the next day, he realized that students didn't have enough technique and that we would need to repaint what they had done in order to make it look more professional.

Alex was concerned, as we all were, that our mural be as professional as possible, especially as it was the first public "permanent" artwork on campus and would no doubt influence future decisions. Painting over the work proved to be quite a disappointment all around. The students who had painted the panel were quite upset that their work would be painted over, although some of them agreed that what they had painted could be improved. Nonetheless, hard feelings emerged between students as images were painted over. At this point, various students took more or less responsibility and ownership. (This was directly related to the amount of time spent painting.)

Following the repainting episode, we had a week of relative calm in painting and excitement in the project. Each day the mural came more to life, and students were encouraged by the numerous visitors and admirers making their way to check on the progress of the work. The media became interested as well, which excited students. The local affiliate of CNN as well as a few local papers covered the story.

As the end of December approached, we confronted our second crisis. We still did not have a final draft of our diversity panel. I became frustrated with Alex for not pulling a draft together, as did the students. On the other hand, Alex felt that students' ideas just couldn't translate visually—or if they did, it would be far too difficult to paint within our timeframe. Therefore, the last week prior to vacation we had to make a decision as to how to proceed. Alex suggested dividing the panel into smaller squares and having children paint self-portraits (or adults copy children's self-portraits onto the wall). After considerable discussion—some heated—students eventually concurred with Alex and quickly became excited by this solution. This also solved the problem of having to work collaboratively, as students could fill in their square when it was convenient.

DECEMBER 22–JANUARY 20

Winter break provided some respite. Students painted their individual squares.

JANUARY 20–FEBRUARY 1

School reconvened and some of the more detail-oriented students attended to touching up the mural. At the same time, the class discussed how to organize the dedication ceremony. It was agreed to have a ribbon cutting and a few speakers, though none of the students wanted to speak publicly. At the time, I was concerned that no one was eager to represent the project by speaking about it at the ceremony. In retrospect, I wonder if it was because the students were not completely comfortable with the collaboration. If this were the case, they might not want to speak for others considering there were so many voices to represent. All students, however, wanted to wear their painter's hats so that they could be easily identifiable to answer any questions guests might have concerning the project.

FEBRUARY 2

The mural dedication ceremony was a wonderful event. The dean spoke and I hosted the program. In a surprise move, the president of the university attended the ceremony and even had words of praise he offered publicly. Well over a hundred guests and media representatives were in attendance. The students were exhilarated. I was relieved!

At the completion of the mural, it was clear that a community was emerging in our class. Members of the class were finding individual voices as well as an identity together as the "arts cohort." It was at this time that I began to understand the nature of what was emerging. Critical voices are fundamental to creating community. At the same time, this implies that our critical voices might not always emerge as the dominant voice of our community, nor our ideas be the ideas that take precedence in a particular circumstance.

The mural provided many opportunities. At one point, I was saddened by one student's angry comment: "Why should I bother to be innovative when I'm likely to be shut down?" This statement reminded me of Herbert Kohl's (1994, p. 2) notion of "not learning," or the beginning of a willful rejection of working within a given system. He writes, "Learning to not learn is an intellectual and social challenge; sometimes you have to work very hard at it. It consists of an active, often ingenious, willful rejection of even the most compassionate and well-designed teaching." All of us have probably engaged in *not* learning at some point in our lives. When it becomes habitual, however, there is more to consider than the "not-learner." We must consider the systems encouraging and enabling the "not-learning" to prosper while at the same time examine what can lead to a loss of critical voice.

Student resistance can at once be powerful and detrimental. It is powerful in that students have raised a voice and taken a stand. Left unchecked, however, resistance can interfere with learning. Sondra Perl (1994) notes that many students "will not risk raising questions or responding honestly if they suspect that their doubts or concerns will be ridiculed, ignored or rejected." "Resistance," writes Beverly Tatum (1992), "can ultimately interfere with cognitive understanding and mastery of material."

Critical voice, as we saw it developing in the mural project, is not a matter of reaction—it is a matter of respectful and sincere give-and-take. Critical voice means giving up of a sense that "I" know what is best and others are, to lesser and greater extents, misguided. Accepting critical voices might mean to give up complete control of how a certain mural panel will look, how a performance guide will turn out, or how a specific class is going to be taught. But without an attention to critical voice, society perpetuates an acceptance of decided oppression.

Our nation is built on a sense of power and elitism. Not only do we have the "haves" and the "have-nots," but built into that system is the tacit notion that "those who have know best." This is where we can see the breakdown of even the most important of all human traits—respect and dignity. When someone has the attitude that he or she knows best and acts accordingly, he or she jeopardizes and marginalizes others. The "others" in this case can

Photo Courtesy of David Ortiz and Nick Obando

react in a number of ways: with a sense of sadness, with a sense of anger, a sense of injustice—even a sense of hate. They might protest, find alternative methods, and be even more determined to make others listen to their voice. When individuals experience a persistent shutting down over and over again, a tension builds up whereby specific acts lose importance in the fight for another cause—that of freedom from "those who know best."

Herbert Kohl (1994) suggests that risk taking is at the heart of moving beyond entrenched systems. "That means that teachers will have to not-learn the ways of loyalty to the system and to speak out, as the traditional African American song goes, for the concept that everyone has a right to the tree of life." When individuals or groups continually are—or perceive themselves as being—put down and/or treated in a manner whereby their voices are not among the powerful or respected, then the hurt, anger, and sadness begin to coalesce into a powerful shape and form. That form can be incomprehensible to others. Specifically, those who perceive themselves in power can't even imagine the rage and reactions of a group of people different from them and vice versa. A system is firmly in place that perpetuates differences and a separation of voices.

To avoid such systematic claiming of one voice over another means to accept, listen, and try to understand a multitude of voices rather than to react to them. It might mean giving up your own voice in acceptance of another or developing a forum for negotiation, such as Alex and I tried with each other when the diversity panel became an issue. This process is necessary toward developing a community in which all members feel a commitment to each other and to the community as a whole. It can only be achieved when all voices are accepted as critical. In this scenario, all voices are respected rather than rejected, and collaboration replaces judgment and competition. The collaboration is rigorous and voices are often challenged. In that rigor it is not unusual for opinions to evolve and beliefs to be broadened.

To create an educational community that values critical voice, we must continually find ways to bridge learners with each other in respectful and profound ways. I remind myself to trust my students and their ability to form critical voices as they respond to each other. They are, given the opportunity, support, and the time, critical thinkers and active participants in our classroom community. This rigorous and collaborative community building will, I hope, transfer to their classroom communities. As a teacher, I have many choices. I might act as a facilitator of learning, but not an owner of the content. My role can be to orchestrate learning rather than dictate ideas or my perception of others' great ideas. This is not to say, however, that I have no control over content. As the instructor, I create the syllabus and do so according to my experiences. I am a critical voice in the process of structuring a place for learning, while at the same time recognizing that trusting in my students' abilities to develop their thinking necessitates respecting that it might differ from my own.

Paying attention to the critical voices in our community offers us pathways to reach beyond society's walls and the limits others have set before us. In our case, the mural provided a pathway to critical voice and understanding. "In fact," Dostoievski reminds us through his underground character, "man is a comical creature: there seems to be a kind of jest in it all. But yet mathematical certainty is, after all, something insufferable. Two times two making four seems to me simply a piece of insolence . . . consciousness, for instance, is definitely superior to two times two making four. Once you have mathematical certainty there is nothing left for you to understand." Listening to the critical voices, on the other hand, opens worlds of understanding, and introduces the possibility that 2×2 will equal something other than 4.

EPILOGUE

Four months after the mural opening and just prior to graduation, I handed out another questionnaire to the arts cohort concerning their reflections on the mural and whether or not they would be inclined to create a mural with their own students. To my surprise, every student wrote that they planned to create a mural. In asking for general reflections concerning the project, many students commented on the sense of collaboration and camaraderie the project engendered. "It was a very special project," one student wrote, "one that taught me about group cooperation, motivation, and cohesiveness." "It was a great cooperative large group exercise which required collaborating and bending individual desires to help the group . . . not easy for many strong egos in our cohort," wrote another student.

In addition to their contribution of the mural to the campus, the arts cohort became the first group of students to sing publicly at a graduation ceremony. A few weeks prior to graduation, they decided they wanted to perform before their peers, parents, and friends. Feeling confident, they went to the provost with their proposal to sing a song of celebration and to request her permission to be a part of the ceremony. It was granted.

Alex continues to paint and is a strong advocate in his community.

A FINAL WORD

I hope this book has encouraged you, or even challenged you, to consider the arts in ways that broaden your teaching tools and languages of learning. I have written it with excitement and conclude it knowing that what I have written is but a slice of what is possible. Perhaps one of the most wonderful aspects of this journey has been knowing that the destinations are limitless.

 QUESTIONS TO PONDER

1. What are your experiences as a student or teacher with collaborative projects? Have the experiences been positive? Negative? Mixed? Do you believe you or your students have learned in collaborative situations?

2. Have you ever experienced resistance to learning, or the feeling of "not learning"? What was that experience like?

3. Do you feel like your voice is a "critical voice"? Do you think that "critical voice" is something important to encourage? Does it depend on specific situations?

 ## EXPLORATIONS TO TRY

1. Develop a relationship with an arts agency in your community. Create a collaborative project with that agency (mural, performance guides, Web site, gallery exhibition).

2. Study the role of graffiti in culture and community. What do graffiti artists have in common? How do they differ? Create a wall for graffiti in your classroom based on the issues important to your students.

3. Revisit the essay you wrote at the end of Chapter 1 outlining your philosophy of education. How would you change it? What aspect(s) of your thinking has evolved?

REFERENCES

Dostoievski, T. M. (1943). Notes from the underground. In B. G. Guerney (Ed.), *A treasury of Russian literature*. New York: Vanguard Press.

Duckworth, E. (1996). *The having of wonderful ideas and other essays on teaching and learning* (2nd ed.). New York: Teachers College Press.

Gallas, K. (1994). *Languages of learning*. New York: Teachers College Press.

Goldberg, M., & Bossenmeyer, M. (1998). Shifting the role of arts in education. *Principal, 77*(4), 56–58.

Greene, M. (1991). Texts and margins. *Harvard Educational Review, 61*(1).

Kohl, H. (1994). *"I won't learn from you" and other thoughts on creative maladjustment*. New York: The New Press.

Little, N. F. (1952). *American decorative wall painting 1700–1850*. New York: Studio Publications.

Meiss, M. (1970). *The great age of fresco*. New York: George Braziller in conjunction with The Metropolitan Museum of Art.

Nieto, S. (1992). *Affirming diversity*. New York: Longman.

Perl, S. (1994). Composing texts, composing lives. *Harvard Educational Review, 64*(4).

Tatum, B. (1992). Talking about race, learning and racism: The application of racial identity development theory in the classroom. *Harvard Educational Review, 62*(1).

Index